Teaching Social Studies
A Literacy-Based Approach

Emily Schell

Douglas Fisher
San Diego State University

PEARSON

Merrill
Prentice Hall

Upper Saddle River, New Jersey
Columbus, Ohio

Library of Congress Cataloging-in-Publication Data

Schell, Emily.
    Teaching social studies : a literacy-based approach / Emily Schell, Douglas Fisher.
        p. cm.
    Includes bibliographical references and index.
    ISBN 0-13-170017-0
    1. Social sciences—Study and teaching—United States.   2. Literacy—Study and teaching—United
States.   3. Teachers—Training of—United States.   4. Interdisciplinary approach in education—United
States.   5. Curriculum planning—United States.   I. Fisher, Douglas.   II. Title.
    LB1584.S354 2007
    300.71—dc22   2006025646

Editor in Chief: Jeffery W. Johnston
Acquisitions Editor: Meredith D. Sarver
Senior Development Editor: Hope Madden
Senior Editorial Assistant: Kathleen S. Burk
Production Editor: Alexandrina Benedicto Wolf
Production Coordination: Techbooks
Design Coordinator: Diane Lorenzo
Cover Design: Kristina Holmes
Cover Art: Corbis
Production Manager: Susan W. Hannahs
Director of Marketing: David Gesell
Senior Marketing Manager: Darcy Betts Prybella
Marketing Coordinator: Brian Mounts

This book was set in Mendoza Roman by *Techbooks*. It was printed and bound by
R.R. Donnelley & Sons Company. The cover was printed by Phoenix Color Corp.

Pearson Education Ltd.   Pearson Education Australia Pty, Limited
Pearson Education Singapore, Pte. Ltd.   Pearson Education North Asia Ltd.
Pearson Education Canada, Ltd.   Pearson Educación de Mexico, S.A. de C.V.
Pearson Education—Japan   Pearson Education Malaysia, Pte. Ltd.

10 9 8 7 6 5 4 3 2 1
ISBN 0-13-170017-0

We dedicate this book to the many students who sit in classrooms throughout this nation and wonder, "What's the big idea? Why do I have to learn this stuff anyhow?" We hope that each student will recognize, understand, and appreciate his or her potential as an important member of society with invaluable contributions to make today, tomorrow, and throughout our future.

And especially for Evan, one of our favorite students in the world.

Preface

R ay Yazzie wrote this about his Navajo people: "A long time ago people used to say that if you remembered the stories that were passed down, they would make you strong. Even just a little portion of the stories would keep you and your children strong so you could face whatever is in the future." This is why social studies is important. It is by passing on the stories and events of our past that we create our future. Through social studies, students learn to make sense of the world. They learn to become committed citizens of this global community; they learn about the events, people, communications, advancements, and conflicts of the past and their consequences on the present; and how to find their own place in history.

We begin to help students make sense of their world by helping them build understanding of themselves, their families, schools, and communities. As students learn about diverse people, places, and events over time and space, their connections to their cities, states, nations, and world emerge. They build these connections with teachers through thoughtful discussions and interactions with the world around them.

It is through the words of the Navajo and Hopi, the Greeks and Egyptians, philosophers, explorers, artists, Founding Fathers and Mothers, pioneers and settlers, war veterans, Civil Rights leaders, migrant farm workers, immigrants, and voters that we will become stronger. Using social studies as a vehicle, these words are communicated through pictographs, cuneiforms, illustrations, oral traditions, poetry, journals, logs, letters, news articles, official documents, songs, speeches, and stories. The words come on stone, papyrus, parchment, cloth, and digital form.

Exploring, interpreting, and using these words require strategic teaching, which means time, preparation, and reflection. Learning from these data cannot happen unless students are continuously engaged in reading, writing, listening, and speaking—all important components of a balanced literacy program. And yet these literacy skills would be meaningless to students if not skillfully contextualized by real content and challenging issues that relate to the world around us. *Teaching Social Studies: A Literacy-Based Approach* presents suggestions for how you and your students can become actively and creatively engaged in that kind of learning—from exploration to application.

INTEGRATING LITERACY AND SOCIAL STUDIES

We recognize (and lament the fact) that teaching explicit social studies as a daily, comprehensive, and coordinated program has become more difficult for many teachers because of a variety of local, state, and federal issues. There is less time to teach social studies, more pressure to raise literacy and mathematics test scores, and fewer resources and professional development opportunities for teachers of social studies. And yet there has never been a time when social studies has been more valuable.

Our desire to help teachers tackle the issues facing social studies education today was the catalyst for writing this text. We address time and accountability issues by proposing an integrated, meaningful approach to planning, teaching, learning, and assessing social studies through literacy skills and literature. After all, most social studies teachers will tell you that history is a story well told, and as historian Barbara Tuchman states, "Tell stories. The pull, the appeal is irresistible, because history is about two of the greatest of all mysteries—time and human nature."

Each chapter focuses on a separate, yet connected facet of social studies education. Collectively, the chapters present readers with information and ideas that broaden their understanding of social studies and suggest strategies for developing a meaningful literacy-based social studies program. We refer to common practices and research about literacy instruction while focusing our attention on social studies instruction with information on teaching history, economics, geography, and civics/government, ensuring students' understanding of the content as well as their development of literacy skills.

- **History's Finer Points** stretch your historical thinking about where we are in education and society today. Each historical note connects to the chapter content and encourages you to delve deeper into historical records to satisfy your own interests, curiosities, and thirst for knowledge.
- **Book Links** provide specific guidance for linking social studies content to motivating, enriching literature.
- **Margin Notes** sprinkled throughout the book present historical notes and context and raise questions for you to consider, discuss, and write about. You might think of these as "sticky notes" that we posted in the book without interrupting the flow of the text. Look for links to the text's Companion Website.

ADDRESSING THE REALITIES OF TODAY'S CLASSROOM

During our many years in education, we have paid close attention to students, teachers, resources, materials, pedagogy, and educational trends. This book represents the best of what we've learned from these experiences.

In preparing and supporting teachers for meeting the challenges of today's classroom, we have paid particular attention to standards and assessment. Although standards vary from state to state, they are an important component of each teacher's program because they specify goals and objectives for student achievement in the area of social studies.

- **Vignettes** in every chapter reflect masterful, integrated teaching found in the real classrooms of committed, successful social studies teachers. These vignettes train your mindset and keep you anchored in the reality of today's students in today's classrooms.

- **Assessment,** whether formal or informal, formative or summative, is addressed throughout the book so that teachers and students recognize the importance of monitoring for comprehension and progress. We know that we cannot afford to wait until the "big test" or final project to determine whether or not the students "got it" or understood the lessons.

- **NCSS Standards** are a special consideration. This book aligns strategies for teaching social studies and literacy integration to these important objectives and outcome goals.

- **Understanding by Design** research of Jay McTighe and Grant Wiggins influences the chapter materials. Learning social studies is complex and ongoing, and we all must make connections between historical events, important decisions, leaders, systems, organizations, ideas, and locations to better understand new situations. Each day brings new challenges that require informed decision making. Our youngest citizens need to learn how we do this.

- **Big Ideas** and **Essential Questions** at the beginning of each chapter drive your thinking and learning throughout this book. As you read and discuss information from each chapter, keep the Big Ideas and Essential Questions in mind. These will help you form your personal philosophies of teaching and learning social studies and challenge you to develop a meaningful instructional program for your students.

PROVIDING TOOLS FOR THE CLASSROOM

The information you find in these pages will do more than inform your teaching. We intend to provide you with tools to take directly into your classroom. We've combined the best approaches to both literacy and social studies teaching and present tried-and-true practices for planning, implementing, and assessing both content areas.

- **Field-Tested Strategies** throughout chapters give you the resources to begin powerful, integrated social studies teaching immediately.

- **Lesson Planning Tools** help you design responsive instruction.

- **Companion Website Margin Notes** direct you to downloadable, standards-driven lessons. Use the existing lessons, keyed to the NCSS Standards, or link out to your own state's standards to create a bank of lessons ideal for your own school district.

For books are more than books, they are the life, the very heart and core of ages past.

Amy Lowell

The integral nature of literacy, literature, history, and learning is undeniable. We hope the powerful possibilities of integrating social studies and literacy teaching, as developed in these pages, allow you to help your students make sense of the world. With your guidance they will learn to become committed citizens of this global community; learn about the events, people, communications, advancements, and conflicts of the past and their consequences on the present; and find their own place in history. Good luck!

SUPPLEMENTS

For the Student

Companion Website. This robust online support system available at **http://www.prenhall.com/schell** offers many rich and meaningful ways to deepen and expand the information presented to you in the text.

- *Chapter Objectives and Overview* provide a useful advance organizer for each chapter's content.
- *Multiple Choice and Essay* self-assessments allow you to gauge your understanding of chapter topics.
- *Web Links* provide useful connections to all standards and many other invaluable online social studies and literacy-related sources.
- *Meeting the Standards* modules provide a chapter-by-chapter matrix that leads you to the exact locations in the text where specific NCSS as well as IRA/NCTE Standards are addressed. Additionally, lessons keyed to the national standards are available for you to download and connect to your own state's standards, providing you with a bank of lessons that align with both state and national standards for your own classroom.
- *Praxis Practice* questions will help you prepare for the Praxis 2 exam.

For the Instructor

Instructor Resource Center. The Instructor Resource Center at **http://www.prenhall.com** has a variety of print and media resources available in downloadable, digital format—all in one location. As a registered faculty member, you can access and download pass-code protected resource files, course management content, and other premium online content directly to your computer.

Digital resources available for *Teaching Social Studies: A Literacy-Based Approach* include:

- A test bank with multiple choice and essay tests.
- PowerPoint presentations specifically designed for each chapter.
- Chapter-by-chapter materials, including chapter objectives, suggested readings, discussion questions, and in-class activities.

To access these items online, go to **http://www.prenhall.com** and click on the Instructor Support button, and then go to the Download Supplements section. Here you will be able to log in or complete a one-time registration for a user name and password. If you have any questions regarding this process or the materials available online, please contact your local Prentice Hall sales representative.

ACKNOWLEDGMENTS

Teaching social studies has always been a challenge for educators. Teaching social studies effectively requires commitment, organization, reflection, teamwork, creativity, time, energy, and patience. Today, we must add "courage" to the list of ingredients that are essential to the development and implementation of a truly meaningful social studies program. This book serves to honor and acknowledge the courageous leaders in education who care deeply about preparing today's youth for their roles, responsibilities, and opportunities as citizens of their communities, states, nation, and the world.

We have been inspired and continue to be motivated by the leadership of such passionate educators as Gary Kroesch (Poway Unified, CA), Dr. Barbara Schubert (St. Mary's College, Moraga, CA), Mark Wolfe (AVID National, San Diego, CA), Dr. Nancy Frey (San Diego State University, CA), Christine Johnson (San Diego Unified, CA), Dr. Michelle Herczog (Los Angeles County Office of Education, CA), Dr. Peg Hill (San Bernardino Office of the Superintendent, CA), Dr. Kevin Colleary (Fordham University, NY), and Andrea Quihuis (Salinas Union High School District, CA). These leaders continue to exercise great strength and courage for the benefit of our students and remind us of Martin Luther King, Jr.'s words: "All the darkness in the world cannot obscure the light of a single candle."

We also continue to learn from and appreciate the hard work and powerful teaching of such amazing and dedicated teachers at Rosa Parks Elementary School (San Diego, CA) as Colleen Crandall, Diana Yemha, Pam Pham-Barron, Adrienne Laws, Jennie Uribe, Hilda Martinez, and Aida Allen, as well as those at Monroe Clark Middle School (San Diego, CA), including Maurice Roundtree, Andy Soto, Francisco Garcia, and Kelly Gelsomino. Our encouragement and ideas remain fueled by such phenomenal teachers as Stephanie Buttell-Maxin (National District, CA), Joan Bray (Carlsbad Unified, CA), Bill Laraway (San Jose Unified, CA), Kate Bowen (Davis Unified, CA), Gigi Kelly (Fullerton, CA), Krista Rose (Fullerton, CA), and Kim Thompson (Mountain View, CA). Over the years, we have loved to see students from our methods courses at San Diego State University flourish in their teaching careers while implementing and adapting much of the information in this book. We salute these new and already-successful teachers, including Sarah Shaw (Fairfax, VA), Jennifer Hofman (San Diego, CA), Amy Vigil (San Diego, CA), and Peter Oskin (Salinas, CA).

These educators represent a larger body of outstanding and dedicated social studies and literacy educators. Together, we look forward to inspiring and supporting a new generation of educators who will join us in creating a stronger social studies and literacy teaching force. In doing so, we will greatly benefit our most precious resources—our youth—and help them ensure the welfare of our ever-changing communities.

We also extend our most sincere appreciation to our editors who guided us through the process of sharing our experiences. Linda Ashe Bishop and Hope Madden of Merrill/Prentice Hall have provided expert leadership, encouragement, support, and most of all friendship through this process. And finally, we must acknowledge the advice and feedback we received from our reviewers. Their time and words made this a much better book: Ernest Barnett, Georgia Southwestern State University; Sara W. Fry, Bucknell University; Thomas B. Goodkind, University of Connecticut; Karen Ivers, California State University, Fullerton; Deborah C. Johnson, Holy Family University; Carolyn Riley, Northern Illinois University; Steven Thorpe, Southern Oregon University; and Saundra Wetig, University of Nebraska at Omaha.

Although we have benefited from the many people who have willingly shared their experiences and advice with us, any errors are our own.

Meet the Authors

Emily M. Schell, Ed.D., is the Principal of Curriculum, Instruction and Assessment at Rosa Parks Elementary School in the San Diego Unified School District. Operated by San Diego State University through the City Heights Educational Collaborative, this large urban school serves 1,500 K–5 students. The school serves as both a professional development school, providing training and field experiences for approximately 80 student teachers each year, and a community school offering unique social and educational programs to a diverse, low-SES, inner-city community experiencing urban renewal. A former classroom teacher, district Social Studies Resource Teacher, and San Diego County Office of Education K–12 History–Social Science Coordinator, Dr. Schell has spent the past 13 years teaching Social Studies Methods courses at San Diego State University. As Visiting Professor, she has supervised student teachers, taught courses in Children's Literature and Curriculum Issues, and served as the Social Studies Professional Development Director for the City Heights Educational Collaborative. She has developed a variety of professional resources, and authored several articles and book chapters about social studies and content area literacy.

Douglas Fisher, Ph.D., is Professor of Language and Literacy Education in the Department of Teacher Education at San Diego State University and the Co-Director of the Center for the Advancement of Reading, Office of the Chancellor, California State University. Doug taught at Rosa Parks Elementary, among other schools. He is the recipient of the International Reading Association's Celebrate Literacy Award as well as a Christa McAuliffe award for excellence in teacher education. He has published numerous articles on reading and literacy, social studies education, differentiated instruction, and curriculum design as well as books such as *Reading for Information in Elementary School: Content Literacy Strategies to Build Comprehension* and *Language Arts Workshop: Purposeful Reading and Writing Instruction*. He has taught a variety of courses in SDSU's teacher-credentialing program, as well as graduate-level courses on English language development and literacy.

TEACHER PREP

MERRILL
PRENTICE HALL

Teacher Preparation Classroom

YOUR CLASS. THEIR CAREERS. OUR FUTURE. WILL YOUR STUDENTS BE PREPARED?

We invite you to explore our new, innovative, and engaging website and all that it has to offer you, your course, and tomorrow's educators! Organized around the major courses preservice teachers take, the Teacher Preparation site provides media, student/teacher artifacts, strategies, research articles, and other resources to equip your students with the quality tools needed to excel in their courses and prepare them for their first classroom.

This ultimate online education resource is available at no cost, when packaged with a Merrill text, and will provide you and your students access to:

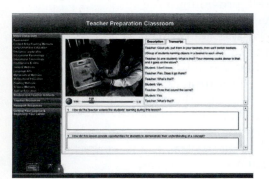

ONLINE VIDEO LIBRARY. More than 150 video clips—each tied to a course topic and framed by learning goals and Praxis-type questions—capture real teachers and students working in real classrooms, as well as in-depth interviews with both students and educators.

STUDENT AND TEACHER ARTIFACTS. More than 200 student and teacher classroom artifacts—each tied to a course topic and framed by learning goals and application questions—provide a wealth of materials and experiences to help make your study to become a professional teacher more concrete and hands-on.

RESEARCH ARTICLES. Over 500 articles from ASCD's renowned journal *Educational Leadership*. The site also includes Research Navigator, a searchable database of additional educational journals.

TEACHING STRATEGIES. Over 500 strategies and lesson plans for you to use when you become a practicing professional.

LICENSURE AND CAREER TOOLS. Resources devoted to helping you pass your licensure exam; learn standards, law, and public policies; plan a teaching portfolio; and succeed in your first year of teaching.

How to ORDER *Teacher Prep* for you and your students:

For students to receive a *Teacher* Prep Access Code with this text, instructors **must** provide a special value pack ISBN number on their textbook order form. To receive this special ISBN, please email: **Merrill.marketing@pearsoned.com** and provide the following information:

- Name and Affiliation
- Author/Title/Edition of Merrill text

Upon ordering *Teacher Prep* for their students, instructors will be given a lifetime *Teacher Prep* Access Code.

Contents

CHAPTER 5
Using Texts for Teaching and Learning Social Studies   112

CHAPTER 6
Effective Uses of Literature to Teach Social Studies   142

CHAPTER 7
Putting the Pieces Together: Curriculum Planning and Organization   180

CHAPTER 10
How Do We Share What We've Learned in Social Studies?

Note: Every effort has been made to provide accurate and current Internet information in this book. However, the Internet and information posted on it are constantly changing, so it is inevitable that some of the Internet addresses listed in this textbook will change.

Teaching Social Studies

A Literacy-Based Approach

What Is Social Studies?

Source: *Anthony Magnacca/Merrill*

Big Idea

Social studies helps students understand the world in which they live by organizing information into concepts that are integrated into a larger story about life.

Essential Question

Who and what defines social studies?

As a first-year teacher, Mr. Morga was very nervous about his upcoming evaluation. He knew that his principal would be coming into his fourth-grade classroom to observe him teaching social studies, but he had some questions. What should he teach when the principal came in to observe? Should he teach a lesson from the textbook or try something more original and engaging for the students? What would the principal look for in a good social studies lesson?

Mr. Morga reviewed his notes from his social studies methods course and finally decided to teach a favorite lesson that he remembered from when he was in elementary school. He found some old newspapers and some starch in the stockroom, bought some balloons, and made plans to have his students create papier-mâché' globes for the observed lesson.

While Mr. Morga's principal observed the lesson, she had a few questions. Why is he teaching this lesson? How does this support evolving student understandings of grade-level standards? Is this good social studies?

Take a minute and ask yourself, what is social studies? Share your ideas with others and consider their perspectives on this topic.

INTRODUCTION

Before you begin to learn how to teach social studies, it is important to understand what defines social studies. In this chapter, we will explore the roots of social studies education in American schools and contrast the history with contemporary definitions and practices of social studies education. As you read, discuss, and learn, please continue to ask, "What is social studies?" and continue to define social studies for yourself and your students.

First, consider taking a stroll into your own past. What do you remember about your social studies lessons when you were in elementary school? When we ask this question of preservice and inservice teachers, their responses usually fall into one of the three following categories.

CATEGORY ONE: THE THREE R'S (READ, RECALL, REGURGITATE)

Which of these categories represents your experience?

In this category, we find few variations on the same theme—a process of reading the textbook chapter, writing the answers to the questions at the end of the chapter, and then taking a test at the end of the unit. This cycle repeats itself over and over within and across grade levels. As a result, teachers associate textbooks, worksheets, and tests with social studies. These are also the teachers who often admit that they do not know much history or geography, and also admit that social studies is not their favorite subject to teach in school.

CATEGORY TWO: FUN, FUN, FUN!

Specific information regarding the contents of history and geography are presented later in this chapter.

Here we have teachers who recall dressing up as historic characters, reenacting historic events, and celebrating holidays with historical significance. These teachers share the details of Thanksgiving feasts they participated in during the first grade. They remember wearing costumes and churning butter during Pioneer Days in third grade. They describe the costumes they wore to school while studying about famous people, ancient Egyptians, or the Civil War. These teachers remember field trips to fire stations, museums, and historic sites. They describe plays, songs, assemblies or guest speakers, and making models or art projects in class. These teachers remember how much fun it was to be a student of social studies because they felt, tasted, created, smelled, listened to, discussed, and "saw" social studies unfold in their classrooms. Many admit that they do not know as much about history and geography as they would like to know, but at least have a positive attitude about learning and teaching the subject.

The memories of these teachers are more vivid and unique to the lessons because they participated in learning experiences. Psychologist Carl Rogers (1969) believed that experiential learning was significant learning because it applied knowledge and addressed the needs and wants of the learner. He reported that experiential learning has a greater lasting effect on the learner than cognitive learning. These teachers' self-reported recollections provide additional evidence of Rogers's theory.

CATEGORY THREE: AMNESIA

Some teachers sit quietly and admit that they cannot remember anything at all about social studies in the elementary grades. Once one teacher makes a statement to this effect, there are echoes: "Oh, good. It's not just me! I can't remember learning anything about social studies either." Although we jokingly label this category "Amnesia," we are not implying that teachers learned something and then somehow forgot or misplaced that information in their memories. We can think of two general reasons

Students of all ages enjoy dressing in historic costumes. As these students reenact 18th century life, what specifically are they learning about early American history?
Source: *Charles Gatewood/PH College*

why some teachers simply do not remember learning social studies until high school or college: (a) Their teachers did not teach social studies, or (b) they learned social studies for the short term, probably to pass a test or write a paper, and therefore do not recall what was taught, learned, assessed, and systematically dumped from memory (see Figure 1.1).

Think of it this way—when you read your e-mail, you open, quickly review, and then delete the messages that are less important to you, right? What do you do with those that you like and those that are important to you? You save them. You go back and read them later. You reply to them and start a thread of messages. You talk about them with others, maybe even forward the message to a friend. You are happy knowing what you have in your mailbox. Now, think about social studies. If you don't like social studies or do not see social studies as important, you will do what you need to do and then delete the information from your mind. Sometimes, we find that we need information that we have deleted from our mailboxes, and then try to recreate or research that information. When it comes to social studies, if students are taught information that they never return to in the future, and foresee no use for, why would they store that information?

We think much of this "learning for the short term" has happened in the teaching of social studies, and even our teachers cannot recall what they studied many years ago. On the other hand, there are some, we firmly believe, who truly never did have social studies instruction because many teachers have not seen the importance and value of this

Figure 1.1

Source: www.cartoonstock.com

subject area. That is a despairing statement in itself. However, when we see what is happening in many elementary schools today with an emphasis on reading and mathematics, we fear that a growing number of students are being denied a comprehensive elementary education that includes social studies.

What other uses of "the 3 R's" do you know?

We use the term "The 3 R's" for category one because we believe that this is an outdated mode of instruction for social studies education. Although some reading, some recall, and even some "regurgitation" is necessary in many social studies programs, these should not be the limitations or the core practices of a meaningful instructional program.

Category two is also assigned a term that is seen as cautionary. Few people disagree with fun, and students are the first to tell you that the more fun they have in school, the better engaged they are in their studies. Teachers, for the most part, are not opposed to fun, either, but recognize their role as professional educators and not as entertainers or activity directors (though some entertaining and directing of activities is necessary in teaching). The problem with many of these category two experiences seen in social studies classrooms is that students walk away feeling good about the fun, but often lose the educational value of the lessons. We have interviewed students who have been able to tell us about the ways foods tasted, how difficult it is to walk on stilts, and how complicated dance steps are after a simulation unit on colonial life. When asked what factors influenced foods of the period (geography and economics), what the roles of children entailed (history and culture), and why dance was so important to some colonists (culture and economics), these same students cannot answer.

Furthermore, many of these students confront high-stakes tests that challenge them to answer questions about trade systems, imports and exports, relationships with Native Americans, laws, religion, and the institution of slavery during the colonial period. Rarely are there questions about daily life, games, foods, and dance. This is not to say that a simulation would not be able to help students learn about such topics as economic systems, laws, and slavery. However, many times the fun takes the place of the specific learning goals for the instructional unit.

Overall, imagine what all of this means for your social studies students. What will your future students say they remember learning from your social studies lessons? These memories are important to surface and discuss as you plan for your work as a teacher of social studies. We have seen many teachers return to what they remember, or replicate what they experienced, when making plans for their own students. In some cases, this is a good thing, as teachers fill their social studies lessons with experiential learning activities and stimulate student interest and understandings while focused on specific learning goals. However, this may also be a bad thing, as teachers use such tactics as scheduling social studies for the last few minutes of the day—oftentimes offering P.E. as a reward in place of social studies if the students are good all day (we have seen this happen!). Sometimes there are negative messages sent from teachers to students when the teacher cares little for the subject and replicates the same boring strategies she recalls from her days as a bored student—usually a repetitious cycle of read-the-text, answer-the-questions, and take-a-chapter test.

Do you know the story of *Goldilocks and the Three Bears?* Well, just like the porridge, the chairs, and the beds, there are some social studies programs that are too _____ (hard, rigid, boring, lackluster, etc.) and some that are too _____ (soft, light, disconnected, "fun and games," etc.). Somewhere in between is a program that is "just right" for you, for your students, and for the goals of authentic social studies programs. In order to determine what is "just right," let's take a look at the definitions and goals of social studies.

How can we make learning fun while not compromising the educational value and effectiveness of social studies lessons?

Many social studies exams require students to list events in relative order: Which came first—the signing of the Declaration of Independence or the Magna Carta?

WHAT IS SOCIAL STUDIES?

How do you define this subject? Initial responses to this question generate such replies as:

- cultures
- history
- maps
- places around the world
- people from long ago
- families
- presidents
- governments
- laws
- famous people
- religions
- holidays

What do you know about each of these topics? Building your background knowledge on each of these subjects is important to be able to teach social studies well.

Further probing elicits such responses as:

- the stories of diverse people from long ago and places far away
- the study of important people, societies, and events
- looking at the ways people live, govern, interact, and survive despite their environments and economic conditions
- respect for various cultural traditions, beliefs, and practices over time and place
- significant people, places, and events that have influenced and shaped our communities and world today
- what allows students to see their roles in the world today and tomorrow

You can find information about the National Council for the Social Studies at the Web Links module in Chapter 1 on our Companion Website at www.prenhall.com/schell or at www.ncss.org.

In all cases, these responses are essentially correct. In fact, there is little that one could say that is not, technically, social studies. The National Council for the Social Studies (1992) has defined social studies in the following way:

> Social Studies is the integrated study of the social sciences and humanities to promote civic competence. Within the school program, social studies provides coordinated, systematic study drawing upon such disciplines as anthropology, archaeology, economics, geography, history, law, philosophy, political science, psychology, religion, and sociology, as well as appropriate content from the humanities, mathematics, and natural sciences. The primary purpose of social studies is to help young people develop the ability to make informed decisions for the public good as citizens of a culturally diverse, democratic society in an interdependent world.

By definition, every subject area and topic qualifies as social studies. And that makes sense, too. If we consider all that exists within and among

A historical photo of an American classroom. How are classrooms today like this and different from this?
Source: *Emily Schell*

societies now and in the past, then we must consider people, places, time, and events. We must consider the range of human activities that make up a society and that differentiate people within and across communities. Throughout time, science, mathematics, and technology have advanced thinking, work, and the daily activities of humankind. Beyond the physical realm are the intellectual, spiritual, and emotional aspects of human beings that also require attention, discussion, and analysis as we study the motivations, achievements, and failures of people, as well as the details of places and events throughout time.

Social studies is huge, expansive, and overwhelming as it encompasses a broad range of topics and concepts that reflect people, places, and events of the past as well as the present. These topics and concepts reflect life, or social systems, and therefore become all-inclusive. Naturally, this only frustrates a teacher looking for a discrete set of knowledge and skills upon which to develop lesson plans, instructional units, and assessments.

Social studies therefore requires specificity for teaching and learning at each grade level. The definition presented by the national organization of social studies professionals recommends that social studies programs be coordinated and systematic, drawing upon the many disciplines. The National Council for the Social Studies (NCSS) and most states have developed coordinated programs through their social studies content standards and frameworks. Content standards isolate and connect eras, people, places, events, and themes in order to narrow that

How will you explain what social studies is to your students?

You can find your state-specific social studies content standards on your state Department of Education website. For more information, visit the Web Links module in Chapter 1 on our Companion Website at www. prenhall.com/ schell.

wide range for students and teachers at each grade level. Consider, for example, the national social studies standards (NCSS, 1994), which are organized into 10 thematic strands:

1. Culture
2. Time, Continuity, and Change
3. People, Places, and Environment
4. Individual Development and Identity
5. Individuals, Groups, and Institutions
6. Power, Authority, and Governance
7. Production, Distribution, and Consumption
8. Science, Technology, and Society
9. Global Connections
10. Civic Ideals and Practice

These themes provide opportunities for teachers at various grades to focus their instruction on these essential components of an authentic social studies program with specific historical, geographic, or economic examples, which are presented more clearly in Curriculum Standards for Social Studies (NCSS, 1994). Coordinating these themes across grade levels will ensure that specific content is not repeated, but enhanced grade after grade. Further exploration of these themes and social studies standards are found in Chapter 3.

The National Standards for History (National Center for History in the Schools, 1996) present topical standards in kindergarten through Grade 4:

- Topic 1: Living and Working Together in Families and Communities, Now and Long Ago
- Topic 2: The History of the Students' Own State or Region
- Topic 3: The History of the United States: Democratic Principles and Values and the Peoples from Many Cultures Who Contributed to Its Cultural, Economic and Political Heritage
- Topic 4: The History of Peoples of Many Cultures Around the World

and chronological history for Grades 5–12:

- Era 1: Three Worlds Meet (Beginnings to 1620)
- Era 2: Colonization and Settlement (1585–1763)
- Era 3: Revolution and the New Nation (1754–1820s)
- Era 4: Expansion and Reform (1801–1861)
- Era 5: Civil War and Reconstruction (1850–1877)
- Era 6: The Development of the Industrial United States (1870–1900)
- Era 7: The Emergence of Modern America (1890–1930)
- Era 8: The Great Depression and World War II (1929–1945)
- Era 9: Postwar United States (1945 to early 1970s)
- Era 10: Contemporary United States (1968 to the present)

This chronological presentation allows for the continual study of people, places, and events over time. These history standards are important to analyze in conjunction with national standards in geography (National Geographic, 1994), economics (National Council on Economic Education, 2003), and civics and government (Center for Civic Education, 1994). When asking the question, "What is social studies?" and considering the NCSS definition, we can refine our thinking by understanding what is meant by these core disciplines in social studies—history, geography, economics, and civics and government.

ROOTS OF SOCIAL STUDIES

To best determine how we got to these contemporary definitions of social studies and these standards that frame the knowledge and skills expected of students in our schools, let us review a brief history of social studies in our public schools.

History takes us as far back as we know from historical record and documentation, and we acknowledge that unrecorded historical events happened during the prehistoric period as well. However, the actual formal teaching of social studies, which includes the studies of prehistory as well as history, has a shorter history, as it did not emerge in

As you learn more about this content area, it becomes clear why this is a critical area of instruction for students—democracy itself rests on understanding our role as citizens and how we interact with our environment, economy, and government.

Fourth-grade students learning about statehood recreate and present important events on this California history time line.
Source: *Scott Cunningham/Merrill*

America's public schools until about 1916. Of course we can date the formal teaching of history, geography, and philosophy back to the earliest days of education in our nation; however, the term *social studies* did not enter educational circles until 1916, when Arthur William Dunn edited *Civic Education in Elementary Schools as Illustrated in Indianapolis* and *The Social Studies in Secondary Education: Report of the Committee on Social Studies of the Commission on the Reorganization of Secondary Education of the National Education Association* (Steffey, 1994). These documents presented what became known as the "expanding horizons" approach to teaching history, geography, and the other social sciences through social studies. The basic structure of this social studies approach engaged kindergartners in learning about themselves and their schools; first graders in learning about their families; second graders in learning about their neighborhoods; third graders in learning about their cities; fourth graders in learning about their states; and so on.

As this subject called social studies developed, citizenship was an important feature of the curriculum. Students learned about and practiced their civic roles and responsibilities. In 1921, the National Council for the Social Studies was founded and became the largest professional organization of K–12 history and social studies teachers. As the progressive movement advanced during this time, some reformers sought to replace the traditional methods of harsh discipline, memorization, and passive learning in schools with a more functional, flexible, child-centered social education. Students were asked to consider multiple perspectives on historic events, and to think critically about modern problems. American children were asked to consider themselves as somehow among the builders of this civilization. One textbook writer, Harold Rugg, was particularly influential during this time as he promoted reform in social education through social studies. Rugg presented textbook material that challenged students to think about, discuss, and debate controversial issues pertaining to history. By 1936, Rugg came under attack for his "subversive textbooks" and for "spreading communist lies" while "Sovietizing our children" (Nash, Crabtree, & Dunn, 1997).

During the 1920s and 1930s, educators had largely agreed to promote critical and analytic thinking in social studies. By 1943, the public demand for more specific teachings of traditional history came as a reaction to news articles stating that students were "historically illiterate." After the attacks on Rugg, book burnings, and controversial changes to the teaching of social studies, teachers began to shy away from nontraditional methods and materials.

Then came the post-Sputnik era when the public again demanded improvements to American education. Funds were made available to develop "new social studies" materials, which ushered in an era of *presentism,* or the application of current ideals and moral standards to interpret historical figures and their actions. Relevancy was also used to help redefine social studies. During the 1960s, the public cries for relevance challenged

The NCSS website also provides a number of ideas for teaching social studies.

History Connections

History changed on October 4, 1957, when the Soviet Union launched the world's first artificial satellite. Sputnik was about the size of a basketball and weighed only 183 pounds. This event triggered the U.S.–USSR space race.

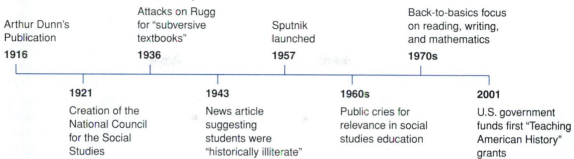

Figure 1.2　Timeline for the development of Social Studies.

1916	1921	1936	1943	1957	1960s	1970s	2001
Arthur Dunn's Publication	Creation of the National Council for the Social Studies	Attacks on Rugg for "subversive textbooks"	News article suggesting students were "historically illiterate"	Sputnik launched	Public cries for relevance in social studies education	Back-to-basics focus on reading, writing, and mathematics	U.S. government funds first "Teaching American History" grants

the studies of ancient periods when there existed modern-day social concerns worthy of study. The 1960s was also a time when the social sciences, which had emerged in the late 19th century as independent academic disciplines, such as economics, political science, and anthropology, began to be challenged for their objectivity.

The back-to-basics movement came in the 1970s, and social studies began to be pushed from the curriculum as reading, writing, and mathematics took a central role in both teaching and testing. Today, teachers continue to struggle to make a place for social studies in an era of high-stakes testing that focuses primarily on reading and mathematics.

Visit the Web Links module in Chapter 1 on our Companion Website at www.prenhall.com/schell.

For the most part, social studies remains part of the core curriculum in most school systems. Historians, social scientists, and educators continue to debate the pros and cons of a social studies curriculum vs. a history-social sciences curriculum. Social studies has been defined as the integrated studies of history and the various social sciences with an emphasis on traditional history and geography. Social sciences are the specific branches of study that deal with humans in the social relations. While social behavior has been studied since ancient times, modern social sciences date back to the 18th century Enlightenment when the scientific method emerged. Social sciences introduced such disciplined studies of economics, anthropology, political science, psychology, and sociology. While educators debate to merits of social studies and history-social sciences, the need for students to learn the basic concepts and important details of social systems remains. A timeline of some of the significant developments in social studies education can be found in Figure 1.2.

A basic and working understanding of the core areas of social studies is essential for the planning, teaching, and assessment in an authentic social studies program. Let us explore

Book Links

Schools and education have changed over time. Some literature that shows these changes include *The Secret School* (Avi), *One Room School* (Pringle), and *One-Room School* (Bial).

these core content areas of history, geography, economics, and civics and government.

HISTORY

Social studies is often challenged by those who prefer a history–social science program in which history plays a major and focused role in the curriculum. Advocates for history education maintain that the explicit studies of history are central and critical to a child's education. History is separated from the social sciences in its defining title of a history-social science program because history is not a science, like anthropology, archaeology, geography, and psychology. In the 19th century, when social sciences entered the educational field, these academic disciplines took their place between the natural sciences, such as biology and physics, and humanities, such as literature and history. After challenges to their objectivity during the 1960s, social scientists began to look to historians and others to strengthen their field. Regardless, there is no doubt that history holds an important and prominent place in every social studies classroom.

History presents the details of the events that have occurred in the past through historic data and the interpretations that scholars bring forward through research, analysis, and conclusion. Although the study of history rests on knowledge of facts, dates, names, places, events, and ideas, true historical understanding requires students to engage in historical thinking (NCHS, 1994). The national history standards introduce historical thinking as a way for students to raise questions and to present solid evidence in support of their answers; to go beyond the facts and examine the historical record for themselves; to consult documents, journals, artifacts, historic sites, art works, data, and other evidence from the past; and to do so imaginatively while taking into account the historical context and multiple perspectives of those on the scene at the time.

In other words, history entails a lot of names, dates, and facts, but cannot and should not be seen as a finite and predetermined set of information that awaits passive consumption and regurgitation by the student. Our understandings and interpretations of the past continue to evolve as science and technologies improve, as new information is unearthed and analyzed, and as society acknowledges the perspectives and contributions of those whose voices have been silenced or overlooked. For these reasons, the studies of history requires students to:

- think chronologically;
- comprehend a variety of historical sources;
- engage in historical analysis and interpretation;
- conduct historical research; and
- engage in historical issues analysis and decision making.

Historical thinking, or thinking like an historian, requires understanding point of view, how the economy and geography influences history, and so on.

Were you required to memorize facts such as "On what date did Custer fight the battle of Little Big Horn?" (1876).

Book Links

Most textbooks are rich with historical information. Consider varied texts to enhance students' appreciation, analysis, and understanding of history through such trade books as *The Watsons Go to Birmingham 1963* (Curtis), *Mr. Lincoln's Whiskers* (Winnick), and *When Esther Morris Headed West: Women, Wyoming, and the Right to Vote* (Woolridge).

Source: Copyright © 2001 by Jacqueline Rogers. Reprinted by Permission of Holiday House, Inc.

GEOGRAPHY

In 1980, educators were introduced to the *Five Themes of Geography* as a first step toward improving geographic education in our schools. The themes—location, place, region, movement, and human-environmental interaction—became popular organizing concepts for teachers across

MR. HeLP is a mnemonic used by teachers who teach students about the five themes of geography: M(ovement), R(egion), H(uman-**e**nvironmental interaction), L(ocation), and P(lace).

the grade levels while helping students understand the important dynamics between humans and their physical world:

How can you relate the five themes of geography to you and your students' lives?

- *Location:* Absolute and relative location are two ways of describing the position of people and places on the earth's surface. A grid system representing latitude and longitude describes the absolute location of a place. For example, knowing the absolute, or exact, location of Jamestown tells us where the first permanent English settlement in North America was built. Relative location refers to the interactions among places. It indicates, for example, how a city is dependent on other places for goods, resources, and transportation. The Southern colonies, for example, sent indigo, tobacco, and rice to colonies in the North. Relative location also allows us to give directions such as "the school is north of the fire station" or "the park is two blocks past the grocery store," which indicate a location in terms of its relationship to another place.

- *Place:* All places on Earth have special features that distinguish them from other places. Geographers usually describe places by their physical and human characteristics. San Diego, California, for example, is known for such physical characteristics as sandy beaches, abundant sunshine, and a mild climate. Human characteristics, such as density of population and a diverse ethnic makeup, also play an important role in shaping the image of San Diego.

- *Movement:* Everywhere, people interact with other people. They travel from place to place, they communicate, and they depend upon distant places for products, ideas, and information. A good example of movement exists in the highly urbanized northeast corridor between Boston and Washington, DC. Here, people can quickly fly from one city to another, and farmers can efficiently send products to restaurants and supermarkets by trucks and trains. Throughout the world, people, products, ideas, music, stories, and so on move from place to place. Geography helps us understand the nature and effects of such movement.

- *Region:* Regions are areas on the surface of Earth that are defined by certain unifying characteristics, either physical or human. The peaks and valleys of the Rocky Mountains form a physical region. Large similar crops, such as corn, unite several Midwestern states into another region. Regions provide an organized way to study Earth's landscapes and peoples, and to monitor the way they form and change.

- *Human-Environmental Interaction:* People interact with their environments and change them in different ways. The large-scale agricultural development of the dry Texas Panhandle, for instance, did not occur until the invention of circular irrigation systems that distribute water from underground wells. But such a change has a price: the region's water supply is rapidly diminishing. Geographers examine how human-environment interactions develop, and what their consequences are for people and the landscape.

These themes continue to play an important role in teachers' understandings, curriculum plans, and students' understandings of geography. However, the development of national geography standards (National Geographic, 1994) expanded these themes into 18 specific content standards. The five themes exist within these standards and remain important organizing features for teachers and students; however, the oversimplification of geography through the five themes encouraged the authors of the standards to provide more specificity for the expectations that all students be geographically informed. The 18 geography standards are organized by six essential elements as seen in Figure 1.3.

More information on *National Geographic* can be found at the Web Links module in Chapter 1 on our Companion Website at www.prenhall.com/schell or at www.nationalgeographic.com.

Figure 1.3   Geography standards and essential elements.

Essential Element	Standards
The World in Spatial Terms	1. How to use maps and other geographic representations, tools, and technologies to acquire, process, and report information. 2. How to use mental maps to organize information about people, places, and environments. 3. How to analyze the spatial organization of people, places, and environments on Earth's surface.
Places and Regions	4. The physical and human characteristics of places. 5. That people create regions to interpret Earth's complexity. 6. How culture and experience influence people's perception of places and regions.
Physical Systems	7. The physical processes that shape the patterns of Earth's surface. 8. The characteristics and spatial distribution of ecosystems on Earth's surface.
Human Systems	9. The characteristics, distribution, and migration of human populations on Earth's surface. 10. The characteristics, distributions, and complexity of Earth's cultural mosaics. 11. The patterns and networks of economic interdependence on Earth's surface. 12. The process, patterns, and functions of human settlement. 13. How forces of cooperation and conflict among people influence the division and control of Earth's surface.
Environment and Society	14. How human actions modify the physical environment. 15. How physical systems affect human systems. 16. The changes that occur in the meaning, use, distribution, and importance of resources.
The Uses of Geography	17. How to apply geography to interpret the past. 18. To apply geography to interpret the present and plan for the future.

Book Links

There are lots of children's books that help students understand basic geographic concepts, such as *Geography A to Z: A Picture Glossary* (Knowlton), *My Town* (Treays), *Me on the Map* (Sweeney), and *Maps and Globes* (Knowlton). Other books help students enjoy geography through stories, such as *Where I Live* (Wolfe), *Going Home* (Bunting), *The Coast Mappers* (Morrison), and *The Little House* (Burton).

Information on NCEE can be found at the Web Link module in Chapter 1 on our Companion Website at www.prenhall.com/schell or at www.ncee.net.

ECONOMICS

As with social studies itself, professionals find it difficult to reach agreement on the definition of economic literacy and what economics education should look like in a school curriculum. This is due, in large part, to the varied interests of academics, consumer advocates, and business leaders. The National Council on Economic Education (NCEE) and its state affiliates continue to work with educators and the business community to define, support, and improve the teaching of economics in schools. In 1997, NCEE led the efforts to develop national economics standards, which many states used to integrate economic concepts and skills into their state social studies or history-social science standards. These national standards for economics focus on the essential principles of economics, and include:

- *Scarcity:* Productive resources are limited. Therefore, people cannot have all the goods and services they want; as a result, they must choose some things and give up others.
- *Marginal Cost/Benefit:* Effective decision making requires comparing the additional costs of alternatives with the additional benefits. Most choices involve doing a little more or a little less of something; few choices are "all or nothing" decisions.
- *Allocation of Goods and Services:* Different methods can be used to allocate goods and services. People acting individually, or collectively through government, must choose which methods to use to allocate different kinds of goods and services.
- *Role of Incentives:* People respond predictably to positive and negative incentives.
- *Gain from Trade:* Voluntary exchange occurs only when all participating parties expect to gain. This is true for trade among individuals or organizations within a nation, and usually among individuals or organizations in different nations.
- *Specialization and Trade:* When individuals, regions, and nations specialize in what they can produce at the lowest cost and then trade with others, both production and consumption increase.

- *Markets—Price and Quantity Determination:* Markets exist when buyers and sellers interact. This interaction determines market prices and thereby allocates scarce goods and services.
- *Role of Price in Market System:* Prices send signals and provide incentives to buyers and sellers. When supply or demand changes, market prices adjust, affecting incentives.
- *Role of Competition:* Competition among sellers lowers costs and prices and encourages producers to produce more of what consumers are willing and able to buy. Competition among buyers increases prices and allocates goods and services to those people who are willing and able to pay the most for them.
- *Role of Economic Institutions:* Institutions evolve in market economies to help individuals and groups accomplish their goals. Banks, labor unions, corporations, legal systems, and not-for-profit organizations are examples of important institutions. A different kind of institution, clearly defined and enforced property rights, is essential to a market economy.
- *Role of Money:* Money makes it easier to trade, borrow, save, invest, and compare the value of goods and services.
- *Role of Interest Rates:* Interest rates, adjusted for inflation, rise and fall to balance the amount saved with the amount borrowed, which affects the allocation of scarce resources between present and future uses.
- *Role of Resources in Determining Income:* Income for most people is determined by the market value of the productive resources they sell. What workers earn depends, primarily, on the market value of what they produce and how productive they are.
- *Profit and the Entrepreneur:* Entrepreneurs are people who take the risks of organizing productive resources to make goods and services. Profit is an important incentive that leads entrepreneurs to accept the risks of business failure.
- *Growth:* Investment in factories, machinery, and new technology, and in the health, education, and training of people, can raise future standards of living.
- *Role of Government:* There is an economic role for government in a market economy whenever the benefits of a government policy outweigh its costs. Governments often provide for national defense, address environmental concerns, define and protect property rights, and attempt to make markets more competitive. Most government policies also redistribute income.
- *Using Cost/Benefit Analysis to Evaluate Government Programs:* Costs of government policies sometimes exceed benefits. This may occur because of incentives facing voters, government officials, and government employees, because of actions by special interest groups that can impose costs on the general public, or because social goals other than economic efficiency are being pursued.

- *Macroeconomy—Income/Employment, Prices:* A nation's overall levels of income, employment, and prices are determined by the interaction of spending and production decisions made by all households, firms, government agencies, and others in the economy.

- *Unemployment and Inflation:* Unemployment imposes costs on individuals and nations. Unexpected inflation imposes costs on many people and benefits some others because it arbitrarily redistributes purchasing power. Inflation can reduce the rate of growth of national living standards because individuals and organizations use resources to protect themselves against the uncertainty of future prices.

- *Monetary and Fiscal Policy:* Federal government budgetary policy and the Federal Reserve System's monetary policy influence the overall levels of employment, output, and prices.

A great deal of sophistication and specificity is involved in the teaching and learning of economics. However, at the earliest grades of social studies, these concepts may be simplified to build a strong foundation for high school courses in economics as well as a strong understanding of historical events. For example, consider these nine basic principles of economics as defined by the California Council on Economic Education:

1. People can't have everything they want, so they choose.
2. If people make a choice, they pay a cost.
3. People make better decisions when they weigh the benefits and costs of alternatives.
4. People respond to incentives in a predictable manner.
5. Exchange benefits the traders.
6. Markets work with competition, information, incentives, and property rights.
7. Skills and knowledge influence income.
8. Monetary and fiscal policies affect people's choices.
9. Government policies have benefits and costs.

History Connections

In 1793, during the "American Plague" (Yellow Fever epidemic) people moved to get away from death. Given their understanding of medicine and disease distribution, why would some people leave their homes?

Depending on the unit of study, students at the earliest grades can recognize that people make choices in their careers, homes, families, hobbies, and so forth. Even as they study more complex histories, such as the settling of new lands, students can identify the incentives that motivated some people to move while others chose to stay. Understanding economics in its simplicity will help you identify the importance of economics in history. Furthermore, your understandings will empower you to teach economic concepts in the context of social studies.

Book Links

To focus students' attention and enhance their understandings of basic economic concepts, read and discuss *Bunny Money* (Wells), *Alexander, Who Used to Be Rich Last Sunday* (Viorst), and *The Story of Money* (Maestro).

Book Links for Nine Basic Principles of Economics

Basic Economic Principles	Key Vocabulary	Suggested Literature for Teaching Economic Principles
1. People can't have everything they want, so they choose.	scarcity, choice, personal responsibility, alternatives	*Bunny Money* (Rosemary Wells); *Faithful Elephants: A True Story of Animals, People and War* (Yukio Tsuchiya); *Alexander, Who Used to Be Rich Last Sunday* (Judith Viorst)
2. If people make a choice, they pay a cost.	opportunity cost, marginal cost, sunk cost, transaction cost	*If You Give a Moose a Muffin* (Laura Numeroff); *A Chair for My Mother* (Vera Williams); *Dandelions* (Eve Bunting); *Oh, the Places You'll Go!* (Dr. Seuss)
3. People make better decisions when they weigh the benefits and costs of alternatives.	goals, alternatives, criteria, relative benefits and costs, choice, reevaluation	*Tops and Bottoms* (Janet Stevens); *My Mom Travels A Lot* (Caroline Bauer); *The Lotus Seed* (Sherry Garland); *Mailing May* (Michael O. Tunnell); *Something Special for Me* (Vera Williams)
4. People respond to incentives in a predictable manner.	property rights, supply, government	*The California Gold Rush* (R. Conrad Stein); *The Great Migration* (Jacob Lawrence); *Coolies* (Chris Soentpiet); *If You Traveled West in a Covered Wagon* (Ellen Levine)
5. Exchange benefits the traders.	domestic and international trade, money, foreign exchange	*Jalapeno Bagels* (Natasha Wing); *Teammates* (Peter Golenbock); *The Story of Money* (Betsey Maestro)
6. Markets work with competition, information, incentives, and property rights.	supply, demand, relative scarcity, relative prices, entrepreneurs, profit, competition, market failures	*Markets!* (Ted Lewin); *General Store: A Village Store in 1902* (Megan O' Hara); *Look What Came from China!* (Miles Harvey); *Sea Clocks: The Story of Longitude* (Louise Borden); *The Silk Route: 7,000 Miles of History* (John Major)
7. Skills and knowledge influence income.	human capital (skills), productivity, supply, demand, relative scarcity, relative wages	*A Day in the Life of a Colonial Wigmaker* (Kathy Wilmore); *Open Hands, Open Heart: The Story of Biddy Mason* (Deirdre Robinson); *Harvesting Hope: The Story of Cesar Chavez* (Kathleen Krull); *I Want to be a Firefighter* (Dan Liebman)
8. Monetary and fiscal policies affect people's choices.	domestic product, economic growth, unemployment rate, new jobs created, interest rates	*A Williamsburg Household* (Joan Anderson); *The Other Side: How Kids Live in a California Latino Neighborhood* (Kathleen Krull)
9. Government policies have benefits and costs.	monetary policy, fiscal policy, price controls, regulation and deregulation, public choice economics, government failures	*For Every Child, A Better World* (Jim Henson as Kermit the Frog in cooperation with the United Nations); *The Journey of Meng* (Doreen Rappaport); *The People Who Hugged Trees* (Deborah Lee Rose); *The Carpet Boy's Gift* (Pegi Deitz Shea)

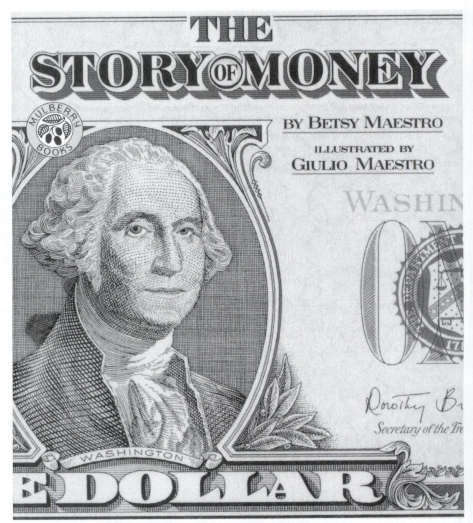

Source: *Cover from* The Story of Money *by Betsy and Giulio Maestro. Cover illustration copyright © 1993 by Giulio Maestro. Reprinted by permission of Clarion Books, an Imprint of Houghton Mifflin Company. All rights reserved.*

CIVICS AND GOVERNMENT

The website for the Center for Civic Education, http://www.civiced.org, contains resources and a professional development calendar.

The national standards for civics and government begin with a rationale for the civic mission of schools (Center for Civic Education, 1994):

> Although it has been argued that the establishment of the proper institutions is sufficient to maintain a free society, Thomas Jefferson, James Madison, John Adams, and others recognized that even the most well-designed institutions are not sufficient. Ultimately, a free society must rely on the knowledge,

skills, and virtue of its citizens and those they elect to public office. Civic education, therefore, is essential to the preservation and improvement of American constitutional democracy.

An educational program that includes civics and government helps students develop the knowledge and skills necessary to be informed, responsible citizens. Students learn what it means to participate in political and social life as competent citizens. The fundamental values and principles of America's constitutional democracy are studied, analyzed, and practiced by students. Students learn about the many institutions that help shape civic character and commitments, such as the family, religious institutions, the media, community organizations, and schools.

Government is studied through history, current events, and political systems. Teachers often teach about government by comparing and contrasting classroom or school rules and procedures. Helping students recognize and understand the individual citizen's roles and responsibilities in government is an ongoing challenge that requires consistent attention across the grade levels. Civics and government cannot be boiled down to voting and elections, but requires students to understand the rights and dignity of others in society.

The national standards for civics and government require students to address the following important questions at kindergarten through Grade 4:

- What is government and what should it do?
- What are the basic values and principles of American democracy?
- How does government established by the Constitution embody the purposes, values, and principles of American democracy?
- What is the relationship of the United States to other nations and to world affairs?
- What are the roles of the citizen in American democracy?

At Grades 5–8, the standards require students to answer these questions:

- What are civic life, politics, and government?
- What are the foundations of the American political system?
- How does the government established by the Constitution embody the purposes, values, and principles of American democracy?
- What is the relationship of the United States to other nations and to world affairs?
- What are the roles of the citizen in American democracy?

As you can see, some questions are repeated. Closer analysis of the standards will show that students study more sophisticated concepts under these overarching questions in the higher grade levels.

Book Link

Fill your classroom with books that help students understand their roles as citizens and how our government works. For example, *Chickens May Not Cross the Road: and Other Crazy But True Laws* (Linz), *Woodrow, the White House Mouse* (Barnes), *How the U.S. Government Works* (Sobel), and *A Kids' Guide to America's Bill of Rights: Curfews, Censorship, and the 100-Pound Giant* (Krull).

SOCIAL STUDIES SKILLS

While integrating many of the areas of history and the social sciences, NCSS proposes that teachers focus on the purposes of social studies—to promote civic competence and to help students make informed decisions for the public good. This allows for teachers to present more than facts and ideas, while equipping students with real life skills.

The content of social studies lessons might focus on one or more of the following:

- an era, such as the Middle Ages or the 1960s; or
- people, such as explorers or immigrants; or
- a place, such as Mount Rushmore or Italy; or
- an event, such as the signing of the U.S. Constitution or the French Revolution.

However, social studies includes a body of skills as well as content knowledge. Teachers are therefore encouraged to integrate social studies knowledge, skills, and attitudes in presenting instructional units and lessons. For example, students are expected to read information from maps, charts, and graphs. Also, students are expected to analyze and evaluate information, opinions, and arguments. They are expected to weigh the costs and benefits of decisions played out in history as well as contemporary life.

The skills that should be promoted in effective social studies programs include the following:

- acquiring information and manipulating data;
- developing and presenting policies, arguments, and stories;
- constructing new knowledge; and
- participating in groups.

These skills should be effectively integrated into the teaching of topical, thematic, or concept-driven units. While some explicit instruction

History Connections

On December 7, 1941, Japan bombed Pearl Harbor. World War II cost the United States a million casualties and nearly 400,000 deaths. What would you consider to be the benefits of the United States engaging in World War II?

in these skills is necessary, they should not be the focus of the instruction unit. Instead, an instructional unit focused on an era, event, or theme should develop and utilize students' abilities to acquire, read, analyze, discuss, and use information to better understand the era, event, or theme. Students should use the writing process to classify, interpret, summarize, evaluate, and present information that reflects good reasoning and decision making. Students should have opportunities to conceptualize and categorize information, identify cause and effect, and develop theories. They should develop their thinking, reasoning, leadership, and communication skills through group participation (NCHS, 1994).

SOCIAL STUDIES FOR THE 21ST CENTURY

With a great deal of history and controversy about social studies, social sciences, and history, teachers have much to consider as they plan for effective instruction. Approaches and understandings of this content area vary, but remain part of the core content for every student. Regardless of the disagreements over how to best define social studies, there remains a basic need for today's students to better understand who they are, where they are, why geographic, economic, social and political systems exist, how we came to be who and where we are today, and why all this makes a difference. Whether a teacher uses a 21st-century lens to explore, analyze, interpret, and evaluate the past or chooses to "transport" her students to the distant past to understand the context of the time, people, and place, the importance of teaching social studies is addressed.

Current scholarship in social studies allows for varied and conflicting forms of historical evidence to determine what happened in the past. This leads to great discussion, debate, and curiosity. Allow your students to explore the various forms of evidence, consider alternate opinions, and generate theories of their own while using the data available. Social studies is *not* just a matter of finding the correct answers. Social studies is about connecting students with their worlds—past, present, and future.

Conclusion

Social studies is a complex area of study that involves history, geography, economics, and civics/government. Although social studies education is at risk of being reduced or eliminated in some elementary and middle schools, students who engage in this area of the curriculum are better prepared to contribute to society and are better thinkers about the world around them. A comprehensive social studies education is

Why would leadership be an important skill for students to learn? How can social studies education contribute to leadership skills?

Using a 21st century lens, a teacher might ask, "How would you feel if you were just sold to a plantation owner because he was the highest bidder at a slave auction?"

Transporting students to the past, a teacher might say, "Imagine that you are living in the year 1655. You are 21 years old, and you lived in a small West African village until 3 months ago when you were captured, chained, and sold to a slave trader. Now you're standing on an auction block. What are you thinking and feeling? What do you think will happen to you next?"

vital and must be provided in ways that engage students in historical thinking and analysis.

History's Finer Points

History and social studies textbooks read a bit differently today than they have in the past. Consider, for example, these passages from outdated texts:

> We see that history proper concerns itself with but one highly developed type of mankind; for though the great bulk of the population of the globe has ... belonged, and does still belong, to other types of mankind, yet the Caucasians form the only true historical race. Hence we may say that civilization is the product of the brain of this race. (*Outlines of the World's History*, 1874)

> In time many people came to think that it was wrong to own slaves. Some of them said that all the Negro slaves should be freed. Some of the people who owned slaves became angry at this. They said that the black people were better off as slaves in America than they would have been as wild savages in Africa. Perhaps this was true, as many of the slaves had snug cabins to live in, plenty to eat, and work that was not too hard for them to do. Most of the slaves seemed happy and contented. (*My Country*, 1948)

Document-Based Question: Can we continue to teach the same today as we have in the past when basic scholarship in this field has advanced so greatly?

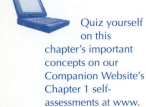

Visit the History's Finer Points module in Chapter 1 on our Companion Website at www.prenhall.com/ schell to answer this question.

Quiz yourself on this chapter's important concepts on our Companion Website's Chapter 1 self-assessments at www. prenhall.com/schell.

Questions to Consider

1. What are the components of an effective social studies curriculum?
2. How do the content standards contribute to lesson planning?
3. Why do students need an education that includes social studies?

Exercises

1. Interview at least three teachers about their beliefs relative to social studies education. Analyze these beliefs. What do these teachers believe about this subject area?

2. Discuss the risks of not having a comprehensive social studies curriculum with someone outside of education (your parents, a neighbor, someone at work). What do they see as the potential harm of losing this core curriculum area?

References

The Bradley Commission on History in Schools. (1988). *Building a history curriculum: Guidelines for teaching history in schools.* Westlake, OH: National Council for History Education, Inc.

California Council on Economic Education. http://www.ccee.org/new2.htm

The Center for Civic Education. (1994). *National standards for civics and government.* Calabasas, CA: Author.

Nash, G., Crabtree, C., & Dunn, R. (1997). *History on trial: Culture wars and the teaching of the past.* New York: Alfred A. Knopf.

National Center for History in the Schools. (1996). *National standards for history.* Los Angeles, CA: National Center for History in the Schools.

National Council for the Social Studies. (1992). *Curriculum standards for social studies.* Silver Spring, MD: Author.

National Council on Economic Education. (2003). *Voluntary national content standards in economics.* New York: Author.

National Geographic Society. (1994). *Geography for life.* Washington, DC: Author.

Rogers, C. R. (1969). *Freedom to learn.* Columbus, OH: Merrill.

Steffey, S. (1994). *If this is social studies, why isn't it boring?* York, ME: Stenhouse.

Children's Literature

Anderson, J. (1990). *A Williamsburg household.* New York: Clarion Books.

Avi. (2001). *The secret school.* New York: Harcourt.

Barnes, P. (1998). *Woodrow, the white house mouse.* Alexandria, VA: Vacation Spot.

Bauer, C. (1981). *My mom travels a lot.* London: F. Warne.

Bial, R. (1999). *One-room school.* New York: Houghton Mifflin.

Borden, L. (2004). *Sea clocks: The story of longitude.* New York: Margaret K. McElderry.

Bunting, E. (2001). *Dandelions*. Marlton, NJ: Voyager Books.

Bunting, E. (1998). *Going home*. Marlton, NJ: HarperTrophy.

Burton, V. (1978). *The little house*. New York: Houghton Mifflin.

Curtis, C. P. (1997). *The Watsons go to Birmingham 1963*. New York: Yearling.

Garland, S. (1997). *The lotus seed*. Marlton, NJ: Voyager.

Golenbock, P. (1992). *Teammates*. Marlton, NJ: Voyager Books.

Harvey, M. (1999). *Look what came from China!* New York: Franklin Watts.

Hensen, J. (1993). *For every child, a better world*. New York: Golden Books.

Knowlton, J. (1997). *Geography A to Z: A picture glossary*. Marlton, NJ: HarperTrophy.

Knowlton, J. (1986). *Maps and globes*. Marlton, NJ: HarperTrophy.

Krull, K. (1999). *A kids' guide to America's bill of rights: Curfews, censorship, and the 100-pound giant*. Marlton, NJ: HarperCollins.

Krull, K. (1997). *The other side: How kids live in a California Latino neighborhood*. New York: Houghton Mifflin.

Krull, K. (2003). *Harvesting hope: The story of Cesar Chavez*. New York: Harcourt.

Lawrence, J. (1995). *The great migration: An American story*. Marlton; NJ: HarperTrophy.

Levine, E. (1992). *If you traveled west in a covered wagon*. New York: Scholastic.

Lewin, T. (1996). *Market!* Marlton, NJ: HarperCollins.

Liebman, D. (1999). *I want to be a firefighter*. Westport; CT: Firefly Books.

Linz, K. (2002). *Chickens may not cross the road: and other crazy but true laws*. New York: Houghton Mifflin.

Maestro, B. (1995). *The story of money*. Marlton, NJ: HarperTrophy.

Major, J. (1999). *The silk trade route: 7,000 miles of history*. Tarzana, CA: Sagebrush.

Morrison, T. (2004). *The coast mappers*. New York: Houghton Mifflin.

Numeroff, L. (1991). *If you give a moose a muffin*. Marlton, NJ: Laura Geringer.

O'Hara, M. (1998). *General store: A village store in 1902*. Markato, MN: Capstone Press.

Pringle, L. (1998). *One room school*. Honesdale, PA: Boyds Mills Press.

Rappaport, D. (1991). *The journey of Meng*. New York: Dial.

Robinson, D. (1998). *Open hands, open heart: The story of Biddy Mason*. Gardena, CA: Sly Fox.

Rose, D. (2001). *The people who hugged trees*. Lanham, MD: Roberts Rinehart.

Seuss, D. (Geisel, T.) (1990). *Oh, the places you'll go!* New York: Random House.

Shea, P. D. (2003). *The carpet boy's gift*. Gardiner, ME: Tilbury House.

Sobel, S. (1999). *How the U.S. government works*. Hauppodge, NY: Barron's Educational Services.

Soentpiet, C. (2003). *Coolies*. New York: Puffin.

Stein, R. (1995). *The California gold rush*. Chicago: Children's Press.

Stevens, J. (1995). *Tops and bottoms*. New York: Harcourt.

Sweeney, J. (1998). *Me on the map*. Cleveland, OH: Dragonfly Books.

Treays, R. (1998). *My town*. Tulsa, OK: Educational Development Corporation.

Tsuchiya, Y. (1997). *Faithful elephants: A true story of animals, people and war*. New York: Houghton Mifflin.

Tunnel, M. (2000). *Mailing May*. Marlton, NJ: HarperTrophy.

Viorst, J. (1987). *Alexander, who used to be rich last Sunday*. New York: Aladdin.

Wells, R. (2000). *Bunny money*. New York: Puffin.

Williams, V. (1982). *A chair for my mother*. Marlton; NJ: Greenwillow.

Williams, V. (1986). *Something special for me*. Marlton, NJ: HarperTrophy.

Wilmore, K. (2000). *A day in the life of a colonial wigmaker*. New York: PowerKids Press.

Wing, N. (1996). *Jalapeno bagels*. New York: Atheneum.

Winnick, K. (1999). *Mr. Lincoln's whiskers*. Honesdale, PA: Boyds Mills Press.

Wolfe, F. (2001). *Where I live*. Toronto: Tundra Books.

Woolridge, C. (2001). *When Esther Morris headed west: Women, Wyoming, and the right to vote*. New York, Holiday House.

Chapter
2

Why Teach Social Studies?

Source: *Stephen McBrady/ PhotoEdit Inc.*

Big Idea

Social studies is an important part of every child's education.

Essential Question

What makes social studies so important?

Compare and contrast the following two journal entries made by two different student teachers based on reflections made during their observations in elementary classrooms:

Create a Venn Diagram or T-chart to summarize, compare, and contrast these student teachers' reflections.

NOVEMBER 25TH

Today I observed another successful language arts lesson. The students in this second-grade class are accustomed to reading the title, author, and body of a piece of text, then discussing the main points of the story. Today's reading was about a young girl of Chinese heritage who shared dinner at the home of a friend whose family is of Mexican heritage. I kept waiting for the teacher or the students to connect the events of this story to that of the first thanksgiving feast at Plimoth. During the entire lesson, no one noted any of the many similarities or connections. I realized that this teacher never taught her students about Thanksgiving, which is an historic event that I remember learning a lot about in elementary school. I asked the teacher about this and she replied, "With such a district focus on reading, I do not have time for social studies." I was left wondering what these students know about our nation's history and what they thought about during their celebrations of Thanksgiving at home last week.

MAY 15TH

I have a lot of homework to do! Today I observed a lesson on heroes in a second-grade classroom. I think these students might know more about history than I do. First, the teacher read a fun and interesting picture book titled, *Thank You, Sarah: The Woman Who Saved Thanksgiving* (Anderson, 2002). The students had a lively discussion about the story. One student said that Sarah Hale reminded him of Esther Morris who helped women get the vote in Wyoming. Later, I asked the teacher who Esther Morris was and how that student knew about her. The teacher said they had read a book about Morris earlier in the year when they studied the election process, and students learned about voting rights.

After the book discussion, the teacher created a graphic organizer on the white board by writing the word "courage" at the center of a web. She asked students if they could name other people, like Sarah Hale, who used courage to make a positive difference in this world. At first, I expected students to call out, "my mom" or "my dad." Instead, they named George Washington, Amelia Earhart, Harriet Tubman, Rosa Parks, Cesar Chavez, Martin Luther King, Jr., the Wright brothers, Jackie Robinson, Christopher Columbus, Georgia O'Keeffe, Amelia Stewart Knight, and Gandhi. Gandhi! How do second graders know about Gandhi? And Georgia O'Keeffe? It became very clear to me that these students are very interested in learning about life and quite knowledgeable about history—in all of its diversity. Social studies has a prominent place in this classroom, and these students are very fortunate to have a teacher who provides opportunities to learn about real people and important events. I think it takes a lot of courage for teachers today to teach social studies. This teacher's name belongs on that web with Jackie Robinson and Amelia Earhart!

BUILDING A CASE FOR SOCIAL STUDIES IN THE CLASSROOM

What motivates a teacher to teach social studies? What are the benefits of teaching social studies? Why are some teachers more effective in teaching this content area than others? These are important questions for you to consider.

Speaking with teachers who are not motivated and who do not find time to teach social studies, you might hear one of the following excuses:

- My district puts so much emphasis on literacy and math that I simply do not have the time to teach social studies. I'm told to spend 3 1/2 hours on reading and 1 1/2 hours on math. Then there is not much time left and I still have science, physical education, art, and health to think about!

- I never liked social studies myself, and so I don't spend a lot of time on it. There are other teachers who like teaching social studies and do a much better job. The students know it's not my favorite subject.

- The textbook is too hard for students to read, and I don't have enough time to create lessons and gather materials for everything I'm supposed to teach. So I just skip it. When I get more time and a better textbook, maybe I will teach more social studies.

Figure 2.1

Source: www.cartoonstock.com

- I did not learn a lot of this information when I was in school. I have to read ahead and learn more about this history and stuff. Then I will get around to teaching it. I can't teach information that I don't know, right? What if the students ask questions and I don't even know the answers?

- We don't assess students in social studies. So why should I teach a subject that no one else cares about? If anyone in our district, state, or nation cared about social studies, we would have high-stakes tests at each grade level, right?

Unfortunately, these are the kinds of comments that are heard in elementary schools across the nation. A focus on literacy and mathematics has dominated the curriculum since the Back to Basics movement in the 1970s. So, this is not necessarily a brand new concern or issue. With

Information on the history of the social studies educational movement can be found in Chapter 1.

Book Links

Biographies, poetry, and historical fiction can bring historical characters to life in your classroom. Identifying themes, such as courage, can generate informed discussions after students read such titles as *Thank You, Sarah: The Woman Who Saved Thanksgiving* (Anderson), *George Washington's Teeth* (Chandra), and *Who Was Amelia Earhart?* (Jerome).

increased, high-stakes testing in literacy and mathematics in recent years, however, the concern has become even greater. In the growing absence of social studies, what are the consequences? What evidence do we have to show that a weak, limited, or absent social studies curriculum is worth our time and attention? These are more important questions to consider as you continue to learn what social studies is, how it can be taught, and why it is an essential component of a student's education.

We have had our own students—at the elementary, middle school, and college levels—ask, "Why do we have to learn this?" One fifth-grade student even added, "All these people are dead, you know!" Several students in our social studies methods courses at the university have added, "No one teaches social studies anymore, anyhow."

Walter Parker (2000), Professor and Program Chair for Social Studies Education at the University of Washington, responded to teachers when confronted with the question, "Why teach social studies?" by saying:

- Without history, there can be no wisdom;
- Without geography, there can be no understanding of people and places—no social intelligence; and
- Without citizenship, there can be no democracy—no government of, by and for the people.

What is your reaction to this message? What do you think about the importance of social studies education?

We heard Parker present this statement to a group of teachers in a large urban school district. Unfortunately, the workshop was voluntary and the group was quite small. We had hoped that every teacher in this district would not only hear Parker's message, but take it to heart, expand, and share the message. In fact, we use his statement frequently in our own work and even add:

- Without economics, there can be no reasonable decision making; and
- Without social studies, there can be little use for literacy.

This last statement leads us back to our beginning. Why did we decide to write this book? This is our opportunity to advocate for a more

Thomas Jefferson—historical archives
Source: *Library of Congress*

informed citizenry—students who not only possess the skills and motivation to read, write, listen, and speak well, but students who recognize
their potential as citizens of their communities. Without past and
present understandings of law, politics, society, business, cultures,
economics, and geography, how will today's students effectively shape
tomorrow's world? Parker's message is not just for you, the teacher,
but it is intended for you to share each and every day with your students as well.

Parker's ideas echo the words of our founders who debated and ultimately framed public education in America. Thomas Jefferson wrote,
"I know of no safe depository of the ultimate powers of society but the
people themselves; and if we think them not enlightened enough to exercise their control with a wholesome discretion, the remedy is not to
take power from them, but to inform their discretion through instruction" (Carroll, 1997). Jefferson went so far as to propose that students
at the elementary stages of education learn to read by reading history
(see History's Finer Points in this chapter).

Kevin Colleary, a social studies professor at Fordham University, explains that social studies instruction helps students begin to understand
their relationship to other people, and to social and political institutions. He believes that through social studies, students learn to build
respect for those who are different from themselves and begin to learn

ways to take action to change their world. Colleary (2004) contends that these important foundations for life may not occur in other curricular areas, and therefore teachers must be diligent in offering explicit social studies instruction for all students.

James Banks, Professor at the University of Washington and Director of the Center for Multicultural Education, also states that social studies is important because its goals include helping students become effective citizens in our diverse nation and world. He notes, "To become productive citizens in a pluralistic democratic society, students must acquire the knowledge, attitudes, and skills needed to work effectively with individuals from different racial, ethnic, cultural, language, and religious groups" (2004, p. 1). Banks, widely known for his research and expertise in multicultural education, states that diversity offers both opportunities and challenges to our nation and to our social studies teachers. Through the teaching of social studies and the inclusion of diverse voices from history, students are better able to recognize stereotypes, misconceptions, and negative attitudes toward racial, ethnic, and social-class groups. As a result, research shows that students who are engaged in studies using multicultural texts, other teaching materials, and cooperative learning structures with other students from diverse backgrounds develop more democratic racial attitudes and choose more friends from outside racial, ethnic, and cultural groups (Slavin, 2001).

When school is viewed as a microcosm of society at large, as a place for students to develop social skills, gain an understanding of how the world works, and learn how to contribute to society in positive, meaningful ways, there is no question that social studies is an important part of children's education. National education reform goals established through an Education Summit in 1989 included the following goal:

> American students will leave grades four, eight, and twelve having demonstrated competency in challenging subject matter including English, mathematics, science, history, and geography; and every school in America will ensure that all students learn to use their minds well, so they may be prepared for responsible citizenship, further learning, and productive employment in our modern economy.

In 1994, the U.S. Congress added foreign languages, civics and government, economics, and arts to the list of subjects in which students will demonstrate competency. These goals responded, in part, to reports that students seldom performed community service and voter turnout among 18-to-20-year-olds was low. Achievement data that was presented in reading, mathematics, and science to highlight the importance of this goal was not, interestingly enough, available in social studies. Another of the six goals agreed upon by our nation's governors and educational leaders during the 1989 Education Summit included:

You can find information about Dr. Banks and the Center for Multicultural Education at the Web Links module in Chapter 2 on your Companion Website at www.prenhall.com/schell.

History Connections

1994 was also the year that the U.S. government privatized Internet management. How different might the world be had this not occurred?

Every adult American will be literate and will possess the knowledge and skills necessary to compete in a global economy and exercise the rights and responsibilities of citizenship.

Again, we see the important connection between literacy and social studies highlighted during the age of educational reform.

Our nation's governors, in cooperation with the White House and Congress, adopted these six National Education Goals in attempt to revitalize and improve public education in the U.S. These goals were folded into President Bush's America 2000 proposals in 1990–1992 for educational reform, and also President Clinton's Goals 2000: Educate America legislation in 1994. Clinton's plan presented eight educational goals and kept the goals of student achievement and citizenship, including:

By the year 2000, all students will leave grades 4, 8, and 12 having demonstrated competency over challenging subject matter including English, mathematics, science, foreign languages, civics and government, economics, arts, history, and geography, and every school in America will ensure that all students learn to use their minds well, so they may be prepared for responsible citizenship, further learning, and productive employment in our Nation's modern economy.

Additionally, the goal of literacy and lifelong learning was presented as:

By the year 2000, every adult American will be literate and will possess the knowledge and skills necessary to compete in a global economy and exercise the rights and responsibilities of citizenship.

These goals became supported with funding, specificity, and accountability through the Improving America's Schools Act of 1994 and later the No Child Left Behind (NCLB) Act of 2001. Although the United States maintains a decentralized education system, as established through the 10th Amendment to the U.S. Constitution, which states: "The powers not delegated to the United States by the Constitution, nor prohibited by it to the States, are reserved to the States," federal and state leadership continue to insist upon the inclusion of social studies for the purposes of student academic achievement, citizenship, and literacy.

The website www.congress.org provides information about current bills being considered, the names and addresses of current members of congress, and a "soapbox" where people can share their thinking about current events.

In Chapter 1, we provided the website for information about NCLB. Links to the criticisms of NCLB can also be found at the Web Links module in Chapter 2 on our Companion Website at www.prenhall.com/schell.

Book Links

Books can help students understand people who have stood up for their rights and the rights of others, including *Harriet and the Promised Land* (Lawrence), *Rosa* (Giovanni), *Martin's Big Words: The Life of Dr. Martin Luther King, Jr.* (Rappaport), and *Gandhi* (Demi).

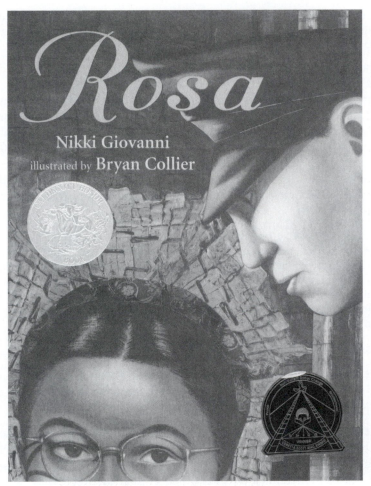

Source: *Cover from* Rosa *by Nikki Giovanni.*

OUR NATION'S REPORT CARD

Since 1969, the National Assessment of Educational Progress (NAEP) has provided data on student achievement in our schools. Also known as "the nation's report card," the NAEP tests are coordinated under the direction of the U.S. Department of Education and the National Center for Educational Statistics. NAEP tests are developed using approved frameworks for each of the 11 specified content areas. In the field of social studies, NAEP tests are administered in the areas of U.S. history, geography, and civics. Each of these tests is administered to students at grades 4, 8, and 12. Beginning in 2006, a NAEP test in economics will be administered at the 12th grade. By 2010, a 12th-grade test in world history is also expected.

Figure 2.2   Recent NAEP data.

Grade Level	At or Above Proficient in U.S. History (1994; 2001)	At or Above Proficient in Geography (1994; 2001)	At or Above Proficient in Civics (1998)
4	17%; 18%	22%; 21%	23%
8	14%; 17%	28%; 30%	22%
12	11%; 11%	27%; 25%	26%

These tests are administered in 4- to 7-year cycles, provided there is funding for these "other subject areas." This way, each content area is not assessed each year. Students are randomly selected for NAEP assessment from both public and private schools, and since states have their own curriculum standards and frameworks, these assessment data do not always reflect what students are learning in their classrooms. Still, long-term growth indicators of what general knowledge students display about U.S. history, geography, and civics are worth discussion (see Figure 2.2).

What conclusions can you draw from the NAEP data? The reports yield important data that we believe helps build an argument for increased and improved social studies programs, such as:

- Although most students have a basic knowledge of civics, it is apparent that their understanding of civics could be strengthened. For example, at the fourth-grade level, 74 percent of the students knew that in the United States, laws must be applied to everyone equally. Only 15 percent were able to name two services that the government pays for with taxes.

- At the eighth-grade level, 81 percent of the students identified Martin Luther King as someone who was concerned about the injustice of segregation laws. Only 6 percent were able to describe two ways that countries benefit from having a constitution.

- At the 12th-grade level, 90 percent of the students understood that Social Security is an issue of primary concern to the elderly. Only 9 percent of the students could list two ways that democratic society benefits from the active participation of its citizens.

- At grade 4, a large majority of students had teachers who reported having them read from a textbook on a daily basis or weekly basis. Reading from a textbook daily was associated with higher scores in the assessment than was doing so weekly or monthly.

- At grade 8, students whose teachers reported using primary historical documents—such as letters, diaries, or essays written by historical figures—once or twice per week had higher scores than those whose teachers reported doing so less frequently or never.

Detailed information about the tests, disaggregated data, and results can be found at the NAEP website, accessible via the Web Links module in Chapter 2 on our Companion Website at www. prenhall.com/schell.

History Connections

As popularized in the film *Good Night and Good Luck* (2005), in the early 1950s the media was generally fearful of questioning the tactics of Senator Joseph McCarthy of Wisconsin, because they might be tried as Communists for simply asking questions. McCarthy's threat of Communism created paranoia in the United States. CBS reporter Edward R. Murrow and his producer Fred Friendly decided to take a stand, challenge McCarthy, and expose him for the fearmonger he was.

- Eighth- and twelfth-graders who never or hardly ever studied countries and cultures had lower scores, on average, than students who did so at least once or twice a month or more.

Some argue that students who do not receive explicit instruction in social studies will "pick it up" through the media, including books, television, and movies. However, NAEP data (and better understandings of what social studies really is) serves to contradict that belief. More specifically, we worry that students who are not taught historical analysis and thinking skills will be reduced to consumers of information that has been filtered by the media.

We believe that these and other data clearly indicate that more time, attention, leadership, and resources should be focused on improving student achievement in social studies across the grades and throughout the nation.

BUILDING A CASE IN THE COMMUNITY

Why is it necessary to convince legislators, community leaders, and educators that teaching social studies is vital to the education of students? The work of many professional organizations has turned to lobbying for both curricular acknowledgment and resources. For example, the absence of an accountability system for social studies in the No Child Left Behind legislation has caused professional organizations to ask, "Why?" This legislation requires statewide assessments and student proficiency in literacy, mathematics and science, but leaves one core content area behind.

As educators speak against local, state, and national practices and policies that eliminate or diminish social studies, they argue that our students need the following:

1. *Balance.* A well-rounded, balanced curriculum includes more than reading, writing, and mathematics. As many students rise through the grade levels in an education system that focuses primarily on two subject areas, they are the first to say, "I'm bored" and ask, "Is this all there is?" or "When will I do more than read, write, and calculate?" A balanced curriculum includes not only social studies and science, but also music, drama, art, dance, physical education, health, technology, and more (McDonald & Fisher, 2006). Without "real content" (as social studies is often called), what good are literacy and mathematical skills in this world for which we are preparing our students?

2. *Knowledge.* If our students are to make informed decisions for the public good, how will they ever understand "public good" without social studies? How will they make informed decisions without

Geographic, economic, and historical understandings become represented in this fourth-grade artist's rendering and presentation of Mission San Buenaventura.
Source: *Emily Schell*

knowledge about how others have responded to issues in the past? Knowledge is required of students to participate in today's economy. Knowledge is useful for students who interact with the environment to find places, understand ecosystems, and make choices about conservation. Knowledge of society's laws and mores helps our youth make the right decisions before facing the consequences of breaking them. Knowledge of one's own history and culture allows for better understandings of others' histories and cultures as well.

3. *Useful Skills.* The skills embedded in a good social studies program empower a student to locate, analyze, and evaluate information carefully, separate fact from opinion, compare and contrast data, discuss ideas intelligently, present information, and work collaboratively with others. Social studies helps students learn how to effectively read maps, charts, and graphs for information, and it encourages students to make decisions, choose carefully, and take action. These skills are crucial for students' success in life as they face choices about work, family, friends, and life. Ultimately,

these students exercise their skills when they vote for our community, state, and local leaders and policies. Without social studies, what skills and criteria will today's youth use when they go to the polls?

4. *Citizenship.* What does it mean to be a citizen of one's classroom, school, local community, nation, and global community? If we leave these questions out of our curriculum, and if students are not provided an educational forum to learn, discuss, and debate the roles and responsibilities of citizenship, what might we expect of these citizens? Beyond voting, citizens maintain a plethora of rights and responsibilities in American society. By studying the past, we can learn how these rights came to be, we can learn what happens when people's rights are restricted, and we can learn how to uphold our rights through responsible citizenship. If not during social studies instruction, then when will our students learn these important concepts?

School boards are elected by the community and are charged with overseeing the operation of public schools. For more information about school boards, see the Web Links module in Chapter 2 on our Companion Website at www. prenhall.com/schell.

Recently, we were asked to present information to a local school board about social studies. Naturally, as advocates for social studies, we jumped at the opportunity. The school board had just elected new members and decided to hold special board meetings for each of the five core content areas (English language arts, mathematics, science, social studies, and visual and performing arts). For each meeting, the district hired a specialist to speak about what should occur in K–12 classrooms, then the district officials reported what was happening in classrooms, and finally the public was invited to make comments before the school board decided on any action. Prior to our meeting about social studies, the meetings about science and mathematics had been well attended and lasted for several hours before the board finally halted public comments and took action. When the social studies meeting was held, only a handful of people attended, and the meeting ended before its scheduled 2-hour time limit. We had taken the time to prepare and present at this meeting because we feel passionate about the importance of social studies. We were disappointed, though not surprised, at the minimal support (or even outrage) exhibited by the community. Social studies has become so minimized in this district that teachers find it difficult to muster up support in this or any public forum.

We share this anecdote because you are entering your career as an educator. You will make decisions about what is important to you and to your students. These decisions will be reflected in your daily lesson plans, your ongoing unit plans, and your voice at staff meetings, district meetings, and professional conferences. If you recognize the importance of informed and decisive citizens who serve the public good, then you will teach for and model this through your actions as an educator. Consider the following avenues for building your knowledge, skills, and opportunities to advocate for strong social studies programs:

- Volunteer to serve as the site or district lead teacher or department chairperson for social studies;
- Gather, share, and facilitate discussions about social studies lessons, resources, programs, assessments, and so on;
- Participate in district workshops, institutes, and conferences at the local, state, and national levels that support social studies education;
- Present your great ideas and students' work at staff meetings, parent meetings, workshops, and conferences;
- Start an after-school club for students interested in social studies and arrange for speakers, field studies to historic or public sites, and participation in cultural events;
- Explore travel opportunities (contact companies such as World Strides and Educational Field Studies) as well as local field studies to historic sites for your class or grade level;
- Start a book club that features historical fiction, nonfiction, biographies, and other social studies titles;
- Subscribe to professional journals and social studies publications, such as *National Geographic, Smithsonian,* and *Time* (as well as the publications for children);
- Start a professional library at your school site that features professional journals, such as *Social Studies and the Young Learner, Social Education, History Matters!,* and *Magazine of History,* as well as readings that promote the teaching of social studies;
- Join professional organizations, including the local affiliations to the National Council for the Social Studies, your state geographic alliance, local economic education organizations, and more;
- Bookmark websites that will keep you informed about this field, such as NCSS (www.ncss.org), NCHE (www.garlandind.com/nche), Center for Civic Education (www.civiced.org), National Geographic (www.nationalgeographic.com), and the History Channel (www.historychannel.com);
- Celebrate "Make History Strong in Our Schools Day" on April 19 to raise awareness about the importance of social studies education;
- Celebrate Geographic Awareness Week (third week in November) to raise awareness about the importance of social studies education;
- Provide opportunities for your students to showcase and celebrate their social studies knowledge and skills through class, school, and district events as well as organized student programs, such as

National History Day, National Geographic Bee, Project Citizen, Mock Trial, or We the People;

• Volunteer to participate in district committees that relate to social studies, including committees for textbook adoption, assessment development, and so forth.

Through your teaching, sharing, and questioning among colleagues and in political circles, you can and will make a difference. The best advocates we have for social studies are the students themselves. However, in the absence of social studies, we have seen fewer students participating in community events such as Renaissance Faires, History Day competitions, and Geography Olympiads. Consider ways to present historical plays, simulated events, and real issues to parents and the community. Explore opportunities to showcase student work on your school website or in other public venues. Show what good social studies looks like in your classroom and can look like in others'.

History Day projects reflect students' thematic research and understandings based on primary sources, chronology, and historical interpretation.
Source: *Emily Schell*

APPEALING CONTENT

Frequently, we hear from teachers who want to know what to do now that their principal or district official has stated, "No more social studies." Yes, this does happen, mostly when administrators or school board members subscribe to the notion that students can only raise their literacy and mathematics test scores when other content areas, such as social studies, are eliminated from the instructional day.

Using the national social studies standards (NCSS, 1992) strands, we suggest that teachers respond by asking these very important questions:

- When will our students study about cultures and cultural diversity?
- When will our students study the ways human beings view themselves in and over time?
- When will students be able to learn about real people, places, and environments?
- How will students learn about identities and individual development?
- Who will teach our students about interactions among individuals, groups, and institutions?
- Who will teach our students about how people create and change structures of power, authority, and governance?
- How will our students learn about how people organize for the production, distribution, and consumption of goods and services?
- When will our students learn about the important relationships among science, technology, and society?
- Who will provide opportunities for our students to study about global connections and interdependence?
- When will our students learn about the ideals, principles, and practices of citizenship in this democratic republic?

Identifying the important themes of social studies is often a better argument than asking these "when" and "how" questions relative to specific histories. It is often these same administrators and board members who recall boring and less meaningful lessons about the Civil War or the history of their state. Reframing the purpose and importance of social studies through these appealing themes embraces the specific content while building a case for informed, critically thinking, socially active students in our classrooms and communities.

In some cases, responses to the foregoing questions might be, "Students can learn about that through their reading." When this door is opened, walk right in! That is what the remainder of this book prepares you for. However, for students to actively engage in their social studies readings (textbooks, documents, articles, poems, picture books, historical novels, etc.), there will need to be space for teaching historical thinking and analysis skills—or, social studies!

Write a letter to the editor of your local newspaper about the importance of social studies education. Even if you don't send it, it's a good way to clarify your thinking on this issue.

History Connections

The "tipping point" for the reelection of Abraham Lincoln as President was the fall of Atlanta. That event galvanized people to vote for Lincoln. The website civilwarmini.com contains Civil War trivia, terms, a primer, and information about "America's greatest catastrophe."

Book Links

Invite students to consider worlds they will never see by sharing any of the following: *To Fly: The Story of the Wright Brothers* (Old), *Teammates* (Golenbock), *If You Were There in 1492: Everyday Life in the Time of Christopher Columbus* (Brenner), *My Name is Georgia: A Portrait* (Winter), or *The Way West: Journal of a Pioneer Woman* (Knight).

Conclusion

Why teach social studies? This is a question for you to answer on your own and continue to ask and answer as you move forward in your career as an educator. Your reasons may change over time, but we doubt you will ever run out of reasons why this important subject area deserves a prominent place in your classroom and in every classroom.

History's Finer Points

Thomas Jefferson argued fiercely for a free, common education for all young citizens. He had much to say about the importance of a general education that included history, geography, and philosophy, including:

The most effectual means of preventing tyranny is to illuminate, as far as practicable, the minds of the people at large, and more especially to give them knowledge of those facts, which history exhibiteth, that possessed thereby of the experience of other ages and countries, they may be able to know ambition under all its shapes, and prompt to exert their natural powers to defeat its purposes.

But all the views of this law relating to popular education none is more important, none more legitimate, than that of rendering the people the safe, as they are the ultimate, guardians of their own liberties. For this purpose the reading in the first stage, where they will receive their whole education, is proposed to be chiefly historical. History, by apprising them of the past, will enable them to judge of the future; it will avail them of the experience of other times and other nations; it will qualify them as judges of the actions and designs of men; it will enable them to know ambition under every disguise it may assume; and knowing it to defeat its views.

Document Based Question (DBQ): How much progress have we made in "preventing tyranny" since Jefferson wrote this?

Visit the History's Finer Points module in Chapter 2 on our Companion Website at www.prenhall.com/schell to answer this question.

Questions to Consider

1. What is your role in advocating for social studies education?
2. Why do students need a comprehensive, well-rounded education that includes social studies, as well as the arts, physical education, and science?
3. What does the NAEP assessment data tell you about social studies education and the future?

Quiz yourself on this chapter's important concepts on our Companion Website's Chapter self-assessments at www.prenhall.com/schell.

Exercises

Consider the following exercises to help build your personal understandings about why social studies should be taught every day and for every child.

1. Analyze several teachers' plans for teaching social studies. Compare and contrast the amount of time spent, the quality of the lessons, and the accountability for student learning.
2. Interview the school principal or instructional leader and ask about the site or district plan that outlines the expectations and accountability for social studies instruction. Develop interview questions such as:
   a. What have you observed in classrooms that pertains to social studies?
   b. What do you look for in a quality social studies program?
   c. How much professional development is designated to social studies?
   d. How would you summarize social studies instruction at your school?
   e. Why do you think social studies is important?
3. Gather and analyze student work in social studies. Answer such questions as:
   a. What knowledge and skills are evident in this student work?
   b. How will this knowledge and these skills be helpful for these students' future?

c. How might I improve on this assignment to make social studies more meaningful for the students?

References

Banks, J. (2004). *What research says about diversity*. New York: Macmillan McGraw-Hill.

Carroll, A. (Ed.). (1997). *Letters of a nation*. New York: Broadway Books.

Colleary, K. (2004). *Social studies every day for every child*. New York: Macmillan McGraw-Hill.

Harrison, M., & Gilbert, S. (Eds.). (1993). *Thomas Jefferson: In his own words*. New York: Excellent Books.

McDonald, N. L., & Fisher, D. (2006). *Teaching literacy through the arts*. New York: Guilford.

National Assessment of Educational Progress (Civics, Geo, US History). Available at: http://nces.ed.gov/nationsreportcard.

National Council for the Social Studies. (1992). *Curriculum standards for social studies*. Silver Spring, MD: Author.

Parker, W. (2000). *Teaching with concepts*. Presented at the San Diego Unified School District.

Slavin, R. E. (2001). Cooperative learning and inter-group relations. In J. A. Banks and C. A. M. Banks (Eds.), *Handbook of research on multicultural education* (pp. 628–634). San Francisco: Jossey-Bass.

U.S. Department of Education. (1994). *Progress of education in the United States of America—1990 through 1994*. Retrieved January 28, 2006, from http://www.ed.gov/pubs/Prog95/index.html.

Children's Literature

Anderson, L. H. (2002). *Thank you, Sarah: The woman who saved Thanksgiving*. New York: Simon & Schuster.

Brenner, B. (1998). *If you were there in 1492: Everyday life in the time of Christopher Columbus*. New York: Aladdin.

Chandra, D. (2003). *George Washington's teeth*. Farrar, Straus and Giroux.

Demi. (2001). *Gandhi*. New York: Margaret K. McElderry.

Giovanni, N. (2005). *Rosa*. New York: Henry Holt and Company.

Golenbock, P. (1992). *Teammates*. Marlton, NJ: Voyager Books.

Jerome, K. B. (2002). *Who was Amelia Earhart?* New York: Grosset & Dunlap.

Knight, A. (1993). *The way west: Journal of a pioneer woman.* New York: Simon & Schuster.

Lawrence, J. (1997). *Harriet and the promised land.* New York: Aladdin.

Old, W. (2002). *To fly: The story of the Wright brothers.* New York: Clarion.

Rappaport, D. (2001). *Martin's big words: The life of Dr. Martin Luther King, Jr.* New York: Jump at the Sun.

Winter, J. (1998). *My name is Georgia: A portrait.* New York: Silver Whistle.

What Do We Teach in Social Studies?

Source: *Scott Cunningham/ Merrill*

Big Idea

Teachers and students should have a clear understanding of what they are teaching and learning before they set out to do so.

Essential Question

What informs our decisions about what to teach?

Ms. Maxin asked Mr. Pham, her new student teacher, to plan to take over social studies in the coming week. Mr. Pham had completed his social studies methods course during the previous semester and had general ideas about what constitutes social studies. However, now that he was student teaching in a third-grade class, he was unsure about what specifically to teach and where to start in his planning. So, he asked Ms. Maxin for some help.

Mr. Pham asked, "What guides your teaching of social studies at this grade level and in this district? Have you mapped out the entire year's social studies curriculum? What have the students learned already this year? Where do they need to be by the end of this school year? Do you prefer to teach social studies separately or to integrate it with other subjects? How much time do you devote to social studies? What textbook and materials are available for my planning and teaching?"

Pleased that he would ask so many important questions, Ms. Maxin sat down and shared her plans, materials, and ideas with Mr. Pham. She started by outlining the state standards for third grade, summarized what students were expected to learn in second grade, described what they needed to be prepared for in fourth grade, and then presented the district's guidelines for teaching standards-based social studies. Next, she showed Mr. Pham her file of books, articles, and notes about research-based practices collected over several years, and explained the notes and tabs that she had made in the social studies teacher's guide. Ms. Maxin also explained the connections between her classroom management system and the third-grade social studies content and skills—focusing students on the importance of making good decisions about their work and behaviors that benefit the common good of the class.

The two teachers worked together to ensure a smooth transition between different teachers teaching to the same set of goals and learning objectives. These goals and objectives were outlined in the state standards, analyzed and reorganized into Big Ideas and Essential Questions by Ms. Maxin and her third-grade colleagues, and mapped out for the school year. Ms. Maxin explained that other teachers were teaching at about the same pace as this class, so Mr. Pham was welcome to observe or learn from teachers in neighboring third-grade classrooms.

Mr. Pham left the meeting both nervous and excited about planning for this important area of the curriculum. He also left with an appreciation for the work already accomplished by Ms. Maxin and the other third-grade teachers at their school site. He had even more questions about this process of analyzing the standards, unpacking them, and determining the Big Ideas and Essential Questions. He wondered if all schools took such an organized and common-sense approach to planning for social studies instruction.

WHAT EXACTLY DO WE TEACH IN SOCIAL STUDIES?

As you have learned from previous chapters, social studies can be seen as overwhelming and all-encompassing. When considering what we teach in social studies, we can begin with the overarching definition that guides our understandings of what we teach at each grade level. The National Council for the Social Studies (1992), a professional organization of social studies educators, defines social studies in the following manner:

> Social studies is the integrated study of the social sciences and humanities to promote civic competence. Within the school program, social studies provides coordinated, systematic study drawing upon such disciplines as anthropology, archaeology, economics, geography, history, law, philosophy, political science, psychology, religion, and sociology, as well as appropriate content from the humanities, mathematics, and the natural sciences. The primary purpose of the social studies is to help young people develop the ability to make informed and reasoned decisions for the public good as citizens of a culturally diverse, democratic society in an interdependent world.

To better understand this definition, we recommend that you divide the statement into three sections:

Although specific state content standards guide the grade-level content, social studies educators must also remember their goals in providing students with access to this information.

1. **Social studies is the integrated study of the social sciences and humanities to promote civic competence.** To begin understanding social studies, we must focus on the term *integrated*. The integration, or bringing together, of the sciences as well as the liberal arts, such as language and literature, suggests a wide and connected body of information to study (Jacobs, 2004). Drawing from this enormous amount of information from virtually all of the academic disciplines, we are directed to a purpose for studying this information—to promote civic competence. What does this mean? To be civic-minded means to take an active interest in the needs and affairs of a community. To have competence suggests having the abilities to do something well. Therefore, to have civic competence means to understand and perform well the duties and obligations of a contributing member of the community. It is through integrated studies and for the

purpose of promoting civic competence that we better understand our role as social studies teachers at each grade level regardless of the topics, themes, concepts, or eras assigned to that grade level.

2. **Within the school program, social studies provides coordinated, systematic study drawing upon such disciplines as anthropology, archaeology, economics, geography, history, law, philosophy, political science, psychology, religion, and sociology, as well as appropriate content from the humanities, mathematics, and the natural sciences.** We like to begin deconstructing this portion of the definition by asking, "What does *not* qualify as a topic of study in social studies?" This description implies that everything under the sun can be used in the teaching and learning of social studies—art, music, math, science, literature, history, philosophy, religion, and more. If social studies is the study of society—its people, land, institutions, and practices—throughout time and place, then it should include every facet of life. However, we draw your attention to the beginning of the sentence in this part of the definition. The definition states that social studies is a school program that is coordinated and systematic. In other words, drawing from the expansive content, schools create programs to organize and systematically teach the content to students. This is where we recognize the value of curriculum frameworks, standards, and guides that are created with the continuum from kindergarten through high school in mind. No teacher can simply teach to all of these disciplines with his or her own determined topics while ensuring that students receive a comprehensive, meaningful social studies education. Organization and coordination are essential.

3. **The primary purpose of the social studies is to help young people develop the ability to make informed and reasoned decisions for the public good as citizens of a culturally diverse, democratic society in an interdependent world.** Finally, the glue that helps unite our understandings for teaching social studies, and the motivation for teaching with a purpose. The words *primary purpose* acknowledge the multiple purposes for learning social studies and highlight the importance of preparing students for the decisions they face as citizens. If we want to learn from the past, contribute positively in the present, and provide for a better future, knowledge and reason must prevail as we recognize that we live in a culturally diverse, democratic society in an interdependent world. Exploration of what is meant by the "public good" in both its historic and its contemporary sense will continually challenge students to learn, critically analyze, and evaluate detailed information in their quest for understanding. Best of all, students become empowered to apply what they have learned through their daily interactions inside and outside of the classroom.

This all-inclusive description of social studies presents teachers with the overwhelming task of teaching "everything" about people, places,

Many teachers are nervous about addressing religion in the classroom. Interestingly, religion has been the rationale for much of what we study in school—from wars to Supreme Court nominations. It is important to understand that in social studies, we teach about religion as it naturally arises in studies of history. Information on teaching about religion can be found in the Web Links module in Chapter 3 on our Companion Website at www.prenhall.com/schell.

History Connections

The first public school in America was established by Puritan settlers in 1635 in the home of Schoolmaster Philemon Pormont. Benjamin Franklin, Samuel Adams, and John Hancock once attended this school.

time, and events. We tell our students that social studies is the study of society, which entails all aspects of life—where it exists, how is has evolved, why some ideas, objects, systems, and lives have survived while others have not, and what this means for our current and future existence as a people. When teachers see that social studies is simply about life, this provides both a sense of security and a sense of anxiety. Security in that we are all participants in "life" and have a large base of knowledge and experience from which to draw. Anxiety because "life" is nonspecific and takes us in a variety of directions, making for nonlinear, multifaceted teaching and learning.

So how do we make sense of social studies and teach in a coordinated, systematic manner that allows students to build a foundation early in life and then add important details in later years? Fortunately, there are several resources that present ideas and guidance for educators (Figure 3.1).

Figure 3.1

Source: www.cartoonstock.com.

NATIONAL FRAMEWORKS AND STANDARDS

The National Assessment of Educational Progress (NAEP) is the only nationally representative and continuing assessment of what America's students should know in such content areas as U.S. history, geography, and civics (since 1976, there has been no NAEP framework or assessment for social studies). The U.S. Department of Education and the National Center for Education Statistics are responsible for carrying out the NAEP project, which is authorized by law, but the National Assessment Governing Board, appointed by the Secretary of Education, is responsible for developing frameworks for each NAEP discipline. These frameworks describe what students should know and be able to do by grades 4, 8, and 12 and become the foundation for the development of NAEP assessments. For example, according to the NAEP framework for U.S. history, students at grades 4, 8, and 12 should be knowledgeable about all periods of U.S. history. The framework presents this recommended coordination of study and measures student knowledge and skills with assessments at these grade levels in three dimensions:

- *Themes:* Four historical themes are the core organizing structure of the framework. These themes are intended to cover all major branches and periods of historical study, and are used to compare assessment data among subgroups:
  1. Change and continuity in American democracy: ideas, institutions, practices, and controversies;
  2. The gathering and interactions of peoples, cultures, and ideas;
  3. Economic and technological changes and their relation to society, ideas, and the environment; and
  4. The changing role of America in the world.
- *Chronological Periods:* Eight chronological periods are used to ensure appropriate chronological coverage in the studies and assessment of U.S. history knowledge. These periods focus attention on major eras and events in our nation's history:
  1. Three worlds and their meeting in the Americas (beginnings to 1607);
  2. Colonization, settlement, and communities (1607 to 1763);
  3. The Revolution and the new nation (1763 to 1815);
  4. Expansion and reform (1801 to 1861);
  5. Crisis of the Union: Civil War and Reconstruction (1850 to 1877);
  6. The development of modern America (1865 to 1920);
  7. Modern America and the World Wars (1914 to 1945); and
  8. Contemporary America (1945 to present).
- *Ways of Knowing and Thinking:* The framework identifies two ways of knowing and thinking about U.S. history, which are used to develop assessment questions:

Figure 3.2   Distribution of study and assessment time across historical themes

Grade	Change and Continuity in American Democracy: Ideas, Institutions, Practices, and Controversies	The Gathering and Interactions of Peoples, Cultures, and Ideas	Economic and Technological Changes and their Relation to Society, Ideas, and the Environment	The Changing Role of America in the World
4	25%	32%	32%	12%
8	30%	32%	25%	13%
12	28%	26%	22%	25%

1. *Historical knowledge and perspective* includes knowing and understanding people, events, concepts, themes, movements, contexts, and historical sources; sequencing events; recognizing multiple perspectives and seeing an era or movement through the eyes of different groups; and developing a general conceptualization of U.S. history.
2. *Historical analysis and interpretation* includes explaining issues; identifying historical patterns; establishing cause-and-effect relationships; finding value statements; establishing significance; applying historical knowledge; weighing evidence to draw sound conclusions; making defensible generalizations; and rendering insightful accounts of the past.

The U.S. History framework even presents suggested weights, or distributions of time, to these areas in the study and assessment of each of these three dimensions (see Figures 3.2, 3.3, and 3.4).

The national standards for teaching social studies, history, geography, economics, and civics each present their own suggestions for organizing

Figure 3.3   Distribution of study and assessment time across historical periods

Grade	Beginnings to 1607	1606 to 1763	1763 to 1815	1801 to 1861	1850 to 1877	1865 to 1920	1914 to 1945	1945 to Present	No Specific Period
4	13%	14%	11%	14%	9%	13%	7%	10%	9%
8	3%	7%	18%	9%	8%	18%	14%	10%	12%
12	1%	8%	9%	11%	7%	11%	32%	20%	1%

Figure 3.4 Targeted distribution of study and assessment time across cognitive domains

Grade	Historical Knowledge and Perspective	Historical Analysis and Interpretation
4	40%	60%
8	35%	65%
12	30%	70%

the content in kindergarten through 12th grade. The national standards for social studies (NCSS, 1994), for example, recommend that teachers integrate important themes in their organization of social studies content. These themes serve as organizing strands for social studies curriculum at every grade level:

1. Culture
2. Time, Continuity, and Change
3. People, Places, and Environments
4. Individual Development and Identity
5. Individuals, Groups, and Institutions
6. Power, Authority, and Governance
7. Production, Distribution, and Consumption
8. Science, Technology, and Society
9. Global Connections
10. Civic Ideals and Practices

For example, a class learning about its state's history and geography (usually at the fourth or fifth grade according to most states' frameworks or standards) might use these themes while studying sequential units that identify the people and development of cultures within and across the state; develop a chronological timeline of historical events that shaped the state over time and show both continuity and change in demographics, industry, and political boundaries; define the environments and how people have interacted with the environments to develop a sense of place throughout the state; explore various individuals, groups, and institutions that have developed and shaped the history of the state; explain the balance of power within the state and its connection to the federal government as well as the roles of individual citizens within local, state, national, and global communities; explore the economy of the state, including the state's imports and exports over time; identify how society has used science and technology to improve and empower society within the state over

How will you use these themes to plan for your teaching of social studies? How are these themes useful in thinking about what you will teach?

The nonprofit group USA History provides a website (linked in the Web Links module in Chapter 3 on our Companion Website at www.prenhall.com/schell) that includes information about each state, such as when the state joined the Union, the capital, and general demographic information. This site also provides information on U.S. presidents.

time; and compare, contrast, and connect all of these elements to the global community in which we live.

Further exploration of these voluntary national social studies standards reveals that the themes are presented as curriculum standards, which are measured by performance expectations embedded in classroom activities at each grade level. These standards provide a statement of what should occur in effective social studies programs.

Similarly, the national voluntary standards for history, geography, economics, and civics and government present specific content and skills recommended for grade levels, or a range of grade levels, in order for students to leave the K–12 school system with a comprehensive education in each of these areas. The authors of these discipline-specific standards are well aware that few states offer courses in any of these areas at each grade level. For the schools that do offer these courses at one or a few grade levels, these national standards become helpful tools in designing those courses. The national standards, in general, have all become helpful tools for states, districts, and other organizing school systems to develop local content standards. For example, in the development of the K–12 California History–Social Science Content Standards (CDE, 1998), the authors reviewed the national voluntary standards and consulted some of those authors to determine what scope and sequence best fit California's educational goals and supported the state's existing framework. Drawing upon the design and scholarship of these national documents, California adopted its own set of standards, which have been highly rated by the Fordham Foundation (Stern, 2003).

STATE FRAMEWORKS AND STANDARDS

In Stern's report (2003), which analyzed and rated the history–social science standards in each U.S. state, he explains that the purpose for creating this report relates to the important responsibilities that rest with the states, districts, schools, and individual teachers when it comes to teaching social studies. There is no federal legislation or system of accountability for the teaching of history and the social sciences. The NAEP tests report progress, but do not mandate or provide oversight for the teaching of this curriculum area. As a result, Stern writes in his report:

> State academic standards, consequently, are key. They spell out the content for which the state will hold its public schools responsible to impart to that state's children. They form the basis for statewide testing—to determine whether youngsters have in fact learned those things. They typically inform teacher training, professional development programs and textbook adoption decisions. They are the one place the state sets forth what it expects its future citizens to achieve in the area of historical literacy by the conclusion of their primary-secondary schooling.

Using set criteria to rate each state's content standards, Stern's analysis and comparison of state standards for social studies can be found in the Web Links module in Chapter 3 on our Companion Website at www. prenhall.com/schell.

Reviewing the criteria used, the ratings for your state, and the general descriptions of what guides each state's teaching of social studies is both interesting and informative. However, to help teachers narrow the focus on what they teach in their state at their grade level, these standards become the guide.

State and district content standards will provide you with a clearer picture of what the grade-level content and expectations are for your students at every grade level. Although you will want to focus your attention on the standards and expectations for your own grade level, you will benefit from seeing where, in the larger scope and sequence of K–12 content and skills, your grade-level expectations fit.

In most cases, a framework describes in general terms what a teacher is expected to teach at the grade level. The standards, then, describe what a student should know and be able to do. Standards are intended to be clear, concise, and measurable. Therefore, we may see content frameworks and standards coexisting in states. From these guides, clear goals and objectives for teaching and learning are developed—usually by the teacher.

How will teachers benefit from understanding the standards at grade levels that they do not teach?

GOALS AND OBJECTIVES FOR TEACHING SOCIAL STUDIES

In most cases, grade-level framework descriptions and content standards still leave a lot of work for the teacher. Take, for example, this information that comes from the Connecticut Framework K–12 Curricular Goals and Standards—Social Studies (1998):

Content Standard 12: Human and Environmental Interaction

Students will use geographic tools and technology to explain the interactions of humans and the larger environment, and the evolving consequences of those interactions.

Performance Standards:

Educational experiences in **Grades K–4** will assure that students:

- explain the characteristics and purposes of maps, globes and other geographical tools and technologies;
- create information from maps, globes and geographic models in graphs, diagrams and charts;
- use maps, globes, graphs, models, computer programs and texts, as appropriate;
- explain how human and natural processes shape places;
- explain ways in which humans use and interact with environments;
- identify locations of various economic activities and understand how physical and human factors influence them; and

- describe how and why physical and human systems function and interact and the consequences of these interactions.

On one hand, your focus has been somewhat narrowed from the broader scope of social studies and geography with these content and performance standards. However, you still have a lot of information to work with in making grade-specific plans for teaching and learning. To begin your process of establishing specific standards-based goals and objectives, it helps to know the structure of your state or district's standards. For example, it will help you to know that the foregoing standard is one of 15 content standards repeated throughout the grade levels K–12. Still, the question remains: How will this K–4 standard help you frame lesson plans for your second-grade class? What added information do you need to develop your plans? We hope that you will review all 15 standards and determine your grade-level goals and objectives with the assistance of colleagues at grades K–4. These goals and objectives might integrate some of the 15 standards so that historical content for your grade level can be taught using geography and economics standards as well. With specific goals and objectives, you are better able to review and align your available resources and materials designated for your grade level and make plans for your instructional units and lesson plans. The standards as stated do not provide enough clarity about what, exactly, you must teach.

Maps, globes, and atlases become important tools for students engaged in thinking, reading, writing, and discussion.
Source: *Emily Schell*

Let's look at another example from the state of Florida. When the state content standards were originally adopted, like Connecticut's standards, they were presented for grade clusters including PreK–2, 3–5, 6–8, and 9–12. For example, one 6–8 grade standard read (FDE, 1996):

Standard 3: The student understands Western and Eastern civilization since the Renaissance (SS.A.3.3)

1. understands ways in which cultural characteristics have been transmitted from one society to another (e.g., through art, architecture, language, other artifacts, traditions, beliefs, values, and behaviors).
2. understands the historical events that have shaped the development of cultures throughout the world.
3. knows how physical and human geographic factors have influenced major historical events and movements.
4. knows the significant historical leaders who have influenced the course of events in Eastern and Western civilizations since the Renaissance.
5. understands the differences between institutions of Eastern and Western civilizations (e.g., differences in governments, social traditions and customs, economic systems and religious institutions).

In efforts to make new and more specific statements of what students should know and be able to do at each grade level, these grade-cluster standards have become benchmarks for learning, or exit standards for each cluster of grades. The original standards were then "unpacked" and clarified for each grade level. They are now presented as Grade Level Expectations for the Sunshine State Standards in Social Studies (FDE, 1999). At sixth grade, for example, the foregoing standard is now seen in the Grade Level Expectations for 6th Grade Social studies as:

The sixth grade student:

Time, Continuity, and Change [History]

- understands ways language, ideas, and institutions of one culture can influence other cultures (for example, trade, religions in the Eastern hemisphere).
- knows ways major historical developments have influenced selected groups over time (for example, the rise and spread of the Muslim religion, the spread of Communism in Asia).
- understands ways technological factors have influenced selected groups over time (for example, agriculture in the Eastern hemisphere).
- knows significant aspects of the lives and accomplishments of selected men and women in the historical period of ancient civilizations to the present day (for example, Confucius, Buddha to Gandhi, Mao Ze-dong, Mother Teresa).
- knows major events that shaped the development of various cultures (for example, development and spread of major religions).

Florida's revised standards utilize the NCSS standards by focusing specific grade-level content on one of the themes found in the national social studies standards.

Mahatma Gandhi—historical archives
Source: *Corbis/Bettmann*

- knows examples of significant achievements in art and architecture (for example, Chinese and Japanese ink drawing, temple complexes in Southeast Asia).
- knows roles of political, economic, and social institutions in the development of selected civilizations (for example, caste system in India).
- understands ways in which cultural characteristics have been transmitted from one society to another (for example, through art, architecture, language, other artifacts).
- knows ways geographical factors have influenced selected cultures (for example, the development of the Tibetan civilization in the Himalayan Mountains, the Great Wall of China, major river systems in the Eastern hemisphere).
- understands selected aspects of political, economic, and social institutions in selected cultures in Eastern civilizations (for example, governments, social traditions and customs, economic systems, religious institutions).

Making connections between content areas with and for students helps them learn and remember information for greater understanding.

Each of these grade-level expectations have refined the original standard so that the teacher has a more focused understanding of what students are expected to know and do. Further revision and refinement of standards in each state and district should assist educators as well as students in better understanding these expectations. At the same time, we should continue to acknowledge the complexity and interconnectedness of social studies as an integration of disciplines that requires both focus and flexibility for effective teaching and learning.

TOPICS, THEMES, AND CONCEPTS

How do you make sense out of a list of standards or a large chronological period that you are required to teach based on your state or district's standards and expectations? How do you organize the large amount of information and address the multifaceted nature of social studies so that you can clearly state what you teach and what students are expected to learn?

For many years, teachers have met this challenge by organizing, planning, and teaching to topics. Topics are clear and descriptive organizers for large amounts of information. Topics direct the teacher's and students' attention and anchor studies in that topic. The Renaissance, for example, is a topic. There are very specific people, places, and events that relate to the Renaissance. Most textbooks follow a topical outline to present information in an organized manner.

Recognizing the integral nature of historical and geographical events, some teachers have turned to themes to help their students see the patterns in the events that fill our social studies curricula. Themes such as immigration, exploration, and revolution allow teachers to teach interrelated topics so that students may learn about patterns in nature, behavior, and outcomes. The national social studies standards are presented with 10 major themes that are recommended for use in developing curriculum plans. In the example of Florida's revision of its original standards, you saw that the grade-level expectations included one of those 10 themes—Time, Continuity, and Change—to unite the more specific topics to be studied by sixth-grade students. The California framework and standards also carry themes for each grade level, including Learning and Working Now and Long Ago (kindergarten), A Child's Place in Time and Space (first grade), and People Who Make a Difference (second grade). These themes provide an umbrella and focus for the specific standards that fall under a theme at each grade level.

Similarly, concepts have been used to teach principles that guide human behavior. Teaching with concepts instills purpose and invites the application of concepts in students' lives and contemporary understandings of their world. Concepts, such as justice, conflict, and compromise, allow students to see patterns throughout time and place while learning about specific people, places, and events.

More recently, teachers have turned to big ideas and essential questions as a method for making meaning from their identified standards and content. Challenging students to either consider or identify core principles, essential truths, or enduring understandings about an event or about periods of history, big ideas become thought-provoking organizers for information learned through social studies. Some teachers present essential questions as a way of empowering their students to

History Connection

During the Renaissance, almonds were valued as fertility charms and lucky things for marriages. In Italy, for example, almonds were distributed to foster a "fruitful union."

For more information on essential questions, see the Web Links module in Chapter 3 on our Companion Website at www.prenhall.com/schell.

Through a Reader's Theater presentation, these fourth-grade students presented various perspectives of people who took great risks during the Gold Rush.
Source: *Emily Schell*

think critically about historical people, places, and events. Essential questions do not yield pat answers, or names, dates, and locations. Instead, essential questions raise awareness and inspire deeper thinking about the topic, which takes students into those many disciplines of social studies. For example, a teacher might ask, "Why do people establish rules or laws?" This question can be answered in a variety of ways and at different grade levels. Students answering this question might draw upon their knowledge of law, social issues, cultural differences, geographic boundaries, economics, and so forth. This question might be asked during a unit about Native Americans, colonization, the Civil Rights Movement, or statehood.

How might the use of essential questions change the way teachers teach and students learn social studies?

As you can see, there are challenges, benefits, and opportunities that accompany the implementation of any of these methods for organizing and teaching social studies curricula. The point is this—presenting the framework descriptions or content standards to teachers and students verbatim does not necessarily guide effective teaching and learning of social studies. Find a method that works best for you and your students and that helps you to better understand what students should know and be able to do. You will find more examples and attention to topics, themes, concepts and big ideas in Chapter 4 of this book.

Conclusion

Knowing *what* to teach is as important as knowing *how* to teach. Teachers use national frameworks and state and district content standards to guide decisions about content. This ensures that there is some consistency from classroom to classroom and school to school within a state or region. Although they do not dictate or script the lessons, standards and frameworks help teachers plan instruction and determine which students still need help in understanding the content.

History's Finer Points

In 1990, the President of the Association of Supervision and Curriculum Development (ASCD), Donna Jean Carter, wrote:

> It's no secret that our nation's young people are sorely lacking in their historical and geographical knowledge of the world and even their country's role in it. For most of my school years I hated history. To me, it was merely a set of isolated facts to memorize with absolutely no relation to my life. Unfortunately, suffering through boring, seemingly irrelevant history classes is an experience shared by many students in the United States. The result is very little learning.

This served as the foreword to Walter Parker's book *Renewing the Social Studies Curriculum* (1991), in which Parker proposed curriculum reform in social studies through attention to essential learnings.

Document-Based Question: Is Carter's experience the same experience of students today? Has much changed since this was written in 1990? Have Parker's proposals to teach with essential learnings affected our schools through curriculum reform in social studies? Why or why not?

Visit the History's Finer Points module in Chapter 3 on our Companion Website at www.prenhall.com/schell to answer these questions.

Questions to Consider

1. What is the role of content standards in teaching social studies?
2. How do the content standards and themes get organized for instructional delivery?
3. What does it mean to provide students with a social studies education?

Quiz yourself on this chapter's important concepts on our Companion Website's Chapter 3 self-assessments at www.prenhall.com/schell.

Exercises

Consider the following exercises to help build your personal under-standings about why social studies should be taught every day and for every child.

1. Find your district or state standards. Ask teachers if they have pac-ing guides—plans for addressing the standards throughout the school year.
2. Analyze several teachers' plans for teaching social studies. Which standards are being taught? How are the 10 themes being addressed?
3. Interview some students about social studies. Ask them what they have learned in social studies lessons and why this information might be important.

References

California Department of Education. (2001). *History–social science framework for California public schools.* Sacramento, CA: Author.

Connecticut State Department of Education. (1998). *Social studies cur-riculum framework.* Hartford, CT: Author.

Florida Department of Education. (1996). *Sunshine State standards.* Tallahassee, FL: Author.

Florida Department of Education (1999). *Sunshine State standards grade level expectations, social studies.* Tallahassee, FL: Author.

Jacobs, H. H. (2004). *Getting results with curriculum mapping.* Alexan-dria, VA: Association for Supervision and Curriculum Development.

National Assessment Governing Board. (2001). *U.S. history assessment framework for the 1994 and 2001 national assessment of educational progress.* Washington, DC: Author.

National Center for History in the Schools. (1992). *Lessons from his-tory: Essential understanding and historical perspectives students should acquire.* Los Angeles, CA: Author.

National Center for History in the Schools. (1996). *Bring history alive! A sourcebook for teaching United States history.* Los Angeles, CA: Author.

National Council for the Social Studies. (1992). *A vision of powerful teaching and learning in the social studies: Building social under-standing and civic efficacy.* Silver Spring, MD: Author.

National Council for the Social Studies. (1994). *Expectations of excellence: Curriculum standards for social studies.* Silver Spring, MD: Author.

Parker, W. (1991). *Renewing the social studies curriculum.* Alexandria, VA: Association of Supervision and Curriculum Development.

Stern, S. (2003). Effective state standards for U.S. history: A 2003 report card. Retrieved January 28, 2006, from http://www.edexcellence.net/FOUNDATION/publication/publication.cfm?id=29&pubsubid=470.

Chapter

4

Teaching Social Studies for Understanding

Source: *Krista Greco/Merrill*

Big Idea

Effective planning and a variety of meaningful strategies can be used to help students understand social studies.

Essential Question

What does it mean to understand social studies?

Compare and contrast the following reflections that were written by two different student teachers after making observations in two different classrooms:

Picture these two classroom scenes in your mind as you read. After reading, describe how you feel about each classroom scenario.

FEBRUARY 10TH

I am so overwhelmed by the information presented in my social studies methods class. After learning about our state content standards, assessments, different approaches to teaching, and the diversity of students with varying intelligences and learning styles and needs, I asked my guide teacher how on earth he is able to teach social studies so well. I know he is a good social studies teacher because the students in our class talk about how much fun they have in the afternoons when I am taking classes at the university. One student told me last week that I miss the best part of the day when I leave. He said the best part of the day is when Mr. Stallo teaches social studies.

So, Mr. Stallo decided that he would start teaching social studies earlier in the day when I was there to observe and participate. He said, "Then, you can answer that question for yourself." He also thanked me for bringing this to his attention. What a nice teacher he is!

Today, I observed my first social studies lesson and now I understand why the students enjoy this part of the day. Mr. Stallo began the lesson by asking students what they would do if their parents came home and announced, "We have sold the house and we are moving to Oregon!" He gave students a minute to think about this, then told them to turn to a partner and share their responses. Mr. Stallo then shared some of the statements and questions that he heard while walking around the room and listening to students. Then he gave students 10 minutes to write in their journals about how they would respond to moving, and what they would pack for the trip. Before students started writing, he added, "Oh, yes. There is not much room for your belongings, so write about what you will bring in a suitcase no larger than this." And with that, he placed a small suitcase on the table in the front of the room. The students gasped, grumbled about the small bag, and then started writing furiously and seemed surprised when the timer sounded after 10 minutes.

Book Links

There are lots of great stories to bring into a unit about pioneers. For example, *The Way West: Journal of a Pioneer Woman* (Knight), *Little House on the Prairie* (Wilder), *Sarah, Plain and Tall* (MacLachlan), *Mississippi Mud: Three Prairie Journals* (Turner), *Roughing it on the Oregon Trail* (Stanley), *A Pioneer Sampler: The Daily Life of a Pioneer Family in 1840* (Greenwood), *Dandelions* (Bunting), and *Daily Life in a Covered Wagon* (Erickson).

Mr. Stallo told the students he looked forward to reading their entries later, but for now he wanted to read them a story. He began reading about 8-year-old Virginia Watson, whose father sold their farm in Illinois in 1848 and told his family they were moving west to Oregon. The story was captivating and included diary entries from the young girl herself. Mr. Stallo told the class that they were beginning a unit about Pioneer America and that during this unit, they would be taking an adventure into the past to learn about why people moved west and what happened to them. He reminded them that they still had the challenge of figuring out why this part of the past was important to study today.

Then, Mr. Stallo announced that students sitting at each table group were going to function as a family living in 1848 for the duration of this unit. He assigned roles randomly so that each group had a father, a mother, and two children. One table group had 5 members, so that group had a grandmother, too! Their first tasks were to map out their travel route, decide which items to pack in a wagon the size of their two tables, and write a letter to someone special explaining what was happening. The groups all put their heads together and started working on their tasks. Mr. Stallo stepped back and watched the students open books and atlases, take out notebooks, and engage in discussions about how to proceed. He winked at me and I could tell that this was going to be an exciting unit with lots of twists and turns ahead!

FEBRUARY 12TH

Today I observed my guide teacher presenting a social studies lesson. She told the students to take out their social studies books and many of the students began to groan and complain. She told them to stop or else she would have to take away minutes from their P.E. period, which was to follow the social studies lesson.

When students opened to the correct page, she read the title of the unit and said, "This is what we are studying today." She wrote some page numbers on the board and told the students to quietly and independently read the five pages, and then answer the questions on the fifth page. She passed out lined paper for their answers and re-minded students to put their names on the paper because it would be collected at the end of the 30-minute period. She explained that they should be able to read the pages in about 15 minutes, and use the last 15 minutes to answer the questions. She asked if there where any questions from the class and one student asked, "What can we do if we finish early?" The teacher said they could have free time on the computer if that happened.

I wonder what these fourth-grade students are learning about social studies in this class. Was the teacher unprepared to teach this today? Is this the way she always teaches social studies? It seems to me that the teacher does not really like teaching this subject.

INTRODUCTION

What are the essential differences between these two examples of social studies lessons? Which would you most want to emulate in your own teaching? If you could sit down with either teacher, what questions would you ask? If you could meet with the students in either of these classes, what questions would you ask?

Ideally, you would ask a lot of questions, and your questions would relate to each teacher's goals and objectives for teaching social studies. Ultimately, you would find that thoughtful planning and preparation are essential for successful teaching, and you would probably find that one or more of the following drives each teacher:

- a philosophy of education
- perceived value of social studies
- understandings of social studies
- knowledge of effective teaching strategies in social studies
- experiences as a teacher of social studies
- experiences as a student of social studies

This chapter will address these areas of inquiry while providing you with a variety of ideas, suggestions, and guidelines for effective teaching and learning of social studies. Although a great deal of research exists on best practices and effective strategies for teaching and learning (Marzano, Pickering, & Pollack, 2001), there is limited research spe-cific to the field of social studies (Shaver, 2004). Research tells us that there are certainly effective strategies used for student achievement in social studies (Steffey & Hood, 1994; Zemelman, Daniels, & Hyde, 1993). However, these strategies must be selected, adapted, and ap-plied for specific use depending on the content, goals, and objectives determined by the teacher as well as the student audience and classroom setting. Shaver (2004) states:

Figure 4.1

"I don't get it! They make us learn reading,
writing, and arithmatic to prepare us for a world
of videotapes, computer terminals and calculators."

Source: *www.cartoonstock.com*

In part because of the scarcity of firm, cumulative findings, research cannot provide mandates for social studies instruction . . . sound instructional decisions must be based on the educational values of the teacher,
the school, the school district, and the community, as well as on district
and state guidelines and mandates. Skilled, thoughtful, and motivated
teachers must adapt and implement techniques or approaches suggested
by research findings to achieve desired student outcomes.

Therefore, you have many decisions to make about the strategies
that you will use for your social studies instruction. Those decisions will
reflect your understandings as well as your appreciation of social studies
and are best made when you draw from a variety of available promising
practices and adapt each to meet your students' needs. It may help to
acknowledge the methods that were successful and unsuccessful when
you were a student of social studies. Chances are you will find that you

remember some fun and engaging experiential activities, such as field trips, projects, simulations, or performances. Or, you recall a lot of reading from your textbook, writing the answers to questions in the book, and recalling lots of facts on tests. In many cases, our students tell us that they simply cannot remember ever learning social studies. Reflect on and share your personal experiences in social studies with others while listening to their memories. We have much to learn from each other about what we found engaging and about what provided an impetus or support for ongoing explorations of social studies. On the other hand, we can learn more about what strategies do not encourage or inform achievement in this subject area.

Once you know *what* you should teach at any given grade level, the next step is to consider *how* you are going to teach the content and skills outlined through state goals, objectives, frameworks, or standards. After personally reflecting about how you learned, and sharing experiences to compare and contrast your own experiences with those of others, you are now ready to learn about and consider more options. Let us explore some of those teaching options throughout this chapter.

PLANNING FOR EFFECTIVE INSTRUCTION

Good teaching requires thorough planning in every subject and across all the subjects. Because time limitations tend to interfere with social studies instruction in many elementary classrooms, efficient and effective planning for social studies instruction is more important today than ever before. Through careful planning, teachers can maximize the minimized time allowed for this subject and create opportunities for teaching social studies content in such areas as reading, language arts, visual and performing arts, and physical education. Suggestions for integrating social studies across the curriculum are presented later in this chapter.

The first step toward effective planning requires you to identify what students should leave your grade level knowing and being able to do. Reviewing your grade-level standards and framework will assist in this process. For most teachers, this is an overwhelming task. Working with grade-alike teachers certainly can help, especially if you are working with veteran teachers who have experienced the pacing of your grade-level social studies content. During this first step of planning, identify large "chunks" or units of instruction that are necessary for you to teach and for students to learn based in your grade-level standards or guidelines. Look for opportunities to combine or overlap material so that there are not too many small and isolated units. For example, you can combine individual units on Africa, Asia, South America, Australia, North America, Europe, and Antarctica into one larger unit on "continents" or with a theme of "Cultures Around the World." Otherwise, your plans will reflect more of a laundry list and less of a cohesive social studies plan.

Take some time to reflect on your own experiences—positive, negative, and indifferent. How did you learn social studies? Possibly, what kept you from learning social studies?

Information on *what* should be taught is discussed in Chapter 3.

Focus on what you want your students to know when they have completed your class—plan with the end in mind.

History Connections

Australian women were granted the right to vote in Federal elections in 1902. That didn't happen in the United States until the passage of the 19th Amendment to the Constitution of the United States, in 1920.

Students, teachers, and parents at Rosa Parks Elementary School celebrate the Vietnamese and Chinese New Year with a lion dance, parade, and firecrackers! Source: *Emily Schell*

After the major units of instruction have been determined for the school year, the next step requires you to "map out" your teaching. Once you know where you are going, creating a map helps you identify how to get there. A curriculum map allows you to plan around obstacles (test periods, school breaks, holidays, special school events), identify the little trips (units) that help you work toward your ultimate goals, and align useful resources, such as the textbook. Another approach is to create a timeline for the school year that shows when you will teach each unit and for how long. This is often called a pacing guide. In most cases, you will want to place your instructional units in a particular order that is organized around chronology, holidays, or skills development.

After the year-long plan for social studies instruction is created, the next step requires you to develop each individual unit. This process begins with the standards or framework descriptions for the identified unit. These guidelines articulate what the students should know and be able to do at the end of the instructional unit, but oftentimes remain subject to interpretation. Therefore, using a process to "unpack" (McTighe & Wiggins, 1998) or "unwrap" (Ainsworth, 2003) each standard helps you analyze each standard to identify more clearly the explicit knowledge and skills necessary for achievement of the standard. For example, the following standard is found in California's second-grade standards (California Department of Education, 2001):

Students demonstrate map skills by describing the absolute and relative locations of people, places, and environments.

This standard can be "unpacked" by separating out the knowledge and skills required of students to achieve this standard. In this case, students must know:

- the definition of absolute location;
- the definition of relative location;
- locations in which people live (e.g., cities, farms);
- locations of places (e.g., United States, White House, Pacific Ocean);
- locations of environments (e.g., Mojave Desert, Rocky Mountains, Amazon rainforests); and
- locations of places in relationship to other places.

Students should also be able to demonstrate these skills:

- map reading;
- identification of place names;
- use of cardinal directions and intercardinal directions; and
- mental mapping of large areas (e.g., continents and oceans).

Identifying the components of a standard in terms of explicit knowledge and skills that are required of the students allows you to plan more clearly and effectively. From these components, you are ready to develop lesson plans that will lead your students toward the assessment and achievement of each standard.

After unpacking several standards that are included in any instructional unit, you are left with a list of knowledge and skills to teach and assess. At this point, there are a variety of considerations about how to frame the information so that you have a cohesive instructional unit. You might ask, "How do I help students make sense of this content and these skills?" or "How can I tie together these facts and skills so they are meaningful to my students?" This is where topics, themes, concepts, and Big Ideas become helpful.

TOPICS, THEMES, CONCEPTS, AND BIG IDEAS

Naturally, we organize information into categories. If we were to just start teaching random and disconnected information, chances are great that little understanding would occur. Therefore, we organize social studies information in topical, conceptual, or thematic categories. Recently, Big Ideas have captured the attention of social studies teachers who seek greater connections between units of study and years of social studies instruction. Let us take a look at these options for planning and teaching.

Topics

It makes sense to inform students that they are learning about a certain topic, such as presidents, Mexico, or the Gold Rush. Topics tend to focus

The North Central Regional Educational Laboratory, a federally funded educational information system, provides podcasts on several topics, including using assessment information to unpack standards. To listen to this podcast, see the Web Links module in Chapter 4 on our Companion Website at www.prenhall.com/schell.

For a web-based lesson on the compass and intercardinal directions, see the Web Links module in Chapter 4 on our Companion Website at www.prenhall.com/schell.

One kindergarten class learned these topics for social studies: Whales, Mexico, Rules, Egypt, U.S. Civil War, and Rainforests. What are the pros and cons of teaching with topics? Are these the appropriate topics for kindergarteners?

on people, places, or events and provide a number of facts for students to learn pertaining to that topic. Topics are clear, direct, and define the boundaries of a particular unit. The use of topics can limit teaching and learning opportunities, as the learning remains focused solely on the particular topic. After one topical unit, another follows. Ideally, the teacher helps students see connections between topical units, but in most cases the units stand alone.

Themes

Thematic teaching serves to expand topical teaching and provide opportunities to include multiple examples under a theme. For example, rather than teach a topical unit on firefighters, the teacher could introduce the theme of Community Helpers, which would include the study of firefighters as well as people who hold other jobs and roles in a community. In this example, students would benefit from seeing that communities also depend on police officers, mail carriers, shopkeepers, librarians, school teachers, trash collectors, and those who provide volunteer service.

Themes also allow teachers to integrate social studies across the curriculum as a theme may be carried into such areas as reading and language arts, visual and performing arts, and science. Carrying the theme of Community Helpers across the curriculum, students might be instructed to read and discuss stories about community helpers, write and illustrate thank-you letters to helpers in their community, paint murals depicting the diversity of helpers, and study the environment to conduct scientific experiments on energy use, pollution, or water quality. Using themes in this way allows for students to see and apply connections between what they learn in one subject area to another. Their understanding of the theme itself becomes enhanced in this way.

The national social studies standards (NCSS, 1994) are presented in 10 themes, which demonstrate the overarching categories for the studies of history, geography, economics, civics and government that span time and place. Those themes as described by NCSS are:

- *Civic Ideals and Practices:* An understanding of civic ideals and practices of citizenship is critical to full participation in society and is a central purpose of the social studies. All people have a stake in examining civic ideals and practices across time and in diverse societies as well as at home, and in determining how to close the gap between present practices and the ideals upon which our democratic republic is based. Learners confront such questions as: What is civic participation and how can I be involved? How has the meaning of citizenship evolved? What is the balance between rights and responsibilities? What is the role of the citizen in the community and the nation, and as a member of the world community? How can I make a positive difference?
- *Culture:* Human beings create, learn, and adapt culture. Culture helps us to understand ourselves as both individuals and members of

History Connections

A librarian in Basra, Iraq, was worried about the library collection and decided to remove the books and hide them. This was reported in the *New York Times* on July 27, 2003, and has since been presented in a picture book, *The Librarian of Basra: A True Story from Iraq* (Winter), and a graphic novel for children, *Alia's Mission: Saving the Books of Iraq* (Stamaty, 2004).

Literature selections help bring social studies themes to life as students see diverse examples of human interactions over time and place.
Source: *Cover from* Alia's Mission: Saving the Books of Iraq *by Mark Alan Stamaty.*

various groups. Human cultures exhibit both similarities and differences. We all, for example, have systems of beliefs, knowledge, values, and traditions. Each system also is unique. In a democratic and multicultural society, students need to understand multiple perspectives that derive from different cultural vantage points. This understanding will allow them to relate to people in our nation and throughout the world.

- *Global Connections:* The realities of global interdependence require understanding the increasingly important and diverse global connections among world societies. Analysis of tensions between national interests and global priorities contributes to the development of possible solutions to persistent and emerging global issues in many fields: health care, economic development, environmental quality, universal human rights, and others. Analyzing patterns and relationships within and among world cultures, such as economic competition and interdependence, age-old ethnic enmities, political and military alliances, and others, helps learners carefully examine policy alternatives that have both national and global implications.

- *Individual Development and Identity:* Personal identity is shaped by one's culture, by groups, and by institutional influences. How do people learn? Why do people behave as they do? What influences how people learn, perceive, and grow? How do people meet their basic needs in a variety of contexts? Questions such as these are central to the study of how individuals develop from youth to adulthood. Examination of various forms of human behavior enhances understanding of the relationships among social norms and emerging personal identities, the social processes that influence identity formation, and the ethical principles underlying individual action.

- *Individuals, Groups, and Institutions:* Institutions such as schools, churches, families, government agencies, and the courts all play an integral role in our lives. These and other institutions exert enormous influence over us, yet institutions are no more than organizational embodiments to further the core social values of those who comprise them. Thus, it is important that students know how institutions are formed, what controls and influences them, how they control and influence individuals and culture, and how institutions can be maintained or changed.

- *People, Places, and Environment:* Technological advances connect students at all levels to the world beyond their personal locations. The study of people, places, and human-environment interactions assists learners as they create their spatial views and geographic perspectives of the world. Today's social, cultural, economic, and civic demands on individuals mean that students will need the knowledge, skills, and understanding to ask and answer questions such as: Where are things located? Why are they located where they are? What patterns are reflected in the groupings of things? What do we mean by region? How do landforms change? What implications do these changes have for people? This area of study helps learners make informed and critical decisions about the relationship between human beings and their environment.

- *Power, Authority, and Governance:* Understanding the historical development of structures of power, authority, and governance and their evolving functions in contemporary U.S. society, as well as in other parts of the world, is essential for developing civic competence. In exploring this theme, students confront questions such as: What is power? What forms does it take? Who holds it? How is it gained, used, and justified? What is legitimate authority? How are governments created, structured, maintained, and changed? How can we keep government responsive to its citizens' needs and interests? How can individual rights be protected within the context of majority rule? By examining the purposes and characteristics of various governance systems, learners develop an understanding of how groups and nations attempt to resolve conflicts and seek to establish order and security. Through study of the dynamic relationships among individual rights and responsibilities, the needs of social groups, and concepts of a just society, learners become more effective problem-solvers and decision-makers when addressing the persistent issues and social problems encountered in public life.

- *Production, Distribution, and Consumption:* People have wants that often exceed the limited resources available to them. As a result, a variety of ways have been invented to decide upon answers to four fundamental questions: What is to be produced? How is production to be organized? How are goods and services to be distributed? What is the most effective allocation of the factors of production (land, labor, capital, and management)? Unequal distribution of resources necessitates systems of exchange, including trade, to improve the well-being of the economy, while the role of government in economic policymaking varies over time and from place to place. Increasingly these decisions are global in scope and require systematic study of an interdependent world economy and the role of technology in economic decision-making.

- *Science, Technology, and Society:* Technology is as old as the first crude tool invented by prehistoric humans, but today's technology forms the basis for some of our most difficult social choices. Modern life as we know it would be impossible without technology and the science that supports it. But technology brings with it many questions: Is new technology always better than that which it will replace? What can we learn from the past about how new technologies result in broader social change, some of which is unanticipated? How can we cope with the ever-increasing pace of change, perhaps even with the feeling that technology has gotten out of control? How can we manage technology so that the greatest number of people benefit from it? How can we preserve our fundamental values and beliefs in a world that is rapidly becoming one technology-linked village?

- *Time, Continuity, and Change:* Human beings seek to understand their historical roots and to locate themselves in time. Such understanding involves knowing what things were like in the past and how things change and develop. Knowing how to read and reconstruct the past allows one to develop a historical perspective and to answer questions such as: Who am I? What happened in the past? How am I connected to those in the past? How has the world changed and how might it change in the future? Why does our personal sense of relatedness to the past change? How can the perspective we have about our own life experiences be viewed as part of the larger human story across time? How do our personal stories reflect varying points of view and inform contemporary ideas and actions? (NCSS, 1994, pp. x–xii)

Use of these themes in teaching social studies does not imply that teachers should teach the theme entirely—providing examples across history and around the world—or select any desirable example for each general theme. These themes should be used while teaching the specific content identified in district or state guidelines.

Concepts

Concepts are very much like themes, though concepts focus student learning on social studies. Like themes, concepts are abstract and encompass a variety of examples, facts, and ideas. Hilda Taba (1967) believes that students seek to make sense of their world and group items together, giving reasons why they belong together, thus generating concepts. Drawing on Taba's work, Parker (2000) describes concepts as the critical attributes shared by a number of examples. In other words, concepts are the important similarities of a set of examples. Each concept, therefore, has a set of examples. Parker promotes concept teaching in social studies to include a set of three or four examples that span time, place, and culture/gender so that students see a concept as universal. Each example, then, has a bundle of facts, information, or data that makes that example unique and specific. In the examples, students become aware of the differences over time, place, and culture/gender, but recognize the common concept that organizes that example into a larger category. Figure 4.2 provides some examples.

Like themes, the use of concepts does not imply that you should teach the entire concept or teach extensively the variety of examples over time, place, and culture/gender. Providing a set of examples as well as nonexamples for the concept may require some teaching, but should not detract from the focused example that supports the district or state guidelines for curriculum at your grade level. Teaching with

Rosa Parks—historical archives
Source: *Courtesy of the Library of Congress*

Figure 4.2   Teaching concepts, examples, and facts.

Concept	Examples	Facts
Community	• tribe • colony • neighborhood	Tribe: • American Indian groups shared ancestry, customs, beliefs, and leadership • Tribes developed their own forms of government • Some tribes cooperated with other tribes while others fought against each other • Shawnee, Wampanoag, Cheyenne, Navajo
Exploration	• Columbus' Voyage • Lewis and Clark Expedition • Space Station	Lewis and Clark Expedition: • 1803–1806 • explored land gained in Louisiana Purchase and as far as the Pacific Ocean • Jefferson named Captain Meriwether Lewis to head expedition • Sacajawea served as Shoshone guide
Technology	• wheel • seafaring ships • computers	Computers: • roots in abacus and calculators • analog and digital • used to process, store, and retrieve information • supercomputers and microcomputers
Leadership	• Cleopatra • George Washington • Rosa Parks	Rosa Parks: • born February 4, 1913 • worked as a seamstress in Montgomery, Alabama • time of segregation • on December 1, 1955, refused to give up seat on a bus, which violated city ordinance • launched bus boycott • became a leader in the Civil Rights Movement

concepts allows for teachers to reinforce and activate prior knowledge in students while also drawing connections to contemporary examples or examples that better relate to students, but are not included in the student textbook or teaching guidelines.

Big Ideas

Children's author Jean Fritz insightfully wrote *What's the Big Idea, Ben Franklin?* in 1976. Her biography for children about the life and accomplishments of Benjamin Franklin challenged readers to think about his many big ideas, such as bifocals, the almanac, use of electricity, and a safer stove to use in homes, before identifying his biggest idea of all. Fritz presented information about Franklin's ideas that met the needs of people living in the 18th century, challenged traditional social roles, and reflected science, literature, and health as well as politics. Fritz concludes that Franklin's biggest idea was that the United States should be a free and independent nation. Her interpretation of big ideas through the accomplishments of Franklin reflects the current interpretation of big ideas in education in that she saw big ideas as important,

Source: *From* What's the Big Idea, Ben Franklin? *by Jean Fritz, illustrated by Margot Tomas, copyright © 1976 by Margot Tomas. Used by permission of Coward-McCann, A Division of Penguin Young Readers Group, A Member of Penguin Group (USA) Inc., 345 Hudson Street, New York, NY 10014. All rights reserved.*

enduring, and transferable. Franklin's work continues to affect our lives as we rely on electricity, fire departments, mail carriers, odometers, and the freedoms guaranteed through the U.S. Constitution.

McTighe and Wiggins (1998) are largely responsible for bringing big ideas into the classroom with their Understanding by Design theory. This theory calls for teachers to plan with the end in mind—beginning their planning process with attention to standards, frameworks and other objectives. During the unpacking process of these content guidelines, they suggest identifying the core concepts or processes that have enduring value beyond the classroom. These "enduring understandings" or "big ideas" are defined as important, engaging, thought-provoking, and transferable within, across, and beyond the curriculum. In other words, the big idea is not only important to understanding the unit of study, but important to understanding additional areas of study and additional areas of life as well. In this sense, many of Franklin's big ideas about science, health, music, and society are enduring and have led to the development of products and institutions, such as fire companies and the U.S. Postal Service. Franklin's work paved the way for scientists and inventors such as Thomas Edison and Alexander Graham Bell. Most importantly, Franklin's ideas, combined with others' ideas at the time, of a free and independent nation have continued to challenge social and political thought and practices since 1776, when independence was first declared. These ideas are not

History Connections

Dr. Martin Luther King, Jr., started college at Morehouse at age 16. His first civil rights action was the Montgomery Bus Boycott, which started on December 1, 1955, and lasted over a year. King's greatest accomplishment is probably the March on Washington on August 28, 1963. The full text of the "I Have a Dream" speech can be found at: www.stanford.edu/group/King.

Martin Luther King, Jr.—historical archives
Source: *Copyright Bob Adelman/Magnum Photos*

static and contained to the 18th century. Americans continue to debate their rights and responsibilities as citizens and work diligently to maintain freedom and independence. The fight to abolish slavery in America contested the interpretation and implementation of the big idea of a free and independent nation, as did the Civil Rights Movement. We continue to see questions and discussions related to this big idea today.

Big ideas can be used to introduce and encompass or connect units of study, or they may serve as goals for students to "uncover" during their studies. Uncoverage of big ideas may occur when thought-provoking questions lead students through inquiry methods to the big idea. In either case, it is important for you to determine what big ideas exist in your curriculum so that you can help students recognize the enduring value of social studies information and skills. Teaching with big ideas can help you create placeholders for new information while accessing prior knowledge in students who have probably encountered examples of that big idea in previous years of social studies instruction or in everyday life.

Teachers throughout the nation have combed their standards and guidelines to identify big ideas to assist in their teaching, as can be seen in Figure 4.3.

Most big ideas exist as statements, but some use essential questions to help students uncover the big ideas in their studies, as noted in Figure 4.4.

When big ideas are used across the grade levels, students begin to develop a stronger sense of social studies while learning specific examples that relate to chronological history, spatial organization of the world, and various systems and institutions. For example, presenting big ideas as questions could look like the ones in Figure 4.5.

You might note that these big ideas and essential questions can be used in a variety of ways across units of study and across grade levels that span periods of time, places, and events. We hope you see how useful big ideas can be in helping students understand the larger purpose and applications of social studies knowledge and skills. For example, you might present the big ideas to your class at the beginning of the school year and display these on the bulletin board, in a chart, or in a

Figure 4.3   Big ideas in geography, history, economics, and government.

Geography	History	Economics	Government
Where people live influences how they live.	All communities have a history.	Limited resources require choices.	Rules and laws are important for everyone.
The exchange of goods, ideas, and values occurs through exploration and trade.	Significant people, ideas, events, and eras shape history.	Positive and negative incentives influence human economic behavior.	Rights have limits.

Source: *San Diego County Office of Education, 2001; Wichita Public Schools, 2004.*

Figure 4.4   Essential questions for geography, history, economics, and government.

Geography	History	Economics	Government
How are people influenced by where they live?	What is the history of your community?	What do people do when resources are limited?	Why do we have rules and laws?
What occurs when people explore and trade?	How is history shaped?	What influences human economic behaviors?	What are rights?

graphic organizer for students to keep in their notebooks and add information over time. A class studying ancient civilizations might use the graphic found in Figure 4.6 to organize, compare, and contrast information throughout the school year.

A simplified example for a primary grade class might look like the one found in Figure 4.7.

Figure 4.5   Big Ideas and questions across grades and themes.

Grade and Theme	Geography	History	Economics	Government
K *Learning and Working Now and Long Ago*	Why do people live in a neighborhood?	Why do we learn about the past?	What kinds of work do people do?	What is a symbol?
1 *A Child's Place in Time and Space*	How do we learn about geography?	What was life like in the past?	Why do people work?	What makes a good citizen?
2 *People Who Make a Difference*	How can we find out about places on Earth?	How can one person make our world a better place?	How do we get the things we need and want?	How does government help people get along?
3 *U.S. and Community History*	How does geography affect communities?	How has life changed for people over time?	How do people in a community meet their needs?	Why do communities need governments?
4 *State History*	How do people adapt to where they live?	Why do people take great risks?	How does technology change people's lives?	What causes a society to grow?
5 *Early American History*	How do different places affect the way people live?	What are some things people are willing to fight for?	Why do new technologies change people's lives?	Why do people form governments?
6 *World History*	What is the importance of physical geography to any civilization?	How do new ideas cause change?	What makes a civilization?	What makes empires rise and fall?

Source: *California Vistas, Macmillan/McGraw-Hill, 2007.*

Figure 4.6 Graphic organizer for comparing information.

	People need food and shelter to survive.	Surplus allows for people to specialize their work.	Trade is important to the success of a civilization.	Land, water, and climate are important to the success or decline of a civilization.	People interact in a variety of ways in a society.
Ancient Egypt					
Ancient Mesopotamia					
Ancient China					
Ancient India					
Ancient Hebrews					
Ancient Greece					
Ancient Rome					

Figure 4.7 Graphic organizer for comparing information.

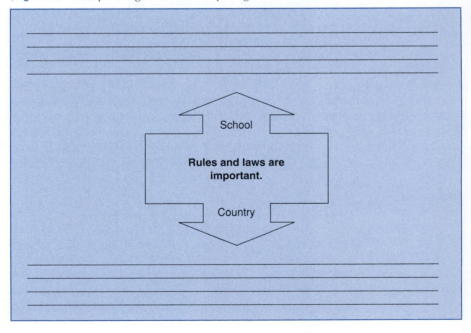

School

Rules and laws are important.

Country

Figure 4.8   Summary of topics, themes, and big ideas.

Grade Level	Topic	Concept/Theme	Big Idea
K	Firefighters	Community Helpers	People work together in a community.
1	Houses	Homes	People adapt to their environments.
2	Ancestors	Families	History tells the stories of people and events over time.
3	Cities	Environments	Where a person lives determined how a person lives.
4	Gold Rush	Immigration	People move to improve their lives or because they are forced.
5	Explorers	Exploration	Exploration leads to the exchange of products, ideas, and information.
6	Ancient India	Ancient Civilizations	Religious beliefs influenced the development of cultures just as cultures influenced the development of religions.

Your teaching units may be based on topics, themes, concepts, or big ideas. Whichever of these approaches you use to develop instructional units, there will still be a large body of information and a number of skills that you seek to teach, practice, and assess during the unit. The remainder of this chapter is devoted to proven strategies that can be adapted for use according to your grade level, content, time, and resource considerations. A summary of topics, concepts, themes, and big ideas can be found in Figure 4.8.

HISTORICAL THINKING AND ANALYSIS SKILLS

In the area of social studies, you must recognize the historic, geographic, social, political, and social context of the topics presented. Otherwise, you risk teaching students to memorize a series of meaningless facts. Understanding social studies education means knowing about, developing, and applying skills that are far more useful than rote memorization. Historical thinking and analysis skills are crucial for student engagement and development of enduring skills that promote critical thinking and informed decision making. The national history standards

A full definition of each of these skills categories as well as K–4 and 5–12 grade standards for each skill can be found in the Web Links module in Chapter 4 on our Companion Website at www. prenhall.com/schell.

(NCHS, 1996) present these five interconnected historical thinking skills in conjunction with the content standards:

- Chronological Thinking
- Historical Comprehension
- Historical Analysis and Interpretation
- Historical Research Capabilities
- Historical Issues—Analysis and Decision-Making

Similarly, California's History-Social Science Standards (CDE, 2001) include a set of Historical and Social Sciences Analysis Skills that are separated for grades K–5, 6–8, and 9–12, but include the same general categories:

- Chronological and Spatial Thinking
- Research, Evidence and Point of View
- Historical Interpretation

Note that these intellectual skills are to be learned through *and* applied to the content standards, and that these skills should only be assessed in conjunction with the content standards. This reminds us of the integral and complex nature of social studies instruction and promotes the teaching of social studies as more than the acquisition of historic facts and other data. How can we help students develop these historical thinking and analysis skills while focused on explicit knowledge demanded in state guidelines? Let us examine some instructional strategies that work in social studies classrooms.

INSTRUCTIONAL STRATEGIES THAT WORK

There exist a variety of strategies for engaging students in social studies. Well-planned lessons and units capture the attention of students from beginning to end by generating interest, creating intrigue or mystery for inquiry-based learning, encouraging connections between students and their studies, and providing opportunities for students to participate in meaningful learning activities that lead to increased knowledge and skills.

Generating Interest

Creative teachers seek innovative and captivating ways to engage students' minds and imaginations. You can capture your students' attention using a variety of "hooks" or anticipatory sets to set the stage for important learning. Consider these ideas to engage and focus students in the topic, relate the information to students' experiences, and motivate learners:

- *Read aloud* an excerpt from a primary source, historical novel, or newspaper article. Careful selection and delivery of the text is crucial. Reading aloud a lengthy, confusing, and potentially boring text

California's standards can be found in the Web Links module in Chapter 4 on our Companion Website at www.prenhall. com/schell.

could have unintended consequences. Find text selections that are highly visual, intriguing, humorous, gross, or relate to the issues that your students face are useful. Introduce the read-aloud appropriately and use your voice to retell a story worth listening to.

- Deliver a first-person *character interpretation*. You can bring to life a person from the past by wearing period clothing or simply adding a period hat or cap. This will require some preparation and practice, but you can effectively engage students by presenting a prepared monologue or by interacting with students noting the differences you see between them and "people of your time." The more you do this, the more students look forward to beginning new units and "meeting" new people from the past.

- *Storytelling* is an effective strategy for gaining attention and focusing students. Fables, cultural tales, tall tales, real-life stories and your own personal anecdotes can be well told to engage student interest and thinking about a topic.

For more information on storytelling, including a rubric to assess your storytelling skills, see the Web Links module in Chapter 4 on our Companion Website at www.prenhall. com/schell.

- *Alter or recreate the learning environment* and place students in new roles to generate interest through participation in studies. For example, when it is time to introduce students to a new unit based on a different country or civilization, rearrange the classroom before students enter. Move the desks to the perimeter of the room and assemble the chairs to look like the interior of an airplane. Greet students at the door with, "Welcome to _____ (your name or the school's name) Airlines. Please take your seat." Immediately, they will know it is time for a new adventure. Simulate a brief flight to transition students from one country to another and provide fun opportunities for students to enjoy "traveling" from one unit, or civilization, to another. Offer in-flight movies, readings, mini lectures, and map activities to prepare students for their new destination while they also enjoy time to chat, snack on peanuts, and wish they had first-class seats (where the service is much better!). Consider recreating the classroom environment to align with your content—form wagon families for pioneer studies, colonies, regions of your state, etc.

- *Conduct a treasure hunt*. Remember receiving a list of treasures to go out and find among various houses in your neighborhood? Introduce the topic, concept, or big idea for the unit, then brainstorm with students the kinds of information they think will be important to find and learn about. For example, in a unit about American Indians, students might identify the following items as helpful for learning about American Indians: food, clothing, houses, games, jobs, and celebrations. This becomes your treasure hunt list. Allow students time to explore the pages in the text or the materials (tradebooks, maps, artifacts, etc.) to find examples of these treasures— a photo of corn, a title that states, "The Powhatan lived in Yahikins," etc. Also, invite students to go home and gather more treasures from these same categories to analyze, compare, and contrast through-out their studies of American Indians. Treasures from home might include magazine articles, family photos, artifacts, or books. Allow students to share (in pairs, table groups, or moving around the room) their treasures with each other from each of the categories and integrate these personal items into their studies of American Indians. Allow students to analyze the similarities and differences between their modern foods, clothes, houses, games, and jobs, and those of American Indians in the past as well as the present.

- *Mysterious artifacts* will gain the attention of students. Replicas, natural items that resemble artifacts, or photographs from book or Internet sources often intrigue students when asked, "What is this? Who would have used this? What would this have been used for? What was it made from?" Even if it is only one artifact that ignites their inquiry, use it to set the stage for wider understandings of people, places, and events that will come in the unit. And, it should help students pay closer attention to the details that over time hold a great deal of information and generate a number of questions in the mind of a historian or archaeologist.

- *Political cartoons* grab the attention of students. Historic as well as contemporary examples of cartoons and comic strips often provide rich mining ground for perspectives, opinions, beliefs, and misconceptions. Share these using the overhead projector and focus students on major, or subtle, issues and information that will be explored in the unit.

- *Predictions* can be used to generate student interest. There are a variety of ways to ask students to predict what they will learn in this unit of study. Provide the topic, concept, or big idea and engage students in a quickwrite exercise or discussions. Offer clues through the unit vocabulary or titles from the chapters. Present a thought-provoking question that relates to the content, such as "How will the United States expand from sea to sea?" before a unit on Manifest Destiny or "What will happen during and as a result of the Civil War?"

- Use a *KWL Chart* for students to complete individually, in small groups, or with the whole class. A KWL Chart is an extremely useful graphic organizer that asks students to specify what they *know* about the topic in one column, what they *want* to know in the second column, and then what they *learned* in the third column. Of course, the third column is not completed until after students have learned the content. The first two columns, however, help students focus on the topic, access their prior knowledge, and negotiate the curriculum by identifying what they want to learn. A skillful teacher will integrate the information from the second column into plans for the unit to empower students and meet their needs. Consider adding a fourth column to create a KWLH Chart if you want students to reflect on

History Connections

John L. O'Sullivan coined the term *Manifest Destiny* in 1845. What was he arguing for? How might that term be used today?

how they learned in addition to what they learned. Use the fourth column to let students identify *how* they learned.

- *Provocative, startling, or upsetting statements* can be used effectively to introduce a theme or topic. For example, introduce a unit on the Constitution and Bill of Rights by stating, "We are going to hold an election in class, but only the girls can vote." To introduce a unit on settling the colonies, announce, "I prefer the classroom next door, so after lunch we will all carry our things over there to take over that room." Work with students to identify the issues they have with your statement and use their often-heated opinions to frame and introduce the unit.

- *Provocative questions* can be used in much the same manner. Introduce students to a curious, overarching, and essential question from or about the unit. Allow students to respond in writing, discussion, drawing, or acting. For example, you might ask students what they do when they encounter someone who looks, sounds, and even smells differently than they do. Simple role-play, a quickwrite, or a small-group discussion would pique their interest and establish a mindset for learning about the explorers' contact with Native Americans, or enslaved Africans' encounters with slave traders and owners.

A quickwrite is an important instructional tool because it allows students to clarify their own thinking as they respond to a writing prompt. It also serves as a quick assessment when used by the teacher to determine if students understand what has been taught.

Inquiry-Based Learning

Questioning and critical thinking promotes reading, research, discussion, analysis, and evaluation among students. Consider introducing your students to instructional units or historic situations through questions or challenges that pique their interest and launch them into inquiry mode. When students believe that their role is simply to consume a set of predetermined facts and regurgitate these facts in the form of a test or essay, they have little interest in their studies and do not retain information for understanding. However, when they are presented with thought-provoking questions, they have a different response.

For example, students studying immigration might be asked, "Why would someone leave their home, their family, and their friends and travel thousands of miles away to a place where the land, language, and customs are completely different?" In response to this question, students should be able to begin their studies of immigrants by recognizing universal concepts of survival, economic struggle, sense of adventure, and escape from undesirable situations.

Questions can serve to access prior knowledge or draw connections between the students and people of the past. In the process, students begin to develop historical empathy as they consider situations from various economic, geographic, historic, and social perspectives. Using the same unit, you might ask, "How would you feel if your parents sent you away to a live with strangers in a new country? Why might they do this?" Students can then discuss, write about, act out, or create projects

To help your-
self learn to
ask better questions,
see the Web Links
module in Chapter 4
on our Companion
Website at www.
prenhall.com/schell.

around these guiding questions before exploring the specified content of European immigration during the late 1800s or immigrant communities in the United States.

Inquiry-based learning means posing questions, seeking answers from a variety of sources and activities, and evaluating responses. A student who continues to wonder about different perspectives, missing information, motivations, historic accuracy, ethical considerations, or biases while reading, listening, and thinking about the information encountered in social studies is a student in inquiry mode. How do we get students into this mode? By modeling effective questioning skills, allowing for thoughtful, informed questions in class, and placing value on the questions that emerge in class. Oftentimes, questions will launch students into areas of study that they would not have approached if their learning were confined to the set of facts distributed through class lectures and materials.

Invite students to develop, document, and share their questions during studies. It is not always necessary to answer every question, but your informal assessment of student progress and student thinking can often occur while listening to or reading students' questions. Allow students to explore and investigate each other's questions during class as well. Teach students how to elevate their thinking and inquiry skills by asking questions that reach various levels in Bloom's (1956) Taxonomy (see Figure 4.9). Instruct and challenge students to ask and answer such questions as:

Evaluation: Do you agree with/that. . . ?; What do you think about. . . ?; What was most important about. . . ?; How would you prioritize. . . ?; How would you have decided to . . . ?; How would you rate. . . ?

Synthesis: What ideas are missing from. . . ?; What might have happened if. . . ?; How did . . . solve the problem of. . . ?; What else might have been done to. . . ?

Analysis: What are the features of. . . ?; How does. . . compare/contrast to. . . ?; What is the evidence that shows . . . ?; How can you classify. . . ?

Application: How is . . . an example of. . . ?; How is . . . related to. . . ?; Why is . . . significant?

Comprehension: How would you describe. . . ?; How might you retell. . . ?; How do you interpret. . . ?

Knowledge: Who. . . ?; When did. . . ?; When did. . . ?; Where was. . . ?; How did. . . ?

If you plan your units using big ideas, pay close attention to the essential questions that will help students uncover those big ideas and direct their thinking and learning. Discussions, projects, and assessments may be developed with the use of good essential questions and promote inquiry-based learning.

Figure 4.9   Bloom's Taxonomy.

Evaluation: compare and discriminate between ideas, determine value of theories or ideas, make choices based on reasoned argument, determine value of evidence, form criteria, make judgments, and detect fallacies

Synthesis: use old ideas to create new ones, produce new information, generalize from given facts, relate knowledge from several areas, predict, and draw conclusions

Analysis: see patterns, organize parts, identify components, distinguish fact from fiction, recognize hidden meanings, and identify components

Application: use information, use methods, concepts, or theories in new situations, and solve problems using required skills or knowledge

Comprehension: understand information, translate knowledge into new context, interpret facts, compare, contrast, order, group, infer causes, predict consequences, paraphrase, and imply

Knowledge: observe and recall of information, remember dates, events, places, understand ways of doing things, learn definitions and specific terms

Some practical strategies for inquiry-based teaching and learning include:

- *Bloom's Levels Question Challenge.* Write each of the levels from Bloom's Taxonomy onto tongue depressors or onto index cards and draw them randomly. Challenge students to write, ask a partner, or provide for the class a question at that level pertaining to the content currently being studied. Continue to require students to generate questions regularly throughout their studies—recording their questions—so that they can understand the benefits of asking all kinds of thoughtful questions.
- *Perspectives.* Identify and assign different perspectives that pertain to the content and instruct students to consider the thoughts, feelings, experiences, and opinions of the people who held these perspectives during the time and events being studied. For example, during a unit about colonial life, assign students the perspectives of men, women, and children of the gentry class (the affluent), middling sort (merchants, tradesmen, large farmers), and lesser sort (small farmers, workers, servants), as well as enslaved Africans. Throughout their studies, students may respond orally or in journal entries about their perspectives on such issues as taxation, religion, and independence.

On January 24, 1848, James Marshall discovered gold at Sutter's Mill. If cholera, exhaustion, starvation, or the onset of winter in the Sierra didn't kill them, the hopeful travelers arrived in the foothills of California only to discover that most of the easy gold had already been claimed. There are websites dedicated to providing information about the Gold Rush—for information, see the Web Links module in Chapter 4 on our Companion Website at www.prenhall.com/schell.

Adding personal information such as this provides students with a model for making personal connections of their own.

• *Solve a problem or mystery.* Explain to the class that they have a problem or mystery to solve and that they will gather information and ideas throughout their studies in this unit to present a solution or answer at the end of the unit. For example, before a unit about interdependence, with young learners, you might explain to the students that there is a farmer who has a problem—he has a lot of corn that he and his family cannot eat. The farmer's family needs money to build a new barn, but does not know what to do. What should the farmer do? Students could then seek to solve the problem while learning about the interdependence of food suppliers and consumers. Some content provides its own mysteries for students to consider and explore, such as the disappearance of colonists at Roanoke, the location of gold in California, or the stories from ancient tombs in China. However, you can generate inquiry through mysteries that you create. For example, explain to students that the class pet (or plant) is missing, but that someone left a map showing its location. As students learn how to read a map, they can apply those skills to discovering the location of their class item.

Making Connections

Teachers relate making connections with effective teaching and learning in social studies (Schell, 2003). They seek opportunities to help students make connections between the content and their own personal lives, make connections across content and grade levels, and connect social studies learning to other areas of the curriculum.

To help students recognize connections between what they are learning and their own lives, you can create opportunities for students to identify examples of when they experienced a struggle, challenge, situation, or feeling in common with the people they are studying. Students are quick to realize that people from the past experienced frustration, fear, excitement, and happiness just as people do today. Bringing human emotion and realistic experiences to students through storytelling, poetry, music, art, and discussions helps forge these connections. Sometimes it is a matter of asking students questions to initiate personal connections, and at other times you might have to facilitate thinking and response by having students write, draw, or discuss with a partner. It will help if you continue to model consideration of personal connections while reading, introducing concepts, and learning about new people, events, and places. Without going off-track with your own personal stories, share with students your connections to people and places from the past. Share your own family histories before asking students to explore theirs. Before learning about pioneers or immigrants, tell about a time you moved from one state to another because of your parent's job.

Here are some strategies to help students consider their personal connections to historic events or other areas of social studies.

- *Four Corners* is a strategy in which you pose a question to students and provide them with four choices—each choice posted in one of the corners of the room. The choices help students rethink and connect to the content. For example, students studying about Columbus' 1492 voyage may have prior knowledge about the age of exploration, explorers, or Columbus to tap into. If not, using this strategy, students can use what they know about human nature to explore information through possible answers. Before, during or after studies, ask students what they think was Columbus' greatest motivation for this journey. Provide four choices for students to consider: (1) Wealth, (2) Fame, (3) Religion, or (4) Adventure. Ask students to select an answer, then go stand in the corner representing what they believe is the correct answer. Once in their corners, instruct students to share their ideas with others in the same corner before each group defends their choice to the others in the room. Whether this activity precedes student learning about Columbus' voyage or not, students will often base their decisions and share opinions that relate to their own knowledge and experiences. Of course, you will want to select situations or choices that relate to student experiences to use for Four Corners activities. Historians would debate the answer to this particular question about Columbus drawing on various resources and contextual arguments. Each would, undoubtedly, defend his or her position reasonably and generate greater interest in the events surrounding Columbus' actual voyage. Similarly, you can recreate this experience in your classroom.

  Four Corners can work with a variety of topics and can be adapted to serve your goals and objectives. Proverbs from various cultures can be displayed in corners for students to select their favorite, or the one that relates most to their life. In their corners, students can share why the proverb is a favorite or how this proverb relates to their lives. Photographs or maps of geographic regions can be posted in corners for students to choose which region they would most like to visit or live in. Once in the corner, they might be instructed to develop a travel brochure for that region or research information about the area. When trying to make connections, provide opportunities for students to make choices and analyze their connections to content through an exercise such as this.

- *Mix and Mingle* is a simple strategy to use when you want students to quietly move around the room, mingle with each other, and share information that relates to the content. At the beginning of the school year, or at the introduction of a new unit of study, students enjoy the opportunity to flip through their textbook to explore the titles, pictures, maps, and other features that they will encounter during their studies. After a few minutes of previewing the text, ask students to find one feature that they are interested in

What did you learn about Columbus' voyage when you were a student? Did you learn that he "discovered" America? Jane Yolen's picture book *Encounter* provides the story from the perspective of a Taino boy and changes our mindset from this explorer's "discovery" to his "encounter" with people already living on the land.

Proverbs are cultural traditions that span the globe and offer advice while expressing obvious truths. You might know "The early bird gets the worm" or "Don't put all your eggs in one basket." How can you use proverbs to help students think critically about social studies concepts?

For resources to help students develop their map-reading skills, see the Web Links module in Chapter 4 on our Companion Website at www. prenhall.com/schell.

History Connections

The pioneer Ezra Meeker became the "Champion of the Oregon Trail" when in 1906, at the age of 76, accompanied by two oxen, a driver and a dog, he made his way from his front yard in Puyallup, Washington, to Washington, DC. His purpose was to preserve and re-mark the Oregon Trail, which was being obliterated by civilization. This man lived to age 98 and made the journey by ox team once more, then by automobile in 1915, and by airplane in 1924!

learning more about. Instruct students to stand, holding their books in front of their chests, facing out and open to the page with their identified feature. With one finger pointing to their favorite feature, ask students to mix and mingle quietly while sharing their favorite item and looking at others' selections. After students have had time to see most or all of their classmates' selections, debrief with students to discuss observations about the selections. You might find that students are interested in learning about topics that you did not intend to cover carefully. Students will appreciate knowing that you pay attention to their interests and acknowledge their opinions.

Aside from selecting features from the text, mix and mingle can be used and adapted frequently to engage students in making and sharing personal connections with the content. For example, students can be asked to identify a person they most admire or would most want to meet from the period they are studying. If learning about careers and workers, young students might be asked what kind of job they would like to have. During the mix and mingle period, students can share their choices and ideas orally, or they can write their answers on an index card to hold in front of their chests while moving about and reading others' cards.

- *Timelines, murals, journals, and memory boxes* are additional ways for helping students connect content over a period of time. When students understand what they learn in social studies, they seek to transfer and apply that information and those skills into new and different settings. Provide avenues for students to compare and contrast historic periods or characters, geographic influences, economic systems, and political dilemmas. Ask questions such as, "What does this remind you of?" or "When did we learn about a similar situation that another group of people faced?" If students have ongoing records of their studies, such as journals or timelines, they can review and connect the information.

- *Scrapbooks, storybooks, or multimedia portfolios* are also used to help students document information during each unit of study and then add to the ongoing project. You can ask students to focus on a person who travels through time or develop a theme over a period of time. For example, each student may create a storybook by pasting his or her photograph into the last page of a bound booklet. Each blank page in the booklet will have a hole that allows you to always see the face of the student in the picture at the back of the book. As students study, for example, about Native Americans, explorers, colonists and pioneers, they can illustrate a page in their booklet framing their own faces with a scene that reflects their studies of different places and different periods of time. The students will enjoy adding more and more stories about their adventures in these places and time periods. Ultimately, they will be able to compare and contrast information about lifestyles over time and space.

Cooperative Learning

A variety of meaningful activities exist for students to participate in learning social studies. Cooperative learning (Johnson & Johnson, 1999; Kagan, 1992) structures and strategies continue to present learning opportunities for students at all grade levels. While cooperative learning activities focus students on learning specific content, they also present opportunities for students to practice and develop their social skills. Here are some ideas for using cooperative learning in your classroom:

- *Think-Pair-Share.* This structure, presented by Kagan (1992), is commonly used at various parts of a lesson. When you want students to answer a question, learn a vocabulary term, analyze a photo, or share ideas, instruct students to first think about their response, then turn to a partner to pair up and compare or share their responses. Finally, call on students to share what they learned from their paired sharing.

- *Cooperative Line-Up.* This is another structure presented by Kagan (1992) and can be used when students need to get up and out of their chairs to organize themselves according to your instructions. For example, if you are reviewing the names of states, ask students to think of the name of a state (or assign) and then line up in alphabetical order according to the name of their state. Once in a line, students can call out the name of their state in order. If you want to press students further, you can ask them to call out the name of a city in that state, or share one fact about the state in another round. Students might identify the name of a historic character or worker before lining up. Students may be lined up in chronological or numerical order depending on your objectives. In some cases, you may want to provide students with information cards to use while organizing. For example, reviewing the steps that led to the Revolutionary War, you could provide students with important dates or important events, which they then represent in chronological order.

- *Jigsaw Reading.* Working together in pairs or groups, students divide the reading into sections so that each person becomes responsible for reading and sharing information with the group. Each student is responsible for learning about the entire reading, so listening to group partners and asking clarification questions are important skills for students to practice.

Cooperative learning activities such as these also provide students an opportunity to practice their social skills such as listening, turn-taking, and sharing.

- *Cooperative Projects.* Assign each group a project to complete requiring the collaborative efforts of all team partners. For example, assign groups to research a historical character or event and design a poster depicting the important features of that person's life or that event. Groups might be assigned to develop and present an oral or dramatic performance. Emphasize the importance of content accuracy as well as the skills necessary to work together.

- *Cooperative Perspectives.* Working in table groups, students are assigned or select a different perspective to represent in discussions. As students learn about a topic through classroom activities, bring the group members together to discuss the different perspectives on the topic. For example, studying about heroes, students can take different perspectives to consider the hero's motivations, fears, supports, and achievements.

Simulations

Interact is a company that develops and sells in-depth simulations that require time, but certainly bring to life many social studies topics and themes. For more information, see the Web Links module in Chapter 4 on our Companion Website at www. prenhall.com/schell.

Simulations are excellent for engaging students in content-specific studies and can be extensive or simplified. A simplified kind of simulation can be found in materials such as *Choosing Your Way Through America's Past* (Walch, 1990) or *Choosing Your Way Through the World's Ancient Past* (Walch, 1991). In these resources, scenarios are read to the class, then students must choose one of two paths before proceeding in the historic adventure. The two groups meet and read material to learn their fate, then face another decision. After each group splits into two groups, the individual groups read on to learn what happens to them. In the end, each group has opportunities to discuss their decisions and their fates, and then learn from those who chose alternate paths. These scenarios represent historical events and engage students by forcing them to make decisions that real people had to make long ago. Along the way, students learn a great deal about the customs, laws, economic situations, and geography that affected people in that place and time.

You can create opportunities for students to be placed in situations where they have to think, discuss, question, analyze, evaluate, and make decisions. Some useful on-line simulations and web-based activities exist that challenge students to make decisions and discover their fates during historic events and periods. These can be used in whole-class or independent learning environments. Furthermore, you can create situations where your students must follow laws or practice customs of the people they are studying. Or, you can go all-out to recreate a historic day or period in your classroom or at your school. Rarely do students forget the day they dressed as pioneers and participated in a wagon train through their neighborhood, or when they portrayed colonial tradesmen, officials, merchants, or slaves and recreated 18th-century life in American colonies.

CREATING ADDITIONAL OPPORTUNITIES FOR SOCIAL STUDIES

When the amount of time dedicated to explicit social studies instruction is limited, look for additional opportunities to engage students in social studies learning. Doing so allows students to see that social studies is not an isolated subject with content and skills that do not transfer or apply in other areas of education and life. Furthermore, students are encouraged to continue thinking about, discussing, and questioning information learned during social studies. Here are some strategies to consider in your classroom:

Read Aloud

Select literature that relates to or supports understandings of social studies topics, eras, themes/concepts, and Big Ideas. Use these during read-aloud periods and align your class discussions to the material introduced during social studies.

For example, during a unit about families, read *Becoming Naomi Leon* (Ryan, 2004) so that students may consider and explore the lives of children raised by a grandparent. There are a variety of issues that confront the main characters in this story reflective of the realities of many families in America today.

Literature Circles

If you use literature circles in your reading program, select books that relate to your social studies content and provide a greater context for the information presented during social studies lessons. Using social studies literature for literature circles allows you to differentiate instruction by providing selections with different reading levels, while focused on the same topic. This also eliminates the need for class sets of core literature, though you will need five or six copies of each title. Literature circles also allow you to develop "expert groups" that can become invaluable resources during the social studies period. In other words, if your class is studying about the Age of Exploration during social studies, and each literature circle group is reading a book about a different explorer from that era, then some students have deeper content knowledge about certain explorers than others. Those "experts" from literature circles can be called on as small-group leaders or in class discussions to share what they know when appropriate. There are a variety of ways to use literature circles to meet your needs in expanding time for social studies.

For example, Joan Lowry Nixon's *Young Americans: Colonial Williamsburg* (2000–2004) series can be used in literature circles by assigning a different book from the series to each reading group.

More information about using literature circles can be found in Frey, N., & Fisher, D. (2006). *Language arts workshop: Purposeful reading and writing instruction.* Upper Saddle River, NJ: Merrill Prentice Hall.

Source: *Book cover from BECOMING NAOMI LEÓN by Pam Muñoz Ryan. Book cover copyright © 2004 by Scholastic, Inc. Reprinted by permission of Scholastic, Inc.*

While studying about Colonial America, students will enjoy the perspectives of children who lived in Williamsburg during the 18th century and will learn more about medical care, smallpox, and the role of women (*Ann's Story: 1747*); slavery, social class, and friendships (*Caesar's Story: 1759*); the Stamp Act, trades, and apprentices (*Nancy's Story: 1765*); crime, punishment, and pirates (*Will's Story: 1771*); freedom of the press and the role of the printer (*Maria's Story: 1773*); and the events that led to the American Revolution (*John's Story: 1775*). Student groups will have characters and settings in common, though the time periods and issues presented in these well-written books vary. Imagine the conversations and engagement during

Fourth-grade students participate in this teacher-facilitated book club featuring a social studies title, *Pascala*.
Source: *Emily Schell*

social studies while reading, discussing, and illuminating these stories during reading!

Book Talks

Inspire students to read great books that relate to your social studies content by frequently providing book talks with your class. You can model this strategy by introducing students to interesting book selections that you have preselected because of their connections to social studies. Rather than introduce them as "good for learning social studies," entice your students by explaining that the book unravels an ancient mystery, or plunges the main characters into a dilemma of historic proportions. Eventually, students will present book talks about exciting selections that they have enjoyed. However, you will want to steer them in the right direction for selecting, understanding and then sharing books.

For example, during studies of the American Revolution, you might present a book talk for *George Washington, Spymaster: How the Americans Outspied the British and Won the Revolutionary War* (Allen, 2004) by stating, "Have you ever written a secret note to your best friend? You wanted the information to be so secret that perhaps you created a special code for just the two of you to use in decoding information. When I was your age, my sisters and I liked to write notes in lemon juice. We dipped a toothpick into a lemon and then used the juice as invisible ink. Then the reader had to hold the letter close to a lightbulb to read the information! Well, I loved reading this book about George Washington and how *he* used lots of creative ways to write and pass secret notes during the most important war of our nation. I grew up thinking that the war was won on the battle fields during the American Revolution. But, after reading this book, I'm beginning to think that we won the war with the help of a lot of spies and a lot of ingenious plans!"

Book Bags

Some teachers send home a book in a bag with a stuffed animal or book-related activity for the family to do at home. Why not send home your social studies in book bags? This will engage the families while allowing them to help expand time, attention, and details to your studies in the classroom. Across the grade levels, you can create book bags as simply as placing a book with an instruction sheet for guided questions, simple activities, and perhaps a map or fact sheet on the area of study in a large, sturdy zip-lock or canvas bag. With a class set of these book bags, students can rotate them regularly, depending on the amount of reading and kinds of activities the bags include.

For example, these are just some of the picture books that may be included in book bags circulated among students during a unit of study about symbols of America:

- *A is for America* (Scillan, 2001)
- *D is for Democracy* (Grodin, 2004)
- *I Pledge Allegiance* (Martin, 2002)
- *The Pledge of Allegiance* (Bellamy, 2000)
- *The Flag We Love* (Ryan, 2000)
- *America Is . . .* (Borden, 2002)
- *The Story of the Statue of Liberty* (Maestro, 1989)
- *America the Beautiful* (Bates, 2004)
- *By the Dawn's Early Light* (Kroll, 2000)
- *Soaring With the Wind: The Bald Eagle* (Gibbons, 1998)

Each book bag could include a few questions for families to discuss after reading the book in the bag, such as:

Understanding how symbols are used in America also helps students understand how authors use symbolism as a literary device.

- What American symbol was the focus of this book?
- What is the meaning and importance of this symbol?
- Where can we go to see or hear this symbol?
- What will we do the next time we see or hear this symbol?
- Why is it important for our nation to have symbols?

Writing Prompts

Frequently, writing prompts are used to warm up thinking and skills before a new topic, or to summarize thoughts and new information after a topic is presented in class. Consider using writing prompts that relate to social studies content when appropriate.

For example, imagine your class is studying about the pioneers who moved west in the mid-1800s. However, during language arts instructional time, you are presenting a lesson on writing friendly letters. Instruct students to imagine that they are traveling to Oregon along that hot, dusty trail and that they have time to write a letter to someone back home. As students learn the format of a friendly letter, allow them to write from an historic perspective. Figure 4.10 contains a student's perspective writing.

Walk and Talk

Oftentimes, your students are walking in pairs from one place to another—the classroom to the cafeteria, the bus to the playground, the library to the auditorium. Pair up students and allow them to hold a quiet two-person conversation while they walk. However, give them a

Figure 4.10   A student letter from the Oregon Trail.

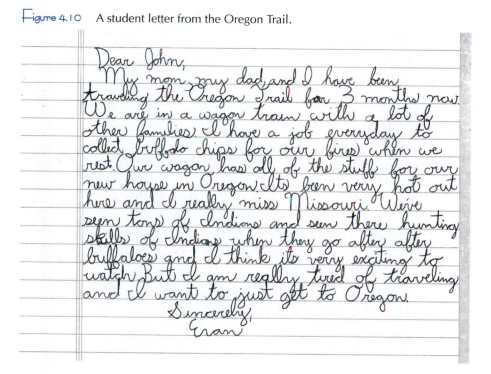

Dear John,

My mom, my dad, and I have been traveling the Oregon Trail for 3 months now. We are in a wagon train with a lot of other families. I have a job everyday to collect buffalo chips for our fires when we rest. Our wagon has all of the stuff for our new house in Oregon. Its been very hot out here and I really miss Missouri. We've seen tons of Indians and seen there hunting skills of Indians when they go after after buffaloes and I think its very exciting to watch. But I am really tired of traveling and I want to just get to Oregon.

Sincerely,
Eran

question to answer or a topic to discuss. These discussion prompts can be generic to social studies, such as:

- What did you learn in social studies this week?
- What questions do you have about the information we are learning in social studies?
- If you could go back in time to meet with any of the people we have studied about so far this year, who would it be? What would you talk about?
- Where in the world would you travel in order to learn more about _____ (communities, democracy, immigration, etc.)?

Or, the prompts may be specific to your studies. For example, during a unit on immigration, you might ask students to discuss with their partners:

- Talk about a time you had to move someplace. Why did you move and where did you go?
- If you had to move to a new country, what would be the most exciting thing to you?
- If you had to move to a new country, what would be your biggest challenge?
- Discuss someone you know or heard about who moved here from another country.
- What would cause you to uproot your entire family and life to move to another country?

This strategy can be used when students are required to walk or jog during physical education as well.

Seize any opportunity to integrate the curriculum—it reinforces student learning and is a good time investment.

Musical Chairs

A lot of period recordings exist as well as songs about historic periods and recordings of songs from periods. Using these recordings during limited social studies time can detract from focused instruction. So, when students need a stretch break, or you have indoor physical education (usually due to weather), use these recordings to play musical chairs. The age-old game requires students to focus their listening skills on the music while walking around a circle of chairs and anticipate when the recording will stop—at which time students dash for a seat in a chair. Because there is one chair fewer than the number of students playing the game, one student loses out and stands out during the next round. A chair is removed and the music continues. A series of rounds are played until there is only one student left. That student is the winner. You might challenge the winner to repeat a verse from the song or try to identify information about the music played during the game.

This is your opportunity to give some background information and added detail to the topics being studied in social studies.

Singing New Songs

Many music programs provide cultural and historical songs for students to learn and sing. Align those songs in your program with your social studies units of instruction. Look for additional songs that will add culture and detail to your social studies and integrate those into your formal music program or into your morning warmup singing. Most students sing a patriotic song each morning following the flag salute, and yet too few associate the song's meaning and context with their studies of American history. Take advantage of these opportunities, as most students enjoy singing and learning new songs!

For example, Forty-niners sang a variety of songs while traveling to California for the Gold Rush, mining in the mountains and rivers, and building communities throughout California. Some of these songs, such as "Sweet Betsy From Pike," have a number of variations since the songs were passed along frequently and oftentimes the words were changed. Still, students learn information from these songs. They learn about the land, experiences of the miners, hopes and dreams, travel routes, etc.

Landscapes and Portraits

Most art programs require students to study and recreate landscapes or portraits. Often, there is a specific grade-level skill associated with these works of art, such as perspective or color in landscapes and detail or use of space in portraits. Sometimes, students are required to analyze examples of artists whose style is emulated in the students' own work. In one classroom, students might create portraits in the poster style of Toulouse-Lautrec, whereas in another classroom students might create impressionistic landscapes in the style of Monet. These lessons can continue to be effective by integrating the period, art styles, and examples from the period or topics studied in social studies.

For example, students in a primary-grade class studying about families might make family members the subjects of their portraits. Older students studying the Constitution might use founding fathers as the subjects of their portraits. The style and skill of the art lesson may still apply. Comparing and contrasting a student-created portrait of George Washington in the style of Picasso to Gilbert Stuart's famous portrait would be exciting!

Acting Up!

Students are good at acting up! If drama is a component of your curriculum, use this opportunity to recreate historic moments that you are studying. An easy way to avoid the full-scale school play is to engage students in impromptu skits or drama exercises that allow them to

You can sometimes find access to songs that can be downloaded for free. See the Web Links module in Chapter 4 on our Companion Website at www.prenhall.com/schell.

You can find copies of many historical documents for use in the classroom. For more information, see the Web Links module in Chapter 4 on our Companion Website at www.prenhall.com/schell.

explore pantomime, monologue, dialogue, scenes, and characterization. Students can write brief narrations to "set the stage" in place of backdrops or costumes. They can act around minimal props, such as a hat, document, newspaper, or artifact. Focus students on a drama skill (voice projection, body language, emotions, etc.) or technique (improvisation, pantomime, tableau, etc.) and then use your social studies content to apply the skill or technique.

For example, while studying a unit about ancient Egypt, and teaching about characterization (skill) and improvisation (technique), you can encourage students to take on the roles of people they are studying. Brainstorm with students the various roles of people who lived during ancient times in Egypt (e.g., pharaoh, queen, scribe, dancer, pyramid builder, slave, farmer, stonecutter, priest, weaver, herdsman). Assign each role to a pair or trio of students and allow those students to discuss with each other what a person in this role might look, feel, smell, think, and act like. Then, set the stage (e.g., you are at the marketplace in the city; you are aboard a boat on the Nile) and call a group of students to come up and take their places. You might want one pharaoh, two weavers, and one dancer, for example. Once their places are established, allow them a few minutes to present an impromptu skit by acting out their role in the designated setting.

Reader's Theatre

A variety of Reader's Theatre scripts are available to purchase through teacher resource networks that can be found in the Web Links module in Chapter 4 on our Companion Website at www.prenhall.com/schell.

Students enjoy participating in (and creating) Readers' Theatres during language arts as well as social studies periods. However, these can become time consuming. Consider adapting lesson plans for drama (acting) and language arts (reading, writing, speaking) to include social studies themes and topics. Look for scripts that support your social studies content.

Students can have fun creating scripts during their writing period by working in pairs or small groups, identifying characters and a setting related to social studies. The students then take turns as one of the characters (or the narrator), adding to the script. One master copy of the script can be circulated among the group as each student adds his or her part. When the script is finalized, the teacher may make copies for each student to practice before the performance.

Games and Sports

Chances are, there is a sports connection to the content being studied in social studies. Almost every culture has a sport or physical game that can be adapted and recreated by students. Periods of history also relate to sports and games that can be played during physical education, but enhanced with attention to social studies lessons. A baseball game becomes more meaningful during studies of segregation (Negro

Book Links

There are a number of excellent books that invite students into the history of sports, including *The Story of Negro League Baseball* (Brashler, 1994), *Wilma Unlimited: How Wilma Rudolph Became the World's Fastest Woman* (Krull, 1996), and *Baseball Saved Us* (Mochizuki, 1993).

Baseball League, Jackie Robinson), equal rights (women's league, Jackie Mitchell, Alta Weiss), or Japanese internment (baseball played in internment camps). Students waiting for a turn at bat or waiting for a fly ball outfield have more to think about than who will win the game.

For example, during studies of ancient Greece, it makes sense to recreate the Olympic games on the playground. Some modifications can be made to turn an orange (or softball) into a shot for shot put, a paper plate into a discus, or a chopstick into a javelin. However, it is the planning and preparation in anticipation for the games that engages students in physical fitness. Each event becomes worthy of discussion as students analyze the necessary skills to succeed in each physical challenge.

Additionally, there are some games that can be adapted to include social studies information. Playing basketball, students might be required to state one fact about _____ (the Bill of Rights; the Civil War; geographic landforms) in order to earn the points after a basket. The game of Duck, Duck, Goose might be adapted to Consumer, Consumer, Farmer. In Four Square, the server might begin by asking a question related to social studies, such as, "What is the name of a Native American tribe from the Southwest?" The student who answers correctly first gets served to that round.

Conclusion

Once you know what to teach, you have to determine the best way to teach. This chapter has presented a wide range of ideas, all based on research evidence and practical implementation, for providing students with access to the wonderful world of social studies. Regardless of the approach we take as teachers, we must remember to teach for understanding.

History's Finer Points

1872 Instructions to the Teachers (from the Mason Street School, San Diego Historical Days Association)

1. Teachers will fill lamps, clean chimneys and trim wicks each day.
2. Each teacher will bring a scuttle of coal and a bucket of water for the day's use.
3. Make your pens carefully. You may whittle nibs for the individual tastes of children.
4. Men teachers may take one evening each week for courting purposes or two evenings a week if they go to church regularly.
5. After ten hours in the school the teacher should spend the remaining time reading the Bible and other good books.
6. Women teachers who marry or engage in other unseemly conduct will be dismissed.
7. Every teacher who smokes, uses liquor in any form, frequents pool or public halls, or gets shaved in a barber shop will give good reasons to suspect his worth, intentions, integrity and honesty.
8. The teacher who performs his labors faithfully without fault for five years will be given an increase of 25 cents a week in his pay—providing the Board of Education approves.

Document Based Question: In what ways have schools, teachers, and students changed since 1872? In what ways have they stayed the same?

Questions to Consider

1. What will you do to plan with the end in mind?
2. Which instructional strategies are you comfortable using?
3. Which instructional strategies would you like to add to your teaching repertoire, and how will you do this?
4. How will you select the reading materials you want your students to use?

Quiz yourself on this chapter's important concepts on our Companion Website's Chapter 4 self-assessments at www. prenhall.com/schell.

Exercises

1. Observe several teachers as they teach social studies. Which strategies do they use? For which students are these strategies most effective?
2. How do teachers vary the implementation of these strategies for English language learners, students with disabilities, students

performing well above grade level, or students who are not motivated to participate in school?

3. Based on the content you plan to teach from Chapter 3, identify the specific instructional approaches you will use to ensure that your students develop a strong understanding of the ideas and information.

References

Ainsworth, L. (2003). *Unwrapping the standards: A simple process to make standards manageable.* Denver, CO: Advanced Learning Press.

Atwood, V. (Ed.). (1991). *Elementary school social studies: Research as a guide to practice.* Washington, DC: National Council for the Social Studies.

California Department of Education. (2001). *California History–Social Science Standards.* Sacramento, CA: Author.

Johnson, D., & Johnson, R. (1999). *Learning together and alone* (5th Ed.). Edina, MA: Interaction Books.

Kogan, S. (1992). *Cooperative learning.* San Juan Capistrono, CA: Kogan Cooperative Learning.

Marzano, R., Pickering, D., & Pollack, J. (2001). *Classroom instruction that works: Research-based strategies for increasing student achievement.* Alexandria, VA: Association of Supervision and Curriculum Development.

McTighe, J., & Wiggins, G. (1998). *Understanding by design.* Alexandria, VA: Association of Supervision and Curriculum Development.

National Center for History in the Schools. (1996). *National Standards for History.* Los Angeles: National Center for History in the Schools.

National Council for the Social Studies. (1994). *Curriculum standards for social studies: Expectations of excellence.* Washington, DC: Author.

Parker, W. (2000, October). *Concept teaching in social studies.* Presentation at San Diego City Schools. San Diego, CA.

Schell, E. (2003). *Exploring teachers' experiences with the Colonial Williamsburg teacher institute.* University of San Diego: San Diego.

Shaver, J. (1991). *Handbook of research on social studies teaching and learning.* Washington, DC: National Council for the Social Studies.

Shaver, J. (2004). *Handbook of research on improving student achievement.* Arlington, VA: Educational Research Service.

Steffey, S., & Hood, W. (1994). *If this is social studies, why isn't it boring?* Portland, ME: Stenhouse.

Taba, H. (1967). *Teacher's handbook for elementary social studies.* Palo Alto, CA: Addison-Wesley.

Walch, J. W. (1990). *Choosing your way through America's past.* Portland, ME: Walch Publishing.

Walch, J. W. (1991). *Choosing your way through the world's ancient past.* Portland, ME: Walch Publishing.

Zemelman, S., Daniels, H., & Hyde, A. (1993). *Bests practice: New standards for teaching and learning in America's schools.* Portsmouth, NH: Heinemann.

Children's Literature

Allen, T. (2004). *George Washington, spymaster: How the Americans outspied the British and won the revolutionary war.* Washington, DC: National Geographic Children's.

Bates, K. L. (2004). *America the beautiful.* New York: Little, Brown.

Bellamy, F. (2000). *The pledge of allegiance.* New York: Scholastic.

Borden, L. (2002). *America is . . .* New York: Margaret K. McElderry.

Brashler, W. (1994). *The story of Negro League baseball.* New York: Ticknor & Fields.

Bunting, E. (2001). *Dandelions.* New York: Voyager.

Erickson, P. (1997). *Daily life in a covered wagon.* New York: Puffin.

Fritz, J. (1976). *What's the big idea, Ben Franklin?* New York: G. P. Putnam Sons.

Gibbons, G. (1998). *Soaring with the wind: The bald eagle.* New York: HarperCollins.

Greenwood, B. (1998). *A pioneer sampler: The daily life of a pioneer family in 1840.* Boston: Houghton Mifflin.

Grodin, E. (2004). *D is for democracy: A citizen's alphabet.* Chelsea, MI: Sleeping Bear Press.

Knight, A. (1993). *The way west: Journal of a pioneer woman.* New York: Simon & Schuster.

Kroll, S. (2000). *By the dawn's early light.* New York: Scholastic.

Krull, L. (1996). *Wilma unlimited: How Wilma Rudolph became the world's fastest woman.* San Diego, CA: Harcourt.

Maestro, B. (1989). *The story of the statue of liberty.* New York: HarperTrophy.

MacLachlan, P. (1985). *Sarah, plain and tall.* New York: HarperTrophy.

Martin, B. (2002). *I pledge allegiance.* Cambridge, MA: Candlewick Press.

Mochizuki, K. (1993). *Baseball saved us*. New York: Lee & Low.

Nixon, J. L. (2000). *Ann's story: 1747* (Young Americans: Colonial Williamsburg). New York: Delacorte.

Nixon, J. L. (2000). *Caesar's story: 1759* (Young Americans: Colonial Williamsburg). New York: Delacorte.

Nixon, J. L. (2000). *Nancy's story: 1765* (Young Americans: Colonial Williamsburg). New York: Delacorte.

Nixon, J. L. (2001). *Maria's story: 1773* (Young Americans: Colonial Williamsburg). New York: Delacorte.

Nixon, J. L. (2001). *Will's story: 1771* (Young Americans: Colonial Williamsburg). New York: Delacorte.

Nixon, J. L. (2004). *John's story: 1775* (Young Americans: Colonial Williamsburg). Williamsburg: Colonial Williamsburg Foundation.

Ryan, P. M. (1996). *The flag we love*. Watertown, MA: Charlesbridge Publishing.

Ryan, P. M. (2004). *Becoming Naomi Leon*. New York: Scholastic.

Scillan, D. (2001). *A is for America*. Chelsea, MI: Sleeping Bear Press.

Stamaty, M. A. (2004). *Alia's mission: Saving the books of Iraq*. New York: Knopf.

Stanley, D. (2001). *Roughing it on the Oregon trail*. New York: HarperTrophy.

Turner, A. (1997). *Mississippi mud: Three prairie journals*. New York: Harper Collins.

Wilder, L. I. (1953). *Little house on the prairie*. New York: HarperTrophy.

Winter, J. (2005). *The librarian of Basra: A true story from Iraq*. San Diego, CA: Harcourt.

5

Using Texts for Teaching and Learning Social Studies

Source: *Patrick White/ Merrill*

Big Idea

Good readers access a variety of texts and use effective strategies to make meaning from those texts.

Essential Question

Why should students use multiple texts in social studies?

Mr. Roundtree projected an image on the screen at the front of the classroom using his laptop and data projector. The image was an icon that he thought would be familiar to most, if not all, of his students. He asked, "What comes to mind when you see this icon?" Students looked at the image of a skateboard with a red circle around it and a red line through the skateboard. They raised their hands and said, "No skateboards!" "You cannot skate in the area where that sign is." "People don't want kids skating in that place." Mr. Roundtree continued to press the students and asked them how they knew what this icon meant, where they have seen this icon displayed, and why we have nonskating areas. At first, he asked these questions to the whole class, and then he asked students to turn to a partner to discuss the icon. Mr. Roundtree circulated around the classroom listening carefully to student conversations. As it turned out, all of the students in his class could identify the image and had seen the image in a public place, and most could explain why these icons existed. Many students also had personal opinions about skating and nonskating areas, which related to their knowledge of state laws and personal experiences. Some students questioned whether or not skaters' rights were being violated, and some raised concerns about skaters' safety as well as nonskaters' safety in the community related to these signs.

Then Mr. Roundtree explained, "Now it is your turn to transform a lot of information and opinions into simple images, or icons, like this. Let's start reading about how people set off in search of spices and gold about 600 years ago. As we read, pay close attention to the images, or pictures, that come into your mind. . . ." Mr. Roundtree then used the data projector to display a section of the text and began reading aloud to his students as they followed along.

Book Links

Use simple books that present signs and icons at all grade levels (even though the books may seem only appropriate for primary grade levels). For example, *I Read Signs* (Hoban), *I Read Symbols* (Hoban), and *Signs on the Road* (Hill). Also, to spice up your studies of exploration and trade from the Golden Age of Exploration, look for these books: *Land Ho! Fifty Glorious Years in the Age of Exploration* (Parker) and *Exploration and Conquest: The Americas After Columbus 1500–1620* (Maestro).

INTRODUCTION

What do you remember about reading and writing in your social studies class when you were a student? You might recall your teacher asking you to take out a big, heavy, boring book with instructions to "*Open your book to page 6,254 and start reading at the first bold heading. Read until you fall out of your chair from boredom.*" Of course your teacher never really said that, but you sure may have felt as if she did. You knew that you had to read to gather information to learn social studies, but you may not have been sure how to do that. As for writing, your experiences were probably limited to writing the answers to the questions at the end of the chapter, which may or may not have included an essay of sorts. Now you are the teacher, and we are going to help you teach your students to read and write for understanding.

READING AND WRITING HELPS STUDENTS UNDERSTAND SOCIAL STUDIES

Most textbook companies also provide a teacher's edition that has a number of teaching ideas based on the content of the book. Several publishers maintain an active website to add current events and updated teaching connections.

Most teachers rely on one or several text sources for their social studies instruction. Although many researchers recommend decreased use of the textbook as the central or sole source for social studies instruction (Zemelman, Daniels, & Hyde, 1993; Steffey, 1994), the textbook remains an important part of most social studies classrooms as it guides student learning articulated by state frameworks and standards. Most new textbooks provide focused content and skills for teachers who struggle to provide standards-based instruction and do not want to develop new curriculum all of the time themselves. Regardless of whether the textbook is used or not, the use of texts in a social studies class is unavoidable if students are to access and understand the course content.

How can we empower students to comprehend and use the various texts they are exposed to in social studies? How can students develop the skills necessary to appropriately evaluate and manage the vast body of information that confronts them in a social studies classroom and textbook? To begin addressing these important questions, let us take a look at how students learn in a social studies classroom with a focus on social studies texts.

As a social studies teacher, you attempt to teach new information, build background knowledge, engage students in critical analysis, and help students generate connections with and across the content. All of this combined with the complexities of social studies texts makes for an almost overwhelming task. However, we can accomplish this task by identifying *how* students will achieve these goals in order to understand the content. First, students must learn to read for information—from contemporary sources as well as historical documents—in order to access prior knowledge and build connections. Beyond that, they must

Figure 5.1

History repeats itself. Which may explain why it's so boring.

Source: © *Mike Baldwin/Comered*

write essays, persuasive arguments, and comprehensive reports to analyze, interpret, evaluate, organize, and summarize the information. Further, students must listen to teachers, guest speakers, and authentic
recordings to build background knowledge, learn new information, and
draw connections across time, across examples, and across content
areas. Students must also answer questions orally, talk with partners
about the content, and give public speeches. Finally, they must interpret
and discuss complex visual information. In other words, the learning of
social studies is complex, and it is language-based.

Students process information by reading, writing, speaking, listening, and viewing. In this chapter, we will explore the various ways that
teachers can facilitate text comprehension. We will focus our discussion
on the range of texts that students typically encounter in the social
studies classroom, including the core textbook, associated literature
selections, primary source documents, and Internet sites. Our goal is to
ensure that students engage with the various texts they are exposed to
and learn from these texts (Alvermann, 2002).

STUDENTS MUST UNDERSTAND HOW TO TRANSFORM TEXT

The Merriam-Webster on-line dictionary indicates that the word
transform means "to change in composition or structure." This dictionary also indicates that the word "implies a major change in form,
nature, or function, as in *transformed* a small company into a corporate
giant." We think that this word and its definition fit just right. Our
work with students learning social studies content from texts suggests
that they must *transform* the text in some way. This transformation allows students to learn with and through the texts. In other words, just
passively reading the text is not sufficient; they must do something with
it—they must transform the text so that it becomes part of them and
their memory (e.g., Fisher & Frey, 2004).

The interesting question, then, is how can we get students to transform texts? We have organized our thinking about this question into two
areas: (1) strategies that require students to transform the text in their
mind; and (2) strategies that require students to transform the text on
paper. We will explore each of these as they relate to social studies texts.

STUDENTS BENEFIT FROM "IN YOUR MIND" STRATEGIES

There are a number of ways that students can transform the text in their
minds, including making connections, engaging in partner conversations, and visualizing.

Making Connections

One of the ways that students can transform the text in their minds is by making connections with the text. Harvey and Goudvis (2000) suggest that there are at least three kinds of connections that students can make: text-to-self, text-to-text, and text-to-world. Of course, students must be taught how to make these connections with their reading materials and must focus on connections that help them understand, remember, and apply the information in the reading.

In terms of teaching these connections, our experience suggests that you should select specific passages and invite students to make connections across the three categories. You should model the type of connection that is useful. For example, you might select the following passage from a sixth-grade social studies text to read aloud while students follow along in the book and then model making connections:

> *Read aloud:* Under Shihuangdi's leadership, unified China grew bigger and stronger. The empire also became increasingly rich as taxes flowed into the capital. As time went by, the government began making even greater demands on its people. (Banks et al, 1999, p. 244)
>
> *Model text-to-self connections:* I remember playing field hockey when I was in high school. When we had good leadership, our team was big and strong. Everyone worked hard to be a part of our team. We took our games seriously and listened to the team captain. When she wanted us to work harder, we did. I have also participated on teams that had poor leadership. We did not want to work hard and as a result, we performed poorly.
>
> *Model text-to-text connections:* So far in this chapter about China, no one has been mentioned as a great leader. I have only read about the changes and turmoil in early Chinese history. Leadership must be important to the success of a nation. This reminds me of someone we read about earlier in the year. His name was Hammurabi and he was a strong leader, too. Shihuangdi also reminds me of some of the Egyptian pharaohs that we read about. I read a book about ancient China last year. I was fascinated reading about the terra cotta army that the emperor had built. I think Shihuangdi was that emperor!
>
> *Model text-to-world connections:* My parents are always complaining about paying high taxes and how it's the fault of the governor and the president. I guess taxing workers is not a new concept. Have empires, or governments, always tried to become rich by taxing the people? I wonder if there is another way for governments to become rich, or wealthy.

Modeling these types of "in your mind" text connections is important for students, but there are other ways to help students learn this process as well. For example, you might provide guiding questions for students to consider in their minds after reading a passage. Read the

Students often need modeling of these types of connections. By thinking aloud the connections you make with a text, you help students learn to incorporate this thinking into their repertoire.

History Connections

Shihuangdi is one of the most notable rulers in China's history. Though he ruled for a brief period of about 15 years, he made lasting changes in the country, which included unifying the written language and monetary system, and building roads and the Great Wall.

following textbook passage from a sixth-grade unit on ancient Greece and think about the kinds of questions you might ask your students to consider in making text-to-self, text-to-text, and text-to-world connections:

> At age 20, Spartan men entered the regular army. The men remained in military barracks for 10 more years. They ate all of their meals in dining halls with other soldiers. A typical meal was a vile-tasting dish called black broth—pork boiled in animal blood, salt and vinegar.
>
> Spartans returned home at age 30 but stayed in the army until age 60. They continued to train for combat. They expected to either win on the battlefield or die, but never to surrender. One Spartan mother ordered her son to "Come home carrying your shield or being carried on it." (Spielvogel, 2005, pp. 126–127)

What questions would you use to invite students to make the connections? Here are a few that we might use:

Text-to-self: Do you have family members or friends who are 20 years old? What would they say if they were required to serve in the army for 40 years? Have you ever tasted food that looks like "black broth?"

Text-to-text: In earlier readings about other ancient civilizations, what did you learn about armies and soldiers? Did other civilizations require men to serve in the army? How does this information compare to other readings about ancient Greece?

Text-to-world: How are armies built today? Is there a need to have large armies in the world today? Where do you read information about armies today?

History Connections

Alexander the Great, who was from Macedonia, was raised in Pella. As a youth, Alexander was taught by Aristotle, who was once a student of Plato.

It is important to remember that not all connections made by students are equal. Making the text-to-self connection, "My parents went to Greece," is probably less helpful in aiding comprehension than a text-to-self connection, "I remember when my dad went to fight in Afghanistan. I bet the kids in Sparta were sad when the Peloponnesian War started." In the first example, the student is making a connection to the general topic of Greece, which might have been useful in first introducing the topic of the unit, but is no longer useful in this focused piece of text. In the second example, the student is making a connection to the specific information presented in the text passage about Greek soldiers. In making this specific connection, the student is creating a more meaningful connection between his own experience and the content in the text.

Similarly, a student might make the text-to-text connection, "This reminds me of a book I read about Spartan soldiers. It was one of those Eyewitness Books called *Ancient Greece* (Pearson, 2004). One chapter showed how Spartan men trained every day so they would be the strongest army in all of Greece." This connection is more focused and

Alexander the Great—historical archives.
Source: *Getty Images, Inc.—Liaison*

useful to the reader than the text-to-text connection, "I read a story about Greece when I was in second grade." Simply making a connection is not sufficient. The connection must be useful and focused in alignment with the main ideas and purpose of the text. Create opportunities to teach your students how to use this strategy and improve their use of this effective strategy by modeling, questioning, guiding, and evaluating the kinds of connections students make to their texts.

Text connections provide ample opportunities for students to make personal, textual, and real-world connections to the information they encounter in social studies texts. You can facilitate student engagement with texts through guided questioning and conversations. By making these text connections during and after reading, you will help students increase their understanding and guide their thinking when they read independently.

Excellent examples of text connections can be found in the book reviews posted at such websites as www.amazon.com. Well-written reviews—most written by young readers—share various kinds of connections made to the text while explaining why the reviewer enjoyed or did not care for the book.

Book Links

Books from the Eyewitness Books series are excellent additions to every classroom library. Various titles feature engaging information for students of all ages through nonfiction text, photography, timelines, charts, and illustrations. Titles range from *Medieval Life* (Langley) and *Maya, Inca & Aztec* (Baquedano) to *Buddhism* (Wilkinson) and *Civil War* (Stanchak).

Source: Cover from Ancient Greece.

Partner Conversations

Another way students can transform the text in their minds is through partner conversations in which they talk about the reading. We are particularly fond of the work done by the Institute for Learning at the University of Pittsburgh (Michaels, O'Conner, & Resnick, 2002) on accountable talk, which, according to the Principles of Learning, refers to the way students engage in discourse to manipulate information. Using accountable discourse, students listen and respond seriously and directly to each other. When making, supporting, or refuting statements, students are accountable for providing evidence to support their ideas. According to the Institute for Learning

(http:// www.instituteforlearning. org), there are three core principles for accountable talk:

- *Accountability to the learning community:* Accountable talk encourages students to build on the comments of their peers in a respect-
  ful and inclusive manner.
- *Accountability to accurate knowledge:* Students are responsible for
  making sure the facts they use to support arguments are accurate.
  When appropriate, students are encouraged to cite their sources of
  information. This can be as simple as saying, "The last section in the
  chapter stated that. . . ."
- *Accountability to rigorous thinking.* Students are expected to use
  methods of reasoning appropriate to the discipline. In the case of social studies, students should exercise their chronological and spatial
  thinking skills in the context of their conversations and pay attention
  to multiple perspectives, point of view, interpretation, and evidence.

To make partner conversations a natural, consistent, and useful
classroom activity, we suggest you teach students by first introducing
the idea of accountable talk as a whole group activity before moving to
small-group and partner conversations. Your goal is to get students to:

- Press for clarification and explanation.
- Require justifications of proposals and challenges.
- Recognize and challenge misconceptions.
- Demand evidence for claims or arguments.
- Have students interpret and use each other's statements.

Imagine the following scenario in a classroom:

*Mr. Matsumoto asks his third-grade students, "How many of you can
remember a time when you just could not wait to get home and share
some exciting news with a parent or your brother or sister? You raced
into the house or waited anxiously for that person to get home and
when you blurted out your wonderful news, the response was, 'Oh,
that's nice' or something equally unenthusiastic." As students start to
smile and show signs that they can relate to this experience, the teacher
goes on to explain the importance of paying attention to and responding appropriately to the words of another person. Then Mr. Matsumoto
calls a student to the front of the room to role-play and demonstrate
the differences between accountable talk and nonaccountable talk.
This is what happened in the classroom:*

1. *In scene 1, the student says with great enthusiasm, "You'll never
   guess what happened on the playground during recess! The custodian
   went crazy and acted really weird and all the kids were laughing!"
   The teacher responds, "Oh, that's nice."*

In classrooms where
partner talk is used,
more students have
the opportunity to
develop their oral
language skills.

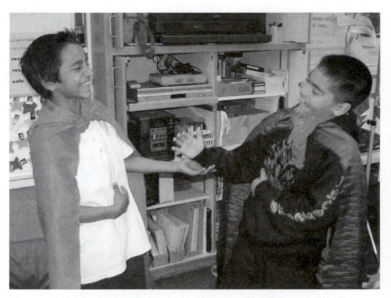

These students practice a scene in their dramatization of a Greek tragedy before presenting to another class.
Source: *Emily Schell*

2. *Then Mr. Matsumoto asks the students what they thought of his response to what the student said. The class concludes that the teacher was not listening. "Right!" says Mr. Matsumoto. "That is not accountable talk."*

3. *In scene 2, the student repeats, with enthusiasm, "You'll never guess what happened on the playground during recess! The custodian went crazy and acted really weird and all the kids were laughing!" The teacher responds politely, "Really? Tell me more about this. What exactly did the custodian do that made you think he was crazy? Why did students laugh at him?"*

4. *Mr. Matsumoto asks the students what they noticed about this response. The class discusses how the teacher asked for more information pertaining to the student's claim. The students explain that they could tell he listened this time to the student by the way he asked questions that related to the student's story, and asked them politely. "This," says Mr. Matsumoto, "is accountable talk."*

The teacher then presents students with a chart (see Figure 5.2) that will remain posted in the classroom for students to use when they engage in accountable talk. He reviews the chart, stopping after each skill to invite additional students to role-play scenes that demonstrate that skill for accountable talk. He asks for two students to read the chart skill and then demonstrate first what is not accept-

able for that skill and then what is acceptable for that skill. Mr. Matsumoto concludes by explaining to students that they have a lot to learn from each other, and that accountable talk helps them to be better listeners, speakers, and learners. He tells the class that they will continue to use these skills to develop accountable talk in their classroom—in large-groups, small-groups, and especially paired discussion. "Don't be surprised," he adds, "if this becomes your homework as well!"

The use of technology can enhance your progress and assessments of students engaged in accountable talk while allowing students the benefit of self or peer evaluation as well. iPods or other recording devices can be used to record student conversations that are then played back for your assessment or as models in the classroom. Some classes

Figure 5.2   Accountable talk chart.

Accountable Talk Skill	Acceptable	Not Acceptable
Clarify and Explain	Asks clarification questions related to the ideas and information shared. Asks for better explanations. Asks until the information and ideas of the speaker are clear and understandable.	Does not ask questions about ideas or information. Asks simplified or general questions, such as "What do you mean?" Does not have a clear understanding of the information and ideas of the speaker.
Justify Statements	Identifies position or statement proposed by the speaker. Asks the speaker to give an acceptable reason for the position or statement.	Accepts what the speaker thinks or says without asking for reasons behind the ideas or information.
Challenge Misconceptions	Recognizes that information is incorrect or false. Asks questions about how the speaker developed these ideas. Presents opinions or information to refute claims.	Accepts what the speaker says and does not ask any questions about the ideas or information. Assumes that what is said must be true.
Ask for Evidence	Asks where speaker found information. Asks if information came from reliable sources. Asks how the speaker drew conclusions from information sources.	Does not question how the speaker found or used information to make statements.
Use Statements	Interprets the speaker's statements. Uses statements made by the speaker to ask questions. Restates information presented by the speaker in order to clarify information.	Responds to the speaker without reference to statements made or information presented.

maintain their own websites and may add model podcasts to their exhibits of student work. This allows students, educators, and parents/community members to listen to content-rich student conversations as evidence of student learning. Developing an on-line rubric for accountable talk expectations and evaluation will be enhanced with audio-clip examples of students performing at each rubric level.

Although we do not suggest that students just randomly talk about their readings, we also do not suggest that the discussion become too contrived. With proper modeling, instruction, and facilitation, over time, students will hold one another accountable for each of these points as they have meaningful conversations about what they are learning in their texts.

Visualizing

A third way to encourage students to transform texts in their minds is through visualizing. We know that good readers create mental images in their minds as they read. Unfortunately, not all students do this. Further, students are less likely to visualize when the text becomes too technical, too factual, or too foreign. As a result, students are not engaging in one of the most powerful transformation strategies exactly when they need to.

Visualizing has been used to teach all kinds of content, from molecular models in chemistry (Wu, Krajcik, & Soloway, 2001) to geography (Chatterjea, 1999) to literature (Goodman, 2003). Harvey and Goudvis (2000) remind us, "When we visualize, we create pictures in our minds that belong to us and no one else" (p. 97). Teachers can use this approach to transforming text to encourage students to create those mental images and to store those images as representations of the texts that they are reading. Students may need to be reminded to use all of their senses in their visualizations—what they could taste, touch, smell, and hear are as important as what they "see." Inviting students to share their visualizations with partners or the whole class provides students an opportunity to understand that people visualize text in different ways and that there is not one right way to do this.

In Ms. Allen's fifth-grade class, students were engaged in the study of the colonies. After reading a selection of the text, Ms. Allen asked her students to visualize life as a person living in one of the colonies. Some students were asked to visualize life in the northern colonies. Others were asked to visualize life in the middle colonies. Still others were asked to visualize life in the southern colonies. As students shared their thinking, Ms. Allen took notes. She used Inspiration to create a visual representation

Inspiration is a software program used to create graphic organizers, but it also includes icons and animations. For information about this, see the Web Links module in Chapter 5 on our Companion Website at www.prenhall.com/schell.

Book Links

Some excellent books that describe life in the early colonies include *Stranded at Plimoth Plantation 1626* (Bowen), *Molly Bannaky* (McGill), *Mary Geddy's Day: A Colonial Girl in Williamsburg* (Waters), and *Samuel Eaton's Day: A Day in the Life of a Pilgrim Boy* (Waters).

of their thinking and projected the image she created as students shared. By the end of the discussion, this group of fifth graders had a much better understanding of the influence that location and physical setting had on the founding of the original 13 colonies. The images recorded and projected by the teacher were clustered by region, and geography-related features became clarified.

STUDENTS BENEFIT FROM "ON PAPER" STRATEGIES

Just like strategies that students can use in their minds, there are a number of ways that students can transform text on paper, including note-making, using graphic organizers, and writing-to-learn prompts.

Note-Making

We make a distinction between the task students have when they are listening to a lecture or watching a film (note-taking) and the task they have when they are thinking about and recording information from text (note-making). Although both serve as an external storage feature (e.g., Callison, 2003), note-making adds a transformation step that builds comprehension and understanding of the content. In note-making, students take a piece of text and distill its essential features, key ideas, or main points to record in their notes. Over time, and with instruction, students use their notes not only for external storage of information, but also for encoding their ideas (Ganske, 1981). This serves to build connections between the student and the content, or text, and empowers the student to think more critically about the information presented instead of passively accepting and recording facts from the text. Importantly, as Peverly, Brobst, Graham, and Shaw (2003) showed, background knowledge and note-taking are significant predictors of success on tests.

But the question remains, what kind of note-taking and note-making system works best? According to a number of studies, a two-column format such as Cornell Note Taking is effective (e.g., Fisher, 2001). Using this format, students take notes and complete the tasks on the right side of the page while the left side provides a guide and key points. Often, the teacher identifies or prepares the guide and key points for the left side of the student's notebook. These key points help students use their notebooks to quickly find information, locate references, and study for exams. As Faber, Morris, and Lieberman (2000) found, the Cornell Note Taking system increases comprehension (and test scores!). A sample student note-taking page is found in Figure 5.3.

Wolfe (2004) presents another successful strategy to use in note-making, which requires students to "lift a line" from the text as they read and add the line to their notes. Lines may be lifted for various reasons,

Although it is not our primary role as educators, we have to remember that students need experience with testing formats to do well on high-stakes accountability tests.

This note-taking system was developed in 1949 at Cornell University by Walter Pauk. It was designed in response to students' frustration over their poor test scores. The system was meant to be easily used as a test study guide and has been adopted by most major law schools as the preferred note-taking method.

Figure 5.3   Sample note-taking guide.

Name: _____ Period: _____ Chapter: _____ Date: _____	
Big Ideas	Notes
People move to improve their lives or because they are forced. • Southern Colonists • New England Colonists • Middle Colonists	
Terms to know.	
Please define, describe and use the following terms colonist merchant indentured servant enslaved African	
Summary:	
Why did people move to the English colonies in North America in the 17th and 18th centuries?	

Here is an example of lines lifted from a fifth-grade social studies textbook: "Chinese shipbuilders made large wooden ships that could carry heavy cargoes even through rough seas. Their ships had painted dragon eyes to help them "see" in strange waters." (Banks et al, 2007). Can you guess why a student might choose to lift these lines to add to his notes?

including connections made with the content, curiosity about the content or presentation of information, or reactions to the statement. The line may be lifted, added to the student's notes, and then later used for further writing, discussions, or research. If you are using Big Ideas (Wiggins & McTighe, 1998), concepts, or themes in your curriculum and instruction, students may be encouraged to lift lines that support or challenge Big Ideas, concepts, or themes presented within or across units of study.

For example, while studying about American heroes and using the Big Idea "People have worked hard to improve our lives today" or the essential question "How is life different today from life in the past?" students might read about Susan B. Anthony. Reading from the text, a student might lift the following line to add to his or her notes: "*When Susan was born, many families did not believe that girls needed an education.*" During discussions about the Big Idea, the essential question, or the topic of this American hero, the student will be able to refer to this lifted line as a source of information, debate, or inquiry. You might ask this student why this line was lifted, and chances are you will hear

Figure 5.4   Lift a line guide.

(Check the Box That Applies)

Text & Page #	Line Lifted	Supports Big Idea	Raises Questions	Interesting Information	Relates Personally	Confusing Information

such comments as, "I cannot imagine people thinking such a thing! Girls deserve educations the same as boys" or "I think it's great that Susan's father did not think like other people back then. He made sure his daughter and other girls got an education, too."

There are a variety of reasons for students to lift lines from texts. Adapt and use the guide in Figure 5.4 to assist students in paying close attention to text and transferring useful lines into their notes. You can model lifting lines by transferring lines from common texts to an overhead transparency, PowerPoint presentation, or class chart. Use these examples to help students look for lines to lift, think about why certain lines are more important than others, and use these pieces of text for better understandings of the content.

Graphic Organizers

Graphic organizers, such as Venn diagrams, concept maps, semantic webs, compare-and-contrast charts, cause-and-effect charts, and the like, also help students transform information presented in texts (Fisher, Frey, & Williams, 2002). The idea is for students to take the text they are reading and transform it into a graphic representation. This requires considerable thought and planning as well as rereading and critical thinking. In addition to serving as a text transformation activity, graphic organizers are a good way of summarizing information and will aid students in remembering and recalling content (Irwin-DeVitis & Pease, 1995; Wilson, 2002). A sample graphic organizer can be found in Figure 5.5.

We recommend that you identify your goals and objectives for lessons and utilize the appropriate graphic organizer to meet those goals and objectives. For example, if you are teaching a lesson on family history, the development of a community, or the steps leading to the American Revolution, it would make more sense to use a flow chart or storyboard for your graphic organizer, which places events in a sequential order. If your lesson focuses on the characteristics of a culture, the elements of a good leader, or the parts of a neighborhood, it would make sense to use a cluster or web for a graphic organizer, which identifies parts of a topic. Different graphic organizers should be used to emphasize the nature of

Graphic organizers must match the content being studied or they are of little help to students.

Figure 5.5   Graphic organizer (sixth grade world history).

Evidence of Big Ideas Across the Ancient Civilizations

	Physical geography influences the characteristics and success or decline of civilizations.	Enduring civilizations have stable and productive economies that allow for the accumulation of wealth.	Religious beliefs influence the development of cultures just as cultures influence the development of religions.	People's lives are affected by social status, which can be determined in a variety of ways.	All civilizations depend on leadership for survival.
Ancient Egypt					
Ancient Mesopotamia					
Ancient China					
Ancient India					
Ancient Hebrews					
Ancient Greece					
Ancient Rome					

Source: *Big Ideas from* History-Social Science Standards-Based Implementation Model Template, *San Diego, CA: San Diego County Office of Education.*

the content. The most common types of graphic organizers used in the social studies classroom feature:

- cause and effect (chain, chart with columns, T-chart),
- description (cluster, bubbles, web, tree with branches and leaves),
- comparisons/contrasts (Venn diagram, alike and different chart, T-chart),
- hierarchy (pyramid, stacking boxes, ladder),
- sequence or chronology (timeline, flow chart, fish bone)

Book Links

Model text features and transferring the information onto an appropriate graphic organizer with picture books that have social studies themes. For example, read *If You Give a Mouse a Cookie* (Numeroff) to teach about cost-benefit analyses and transfer the story information to a cause-and-effect organizer.

Writing-to-Learn Prompts

Writing is an excellent way to learn. Writing requires that students consider what they already know, what they have read, and what they think. Throughout the social studies curriculum, students are exposed to a variety of writings from and about people and events from the past. Models for a variety of forms and purposes for writing are abundant. We recommend that you identify these examples in your text and through other sources to help students understand that what we know about the past comes from multiple and diverse sources, including letters, diaries, poetry, news articles, telegrams, reports, speeches and notebooks.

With well-constructed prompts, students will transform texts as they respond. We recently had the opportunity to observe an eighth-grade teacher discussing the Civil War with his students. On the board was a writing prompt, which read "You are a Southerner (or a Northerner) in 1861. Write a journal entry that explains your reasons for joining the Confederate (or Union) army." As you can see, this prompt requires that students understand the positions of the North and South, what the Confederate and Union armies were, and why they were fighting. One of our favorite writing prompts/structures is called RAFT (Santa & Havens, 1995). RAFT is an acronym for:

Role—what is the role of the writer?
Audience—to whom is the writer writing?
Format—what is the format for the writing?
Topic—what is the focus of the writing?

Using this framework, students will transform their background and prior knowledge as they respond to the prompt. They will also use their assigned readings, class discussions, teacher lectures, and any

The Library of Congress (www.loc.gov) and the National Archives and Records Administration (www.archives.gov) are excellent and abundant resources for finding examples. Project documents from these sites so students can see the original script and printings as well as the modern translations.

Book Links

Pink and Say (Polacco) offers a tender story about two boys from opposite sides of the battle lines coming together and helping each other.

This fifth-grade writer prefers to construct his historical narrative using the computer.
Source: *Emily Schell*

other sources of information they have to take a perspective as they write. For example, a RAFT outline might read:

R (role) = Sailor in the U.S. Navy, stationed at Pearl Harbor on 12/7/41

A (audience) = American citizens on the U.S. mainland

F (format) = Telegram

T (topic) = We have been attacked!

RAFT assignments empower students to use their historical analysis and thinking skills as they consider multiple perspectives, pose relevant questions, summarize key events, identify and interpret multiple causes of events, distinguish between fact and opinion, and draw conclusions using historical characters and events. Although students may not practice all of these skills simultaneously in transforming texts, integrating a variety of RAFT assignments over time will allow students to practice these skills and demonstrate their abilities to use research, writing, and thinking skills in a meaningful context.

DETERMINE WHEN TO USE CONTENT LITERACY STRATEGIES

As you have learned, there are a number of content literacy strategies that teachers can use to encourage students to transform and understand texts. These transformative strategies can be either "in your

Figure 5.6   Before, during, and after reading strategies.

Before Reading	During Reading	After Reading
Previewing the text	Making connections	Summarizing information
Making predictions	Identifying main ideas	Oral retelling
Establishing purpose	Taking notes	Sequencing information
KWL charts	Making notes	Visual displays
Anticipation guides	Partner conversations	Writing prompts
Quickwrites	Visualizing	Writing questions
	Graphic organizers	
	Questioning	
	Think aloud	

mind" or "on paper." The question remains, how do you know which approach will work best for your students at any given time? Figure 5.6 presents a number of content literacy strategies that are commonly used in the social studies classroom. You'll notice that these have been organized into three categories: before reading, during reading, and after reading. Some of these are familiar to you, as we have already discussed them in this chapter. Others are new and we'll focus on describing those now. Figure 5.6 identifies when we have most commonly seen each strategy used. Of course, expert teachers can modify specific strategies and use them to help students access text at other stages in the reading activity.

Which strategies do you use as before, during, and after your own reading?

Strategies Must Be Implemented During the Before-Reading Stage

Regardless of the specific approach you take, the goal is to activate students' background and prior knowledge. This generates interest and attention—which really matters when you're reading. Have you noticed this? When you are interested and the reading is made meaningful to your life, you pay more attention to it. If you know, for example, that you can use the information in this book to teach social studies well, you'll pay more attention to what you're reading.

Activating background and prior knowledge is the key to before-reading activities. Background knowledge is the information that students already possess because of their lived experiences. Students differ in their background knowledge and their own unique knowledge influenced by their family, their experiences, what they've seen, read, and done, and what they're interested in. Prior knowledge, on the other hand, is the information that has been previously taught, or should have been taught either during this school year or in previous years. In most states, for example, we should be able to expect that students leaving fourth grade

Figure 5.7   KWL chart.

Rosa Parks

What do we know about Rosa Parks?	What do we want to know about Rosa Parks?	What have we learned about Rosa Parks?
• she rode the bus • she worked hard • she got angry • she was tired • she knew Martin Luther King • she is African American	• Why did she ride a bus? • Did she have a car? • Did she really know Martin Luther King? • What job did she have? • Did she have kids? • Is she still alive or dead? • Is she old? • How come she is important?	

have learned about the state in which they live so that in fifth grade the curriculum can focus on concepts about the United States. This is where the content standards come in—the standards articulate what should be learned and when at any given grade level. As a result, students are expected to have a certain and specified amount of prior knowledge when they enter classrooms. Both background and prior knowledge need to be "activated" prior to a reading assignment.

KWL Charts

One way to activate background and prior knowledge is through the use of a KWL chart. Figure 5.7 contains a KWL language chart from a second-grade classroom. The teacher charted students' responses to the following questions

1. What do we know about Rosa Parks?
2. What do we want to know about Rosa Parks?

as part of the class study on people who have made a difference. By activating this knowledge, students were ready to focus on reading *Rosa Parks: My Story* (Parks & Haskins, 1992). At the end of the read-aloud, the teacher asked students the final KWL question: What have we learned about Rosa Parks?

Anticipation Guides

Another way to activate background and prior knowledge is through the use of anticipation guides (Head & Readence, 1986). Anticipation guides are easy to create. They typically involve three to five statements that require students to indicate that the statement is true or false, or that they agree or disagree. Students are provided space to record their

thinking both before and after the reading. Figure 5.8 represents an anticipation guide from a third-grade class studying landforms. The anticipation guide was used to access the third graders' background knowledge about landforms before launching into the unit of study.

Completing an anticipation guide provides students an opportunity to think about the words they are learning, the topics they are studying, and what they already know about the content.

Quickwrites

A third way to activate background and prior knowledge is through the use of quickwrites. Quickwrites require open-ended writing prompts that all students respond to in writing for just a few minutes. Quickwrites engage students in focused and fluent thinking that becomes transferred onto paper through writing. Students are given several minutes of quiet time to think and write simultaneously. Since the time is brief, the prompt cannot be too complex and must focus students clearly on the topic. The intent of quickwrites is to provide opportunities for each student to focus, think, recall prior knowledge, and formulate ideas in writing. The following quickwrite prompts are examples of some used to activate background and prior knowledge:

- Why should people follow rules and laws?
- What are the similarities and differences between ancient and modern Egypt?

Figure 5.8   Anticipation guide.

Before reading A = agree D = disagree	Statement	After Reading A = agree D = disagree
_____	Islands have water on every side.	_____
_____	A mountain is a high landform with steep sides, higher than a hill.	_____
_____	A bay is a body of water partly surrounded by land.	_____
_____	A peninsula is land that has water on all sides but one.	_____

- Describe a key event of the American Revolution and how this event affected the new country.
- How does geography influence humans?

Strategies Are Used in the During-Reading Stage

We have already discussed the majority of strategies identified in Figure 5.6 that are used to increase comprehension while students are reading. Unlike the strategies identified in the "before-reading" section that were used to activate background and prior knowledge, the strategies used during reading focus on comprehension. We teach students to use these strategies to ensure that they are engaged with the text, transforming it as they read, and monitoring their understanding while they do so.

This sounds complicated and it is. The best way that students can learn how to use these strategies during their reading is through modeling and practice. Each of these strategies can be modeled by the teacher and then practiced by the students. For example, asking questions as you read is one way to keep engaged with the text and to monitor comprehension. Good readers do this all of the time. Students need to be taught how to do this.

If you want to model your use of questioning, you might create an overhead transparency of the selected text and display it for the whole class to see. You would read the text aloud, pausing to voice the questions you think about as you read. Of course, you tell the students that we really think of the questions in our minds when we get good at this, but that they're going to practice telling others the questions they think of as they read. You might have students work in small groups. They could read a few paragraphs and then pause and share the questions they've thought about during the selection. Each of the "during-reading" strategies can be modeled and practiced in this way. You should note that students need regular practice using these during-reading strategies and additional modeling each year as the text selections become more difficult.

Strategies Are Used in the After-Reading Stage

Remember that the before-reading strategies were used to activate background and prior knowledge and that the during-reading strategies were used to improve comprehension of the reading materials. The after-reading strategies are used to aid memory. Unfortunately, with the pressures of time and the mass of content that must be covered, some teachers skip the after-reading activities. As a result, students do not have a deep understanding of the content they are learning. Although each of the three stages of reading are important, we argue that after-reading activities really formalize the content, allowing students to store information in their long-term memories.

If you had to write a one-paragraph summary of this chapter thus far, or give a one-minute oral retelling of the chapter, what would you do? If you are like most students, you'd go back to the text to identify key points and details. Of course, returning to the text improves your memory of it.

Students need to learn to comprehend informational texts. This requires that their teachers model thinking strategies useful in reading for information.

Consider how much more you learned about something you read after you read the text. This may be because you did something with the information after reading. Perhaps you talked about what you read with another person, researched additional information about the topic, or wrote about your thoughts in a letter or e-mail message.

The act of writing a summary or retelling a partner, a small group, or the whole class causes the learner to paraphrase, or transform the information from the printed page in their minds and produce something original.

Similarly, sequencing the information presented in the reading requires increased attention and thus learning. Teachers accomplish this in all kinds of ways—from asking students to sequence four illustrations based on the reading, to sequencing main idea sentences, to identifying something from the beginning of the reading, something from the middle of the reading, and something from the end of the reading, to creating timelines. Regardless of the ways in which students sequence information, they are thinking about the information and how pieces of information relate to one another. Again, they are learning.

Visual displays, such as posters created to advertise the reading, graphic organizers of the reading, and enactments (skits and plays), are additional ways to encourage students to remember information from the text. Of course, each of these visual displays requires that students really know the text and be able to do something with it.

As you could have guessed from the opening of this chapter, writing prompts provide another way for students to focus on information after they've finished reading. Again, the writing is based on a prompt, and students are provided time to think and write in response to the prompt.

Finally, teachers are asking students to write sample test questions following their reading. This is an interesting way of showing students that knowledge can be represented in different ways and provides them with test format practice. This test format practice ensures that they have thought about multiple-choice questions, for example, before they're asked to participate in the statewide accountability tests in the spring.

> There is research evidence that rereading improves comprehension, but without a purpose for the rereading, most of us don't do it.

MEET MS. AMATO AND HER CLASS

Welcome to room 302! As we enter the room, we see content standards on the wall and realize that the class is just about to read about the early explorers to what is now America. Every visitor can tell that this fifth-grade class loves their history. When asked why they like social studies so much, Maggie responds, "It's about us, our people, and how we got here." Tino adds, "We get to perform a play about every chapter of the book after we finish the reading."

Ms. Amato has a piece of chart paper on the wall. As she walks over to the chart paper, she invites students to take out their explorer journals. These are writing journals in which students take notes, make observations, and respond to writing prompts. Ms. Amato asks students to respond to the prompt that is on the board. It reads:

Why do people like to explore? What do they hope to gain?

As students write, she makes a three-column KWL Chart titled "Exploration" and writes a large letter K in the first column on the chart paper. As students finish writing, she asks the class, "What do you know about the explorers who came to America?" Students talk with their partners before sharing ideas with the whole class. Their ideas include the following: Christopher Columbus, the three ships came, they wanted money, they wanted to discover America, lots of them died, they killed the Indians. Ms. Amato records all of their ideas on the chart paper. As they run out of new contributions, Ms. Amato writes a large letter W on the chart paper in the second column and asks, "What do you want to know about the explorers?" Again, students talk with their partners before sharing with the whole class. Ms. Amato knows that whole-class conversations do not provide all of her students with enough oral language development and therefore asks all of her students to talk with a partner before sharing with the whole class. The class would like to know: Why did they take risks, who came, how did they get here, how many people explored, was Columbus really the first, how did they live on the ship for that long, who died, and how much money did it cost to be an explorer? As they finish identifying what they want to know, Ms. Amato says, "I hope we'll get to find out all of these answers in our readings. How exciting to figure this all out! Before we read, we need to learn a few vocabulary words. Please turn to the vocabulary section of your explorer journal." The pages in this section are divided into four columns, like this:

Word	Common Definition	Social Studies Meaning	Where I Found It

Ms. Amato identified some words for her students to add to the vocabulary section of their explorer journals, including *compass, sextant, latitude,* and *longitude.* She also reminded the class to add words to their vocabulary journals that they find in their readings and do not know.

As the class opens their social studies books, Ms. Amato reminds the students about taking notes during their reading and that the focus strategy is visualizing. She then provides the class with an example from *Lives of Extraordinary Women: Rulers, Rebels (and What the Neighbors Thought)* (Krull, 2000). As she reads the passage about Isabella I, she pauses periodically and explains what she saw in her mind's eye. At one point, she says, "Can you just see her? She's got beautiful clothes, with all kinds of colors on them, and jewelry all over herself. And there she is, riding on that dirty stinky horse trying to get people to help her set

Source: *Cover art for* Lives of Extraordinary Women *by K. Krull. Copyright © 2000, by Harcourt.*

up the first military hospital." Ms. Amato provides visualizations several times during her short reading and then asks students to read the first section of the chapter to themselves.

When they finish the first section, students explain to their partners what they visualized about the early explorers. They also record notes in their explorer journals and update their vocabulary charts. Then they are back to the reading, repeating the process over and over until they reach the end of the section.

Ms. Amato provides each group with a different after-reading task. One of the groups is to enact the selection for the whole class. Another group is to make a poster of the events from the section. A third group will create a picture-book version of the section, while the fourth group prepares sample test questions based on the selection. Ms. Amato regularly changes the after-reading activities and rotates which group completes each type of task.

Following the short performance of the chapter, students are provided time to update their explorer logs, which are graphic organizers to track which countries sent explorers, when, and where. This process of engaging with the text will continue throughout the year and will regularly be supplemented with class discussions, short informational lectures, visits to the library and Internet sites, and lots and lots of before-, during-, and after-reading activities that ensure that all of the fifth-grade students understand their social studies content.

Conclusion

Reading and writing during social studies is necessary—in fact, critical—if students are to learn the content. There are a number of strategies that we can use to help students make meaning from texts and to transform those texts in order to learn from them.

It is also important to note that we are not suggesting that all of these strategies be used within the same lesson or unit. Although we know that students need to transform the text, they should learn many ways to do so. If we teach students to transform texts, facilitate the process, and provide them the time and space to do so, students will learn to utilize these strategies independently and consistently as they read for information.

History's Finer Points

Literacy is the ability to read and write. Many Islamic countries have known comparatively high levels of literacy during most of the past 12 centuries because of the emphasis on individual readings of the Qu'ran. An Islamic edict to be literate is an individual religious obligation, not a privilege given to a few in the society. In the early American colonies, during the 17th and 18th centuries, literacy was determined by a person's ability to write his or her name. Illiterate people were asked to "make your mark" on formal documents, and an "X" marked the person's signature. The literacy levels in the New England colonies rose as an emphasis was placed on reading the Bible. Following the Civil War in America, the ability to read and write became a condition for voting rights. Later, literacy tests were administered to those interested in joining the U.S. military. Today, literacy is an expectation for all students attending public schools.

Document Based Question: How will you share the importance and power of literacy with your students?

Questions to Consider

1. Why are reading "strategies" an important consideration in the social studies classroom?
2. Which of the strategies presented in this chapter are you comfortable using?
3. Which instructional strategies would you like to add to your teaching repertoire, and how will you do this?

Quiz yourself on this chapter's important concepts on our Companion Website's Chapter 5 self-assessments at www.prenhall.com/schell.

Exercises

1. Choose a book that you will use in your teaching. Identify specific strategies that you will use before, during, and after reading to ensure that students comprehend the text.
2. Observe several teachers and students as they interact with texts. How do the teachers introduce texts? How do they model thinking? How do they ensure that students are able to learn from the texts?

References

Alvermann, D. E. (2002). Effective literacy instruction for adolescents. *Journal of Literacy Research, 34,* 189–208.

Banks, J., Beyer, B., Contreras, G., Craven, J., Ladson-Billings, G., McFarland, M., et al. (1999). *Ancient world*. New York: McGraw-Hill School Division.

Banks, J., Colleary, K., Cunha, S., Echevarria, J., Parker, W., Rawls, J., et al. (2007). *Making a new nation*. New York: Macmillan/McGraw-Hill.

Callison, D. (2003). Note-taking: Different notes for different research stages. *School Library Media Activities Monthly, 19*(7), 33–37, 45.

Chatterjea, K. (1999). Use of visual images in the teaching of geography. *Geographical Education, 12,* 49–55.

Faber, J. E., Morris, J. D., & Lieberman, M. G. (2000). The effect of note taking on ninth grade students' comprehension. *Reading Psychology, 21,* 257–270.

Fisher, D. (2001)."We're moving on up": Creating a schoolwide literacy effort in an urban high school. *Journal of Adolescent & Adult Literacy, 45,* 92–101.

Fisher, D., & Frey, N. (2004). *Improving adolescent literacy: Strategies at work*. Upper Saddle River, NJ: Merrill Prentice Hall.

Fisher, D., Frey, N., & Williams, D. (2002). Seven literacy strategies that work. *Educational Leadership, 60*(3), 70–73.

Ganske, L. (1981). Note-taking: A significant and integral part of learning environments. *Educational Communication and Technology: A Journal of Theory, Research, and Development, 29,* 155–175.

Goodman, A. (2003). Get A.C.T.I.V.E: Engaging middle school readers with text. *Voices from the Middle, 11*(1), 15–23.

Harvey, S., & Goudvis, A. (2000). *Strategies that work.* York, ME: Stenhouse.

Head, M. H., & Readence, J. E. (1986). Anticipation guides: Meaning through prediction. In E. K. Dishner, T. W. Bean, J. E. Readence, & D. W. Moore (Eds.), *Reading in the content areas* (2nd ed.) (pp. 229–234). Dubuque, IA: Kendall Hunt.

Irwin-DeVitis, L., & Pease, D. (1995). Using graphic organizers for learning and assessment in middle level classrooms. *Middle School Journal, 26*(5), 57–64.

Michaels, S., O'Conner, M. C., & Resnick, L. B. (2002). *Accountable talk: classroom conversation that works.* Pittsburgh, PA: University of Pittsburgh, Learning Research and Development Center.

Peverly, S. T., Brobst, K. E., Graham, M., & Shaw, R. (2003). College adults are not good at self-regulation: A study on the relationship of self-regulation, note taking, and test taking. *Journal of Educational Psychology, 95,* 335–346.

Santa, C., & Havens, L. (1995). *Creating independence through student-owned strategies: Project CRISS.* Dubuque, IA: Kendall-Hunt.

Spielvogel, J. J. (2005). *World history: Journey across time: The early ages.* Columbus, OH: Glencoe/McGraw-Hill.

Steffey, S. (1994). *If this is social studies, why isn't it boring?* York, ME: Stenhouse.

Wiggins, G., & McTighe, J. (1998). *Understanding by design.* Alexandria, VA: Association for Supervision and Curriculum Development.

Wilson, E. (2002). Literature and literacy in the social studies classroom: Strategies to enhance social studies instruction. *Southern Social Studies Journal, 28*(1), 45–57.

Wolfe, S. (2004). *Interpreting literature with children.* Mahwah, NJ: Lawrence Erlbaum Associates.

Wu, H., Krajcik, J. S., & Soloway, E. (2001). Promoting understanding of chemical representations: Students' use of a visualization tool in the classroom. *Journal of Research in Science Teaching, 38,* 821–842.

Zemelman, S., Daniels, H., & Hyde, A. (1993). *Best practice: New standards for teaching and learning in America's schools.* Portsmouth, NH: Heinemann.

Children's Literature

Adler, D. (1995). *A picture book of Rosa Parks*. New York: Holiday House.

Baquedano, E. (1993). *Aztec, Inca & Maya*. London, UK: Dorling Kindersley.

Bowen, G. (1998). *Stranded at Plimoth Plantation 1626*. New York: HarperTrophy.

Giovanni, N. (2005). *Rosa*. New York: Henry Holt and Company.

Hill, M. (2003). *Signs on the road*. Danbury, CT: Children's Press.

Hoban, T. (1987). *I read signs*. New York: Greenwillow.

Hoban, T. (1983). *I read symbols*. New York: Greenwillow.

Krull, K. (2000). *Lives of extraordinary women: Rulers, rebels (and what the neighbors thought)*. San Diego, CA: Harcourt.

Langley, A. (2004). *Medieval life*. London, UK: Dorling Kindersley.

Maestro, B. (1997). *Exploration and conquest: The Americas after Columbus 1500–1620*. New York: HarperTrophy.

McGill, A. (1999). *Molly Bannaky*. New York: Houghton Mifflin.

Numeroff, L. (1985). *If you give a mouse a cookie*. New York: Laura Gerringer.

Parker, N. W. (2001). *Land ho! Fifty glorious years in the age of exploration*. New York: HarperCollins.

Parks, R., & Haskins, J. (1992). *Rosa Parks: My story*. New York: Dial.

Pearson. A. (2004). *Ancient Greece: DK Eyewitness Books*. Dorling Kindersley.

Polacco, P. (1994). *Pink and Say*. New York: Philomel.

Ringgold, F. (1999). *If a bus could talk: The story of Rosa Parks*. New York: Aladdin.

Stanchak, J. (2000). *Civil war*. London, UK: Dorling Kindersley.

Waters, K. (1996). *Samuel Eaton's day: A day in the life of a Pilgrim boy*. New York: Scholastic.

Waters, K. (2002). *Mary Geddy's day: A colonial girl in Williamsburg*. New York: Scholastic.

Wilkinson, P. (2003). *Buddhism*. London, UK: Dorling Kindersley.

Chapter 6

Effective Uses of Literature to Teach Social Studies

Source: Karen Mancinelli/ Pearson Learning Photo Studio

Big Idea

Teachers can enhance student understandings of social studies through the effective use of narrative and informational literature.

Essential Question

How can literature enhance a student's understandings of social studies?

Ms. Hess starts reading to her second-grade students: "Making an apple pie is really very easy. First, you get all the ingredients at the market. Mix them well, bake, and serve. Unless, of course, the market is closed. In that case, go home and pack a suitcase. Take your shopping list and some walking shoes. Then catch a steamship bound for Europe. Use the 6 days on board to brush up on your Italian. If you time it right, you'll arrive in Italy at harvest time. Find a farm deep in the countryside. Gather some superb semolina wheat. An armful or two will do. Then hop a train to France and locate a chicken. French chickens lay elegant eggs—and you want only the finest ingredients for your pie. Coax the chicken to give you an egg. Better yet, bring the chicken with you. There's less chance of breaking an egg that way. Get to Sri Lanka any way you can. You can't miss it. Sri Lanka is a pear-shaped island in the Indian Ocean. The best cinnamon in the world is made there, from the bark of the native kurundu tree. So go directly to the rain forest. Find a kurundu tree and peel off some bark. If a leopard is napping beneath the tree, be very quiet."

Ms. Hess stops reading. She hands a cinnamon stick to one student and says, "Smell it! Mmmmmm! Wouldn't you want to grind up that cinnamon and sprinkle the flavor into YOUR apple pie?" The student nods his head while inhaling the stick's scent before passing it on to another student. The teacher then points to the world map that decorates the reading corner and asks, "Who can help us find the country of Sri Lanka on this map? Our main character had to travel all the way to Sri Lanka to pick up the finest cinnamon for her pie." Several students eagerly raise their hands remembering a mapping lesson the day before. One is invited to come to the map. There, the student points to Sri Lanka, and explains that her aunt just returned from vacation there. Next, Ms. Hess hands the student a sticky note with the word "cinnamon" printed on it. The student places the sticky note on the map on the country of Sri Lanka and returns to her seat to hear the rest of the story. The class is participating in a read aloud of *How to Make an Apple Pie and See the World* (Priceman, 1996).

INTRODUCTION

Informational texts are those that are generally considered true, whereas narrative texts tell a story and are often fiction.

Literature, both narrative and informational, is a powerful and essential tool in the social studies classroom. Although most elementary teachers teach both reading and social studies in a self-contained classroom, it is interesting to note how many teachers see these subject areas as mutually exclusive and therefore competitors for teaching time and student learning. Instead, like the author of *How to Make an Apple Pie and See the World*, we suggest that you attempt to do more than one thing simultaneously, have a lot of fun doing it, and end up with delicious results.

Source: *From* How to Make an Apple Pie and See the World *by Marjorie Priceman, copyright © 1994 by Marjorie Priceman. Used by permission of Alfred A. Knopf, an imprint of Random House Children's Books, a division of Random House, Inc.*

INTEGRATE LITERATURE AND SOCIAL STUDIES

Bringing literature into the social studies program or vice versa, teachers like Ms. Hess continue to find success in exposing students to good literature, personalizing history for students, building historical empathy, and adding depth, detail, and a sense of context to the place and period. Literature selections allow you to support your students in better understanding or further exploring their social studies content. One of our favorite quotes to explain why we should integrate literature and social studies comes from historian and writer Barbara Tuchman. She advises us to "Tell stories. The pull, the appeal is irresistible, because history is about two of the greatest of all mysteries—time and human nature." Most students (and most adults as well) love a great mystery. As the story progresses, the plot thickens and the complexity of the situation is often overwhelming. When readers ask, "What next?" or "What will they do?" then they are hooked. Fiction writers have crafted some intriguing stories to achieve these results. However, as history has unfolded, there is little need to "craft" when some of the most amazing stories have occurred in real life and deserve attention from our students. In most cases, these are the lessons our students need to read, hear, and remember. Stories about people, places, and events embrace what Tuchman identifies as time and human nature, and they resonate with students because they explore what it means to be human.

What are your favorite stories that reveal mysteries about time, place, and people? How did you become hooked into those stories?

TEACH HISTORY AS A STORY WELL TOLD

The California History–Social Science Framework (California Department of Education, 2001) recommends that teachers present *history as a story well told*. Educators continue to debate and interpret the meaning of this statement. You may have your own ideas about what this means, and what this looks like in a classroom. When we think of stories well told, we are reminded of stories, in print or through oral tradition, that

Talk with a partner: What does it mean to teach history as a story well told?

- demand our attention,
- explain something important,
- intrigue, inspire, and motivate us to think and act,
- take us to faraway places and times, and
- deserve sharing, retelling, and rereading.

Furthermore, the framework states that teachers should use literature *of the period and about the period* being taught. In some areas of history, there are limited literature selections from or about the period. For example, age-appropriate selections for teaching about early humans and ancient civilizations at grade 6 are limited. Fortunately, in

Alex Allen reads aloud to her class from the picture book *Harvesting Hope: The Story of Cesar Chavez* while her students learn about Chavez and the farm workers' movement.
Source: *Emily Schell*

History Connections

Ts'ai Lun, from China, was the inventor of paper (not papyrus) circa 105 A.D. Previously people wove reeds to make papyrus. What Ts'ai Lun discovered was that plant fibers, separated and suspended in water, would form their own woven mats: paper.

Making connections between current events and historical events helps students develop a sense of continuity while being able to explore differences.

recent years we have seen more selections about these periods fill our libraries. Publishers have responded with historical fiction, nonfiction, and poetry selections about ancient Egypt, Greece, Rome and China. On the other hand, there remains little to select from to support the teaching of early humans, ancient Israel, and India.

In other areas of the social studies content, however, there exists a wide array of literature selections from which to select. There are many biographies about George Washington, Susan B. Anthony, Sojourner Truth, Benjamin Franklin, Martin Luther King, Jr., and other famous American heroes. Since 9/11, many books about American ideals, patriotism, and human nature have been introduced, shifting the focus of children's literature to heroism and character among common citizens. Teachers have used many of these selections, including *America Is . . .* (Borden), *The Man Who Walked Between Two Towers* (Gerstein), and *We the Kids: The Preamble to the Constitution of the United States* (Catrow), to help students understand contemporary issues and relate these to students' own knowledge and experience with historical events.

USE GUIDELINES TO SELECT LITERATURE FOR YOUR SOCIAL STUDIES PROGRAM

When it comes to selecting literature to integrate into the social studies program, there are some guidelines that you will want to follow:

Sojourner Truth—historical archive.
Source: *Courtesy of the Library of Congress*

1. Select books that appeal to you. Otherwise you may never use or promote the reading of the selection.

2. Select books that you think will appeal to your students. Even if the topic fits your curricula, if it is not appealing, it will not be read.

3. Match students' reading levels for your grade(s). Provide selections for reluctant readers as well as advanced readers. Across the grades, provide picture books as well as chapter books from which students can select. Mary Pope Osborne's Magic Tree House series and Jon Sczieska's Time Warp Trio series offer high-interest, low-reading-level books all based in some aspect of social studies. Similarly, adult travel guides and coffee-table books make for high-interest, highly visual reading resources that many students enjoy and learn a great deal from.

4. Seek a balance in topics as well as genres. Although you might have a passion for studying about medieval Europe, look for a variety of topics that will help your students find and develop their own passions for topics or periods in history. Similarly, you may love poetry, but find that some students prefer historical fiction or biographies and can learn more from those. Balance, balance, balance.

5. Look for books that present a different perspective on a person, event or period. For example, *My Brother Martin: A Sister Remembers Growing Up With the Rev. Dr. Martin Luther King Jr.* (Farris) presents interesting stories about this famous American from his sister's perspective.

6. Use this opportunity to add missing voices into the study of people, periods, and events. Most textbooks and general history references present common, well-documented, accepted accounts of historical events that tend to represent the experiences of majorities or those in power. Accounts from those who did not document their histories or those who were not empowered through education, political

Figure 6.1

"Do you fancy a read?
...or shall I put the Jester on?"

Source: *www.cartoonstock.com*

roles, and economic advantages are limited or nonexistent. However, folktales, legends, oral traditions, and other forms of evidence have been used by authors to present accounts that include minority groups and those not typically acknowledged in textbooks. Seek books that address the perspectives, roles, and contributions of women, children, and other minority groups. For example, *We Were There, Too!: Young People in U.S. History* (Hoose) gives rise to the stories of many children who witnessed and participated in historical events.

7. Select books that present a concept or teach a skill, even if the topic has little connection to your social studies topics. For example, a story such as *The True Story of the Three Little Pigs by A. Wolf* (Sczieska) is a hilarious piece of imaginative fiction, but can become a great tool for teaching about different perspectives on events. *The Frog Prince Continued* (Sczieska) also generates laughter from students as the story tells about the not-so-happily-ever-after lives of the frog prince and beautiful princess. This book can be used to help students understand that history is an ongoing story and that there is no "the end" to speak of. Though we might finish learning about the French and Indian War or the Industrial Revolution, there are multiple stories that relate to the "end" of those events.

8. Look for selections that lend themselves to lessons or activities. If you know that you have to teach, say, basic economic concepts to primary-grade students, a book such as *Bunny Money* (Wells) or *If You Give A Moose a Muffin* (Numeroff) will help you teach that resources are finite, people must make choices about spending or using those resources, and that there are costs for the choices we make. Both books also lend themselves to dramatic recreations and the use of realia in telling the story.

PLAN FOR THE EFFECTIVE USE OF LITERATURE TO TEACH SOCIAL STUDIES

As you build your collection, or classroom library, it is important that you plan for the effective use of those titles in achieving your goals to improve students' literacy and their social studies knowledge and skills. It will be useful to have a collection of social studies selections in your classroom library and to use some for read-alouds during the year. However, casual use of social studies literature may not draw students' attention to these rich resources and may not allow you to maximize their effectiveness in supporting social studies achievement.

Consider the following options in order to make the teaching and learning of literacy and social studies work for the benefit of both you and your students.

Read-alouds are an effective way of building student's background knowledge and vocabulary.

DEVELOP LITERACY AND SOCIAL STUDIES SKILLS THROUGH THE USE OF LITERATURE

Integrate reading and social studies altogether into a "block" where literacy skills and literature are aligned to the social studies content for your grade level. In Chapter 5, you were provided with a variety of research-based literacy strategies that have been shown to produce results in student literacy abilities as well as acquisition of content knowledge and skills. When literacy skills are taught in the context of social studies content, students are able to recognize the value and purpose of the skills. Furthermore, they are able to apply the skills in a meaningful context using real-world information and resources.

Sequence Content Information

For example, to best understand the Revolutionary War, students must understand the series of events that led up to the war. For this, the skill of *sequencing* is essential. When students are attuned to cue words such as *first, then,* and *finally* because of a literacy lesson identifying these cue words as tools for *sequencing information* in a text, they can see the purpose of the literacy lesson, immediately apply the skill, and best of all, understand that the Revolutionary War erupted after a series of grievances and failed attempts to compromise. Too often, however, teachers oversimplify the content and lead students to believe that the entire story is this:

> *American colonists and Great Britain did not get along, so they had a war, and the winners got what they wanted. In this case, the American colonists got to become free and independent. End of story.*

Although this is not entirely untrue, there is so much information missing in the "story" that students might develop misconceptions about war, conflict, problem-solving, American colonists, Great Britain, and so on. Aside from the need for students to understand the foundations of our nation, there are greater reasons for teaching this content and these skills in depth.

Uncover Big Ideas with Overarching Essential Questions

Using questions that ask students to recognize bigger overarching principles can help avoid the development of students' misconceptions. Consider using overarching essential questions frequently with literature to uncover those Big Ideas that connect historical stories over time and place.

In our world today, we cannot afford to miss these opportunities to teach students about *collaboration, conflict,* and *compromise* through

Remember, we want to foster critical thinking skills so our questions should often require students to synthesize and evaluate information.

Figure 6.2   From topics to questions.

Topics	Overarching Questions
Rules & Laws	Who needs rules?
	Why do people need rules?
	What happens when rules are broken?
	What is the difference between a rule and a law?
	Who makes rules and laws?
Westward Expansion	Why would people leave their homes and move to a new place?
	How do people move from one place to another?
	What causes a large number of people to decide to settle new lands?
	What were the risks and benefits of moving to a new land?
Early Humans	What do humans need for survival?
	How do people get what they need to survive?
	What happens when people do not get what they want or need?
	What are ideal geographic conditions for a group of people?

real examples. Staying with our content example of the American Revolution, students should be encouraged to explore these overarching questions as they employ their literacy skills and read for information and meaning:

- What motivates people to risk life and limb?
- Who holds the rights to land?
- How do people govern themselves successfully?

Naturally, another topic in social studies would lead to other kinds of overarching questions. Refer to Figure 6.2 to see how overarching questions can change based on topics of study. Generating such questions formally or informally with readers establishes a purpose for reading and appropriately using literacy skills.

Combine Skills Development

Following a lesson on sequencing and using cue words, the teacher might facilitate the process of student-generated overarching questions. For example, after a reading period in which students are using these skills and focused on one or two of those questions, the teacher might complete the lesson by connecting the skill of sequencing with the responses to these overarching questions. To better understand the answers to any of the foregoing questions, students would have to use examples (that relate to the Revolutionary War or not) that place a series of events in order. For example, using the overarching question,

A number of "big ideas" related to social studies content can be found in the Web Links module in Chapter 6 on our Companion Website at www.prenhall.com/schell.

"What motivates people to risk life and limb?" students might respond by stating:

- *First,* Great Britain sponsored colonists to move to America and build up the land. The colonists struggled for several years to make a home in America while Great Britain supported them and developed trade with the colonists. *Then,* the colonists had to pay a lot of taxes placed on them by Great Britain because Great Britain needed money, too. Some of the colonists lost their businesses, farms, or homes because they could not pay the taxes. The colonists tried to make their voices heard in Great Britain, but the King and Parliament would not listen. *Finally,* the colonists felt they had no alternative but to declare independence and go to war. They felt this was their only option left. The colonists worked hard and they wanted to have a reasonable government to protect their homes, families and businesses. That was worth fighting for. Great Britain also felt strongly about their rights and felt that the colonists were acting like spoiled children. They were willing to fight for their investments in America, too.

or

- *First,* the American colonists fought for their independence from Great Britain in the Revolutionary War. Many people lost their lives, but Americans are proud to say that *as a result* they broke free from the tyranny of the king and established self-governance. *Years later,* Americans fought each other in the Civil War. Soldiers in the Union and Confederate armies alike fought for what they thought was best for their country. Many soldiers lost their lives, but *in the end,* the nation was united. *Today,* we are fighting a war against terrorism and many American soldiers have lost their lives. They are fighting for what they believe is right for themselves, their nation, and others around the world. American soldiers are fighting people who also believe they are fighting for what is right.

These responses might result from lessons that include readings from the student textbook or from literature accessed through the library, classroom resources, primary documents, or Internet research.

Although a variety of reading resources are recommended, today's selection of children's literature affords teachers the opportunity to engage students in the stories that tell about our past. Some of our favorites for teaching about the Revolutionary War include:

- *American Revolution, 1700–1800: Chronicle of America* (Masoff, 2000)
- *American Revolution: Eyewitness Book* (Murray, 2002)
- *American Revolution: "Give Me Liberty, or Give Me Death!"* (Kent, 1994)

For a list of children's literature websites, see the Web Links module in Chapter 6 on our Companion Website at www.prenhall.com/ schell.

- *And Then What Happened, Paul Revere?* (Fritz, 1976)
- *In the Path of War: Children of the American Revolution Tell Their Stories* (Alder, 1998)

Sequencing Skills Transfer Into Chronological Thinking Skills

On closure of this particular integrated lesson, we would transition students into a future lesson (that might come the following day) about *chronology*. Sequencing and chronology are similar skills, but specific to different disciplines of language arts and social studies, respectively. Students are primed to learn the similarities and differences in these skills as well as their use and application.

Combining reading skills, literature and social studies provides students with multiple opportunities to apply skills. Although the foregoing example may have been suitable during combined lessons on sequencing and the road to revolution, students will be able to use and enhance their sequencing and chronological thinking skills as they continue learning about the course of the Revolutionary War, as well as the development of a new nation after the war. Of course, further skills will be added to the students' repertoire as they become more proficient readers and better versed in the history of our nation.

Keep in mind that the goal for teaching and learning is understanding. For students to understand these literacy and historical thinking skills, they should be able to flexibly apply the skills in a variety of settings that are new and unanticipated (Wiggins & McTighe, 1998). Such opportunities for skills application occurs when students are engaged in the text, discussion, and research of a topic or issue that is interesting, motivating, or controversial. Social studies topics and issues offer exactly that.

USE READING INSTRUCTION APPROACHES TO TEACH SOCIAL STUDIES

Utilize reading selections that support the social studies content for read-aloud, shared reading, literature circles, or independent reading during the reading period. In some situations, schools have designated a reading block period and discourage teachers from integrating the teaching of other subjects during the reading block. This does not mean that the reading selections used during these reading periods cannot align to the topics and concepts being taught and learned during the social studies period. In fact, it makes sense that teachers use this opportunity to deepen students' understandings of a particular social studies topic, era, or event through the use of literature. This can be accomplished in several ways.

What stories do you recall from read-alouds by your teachers? What made that experience memorable?

Links to these informational sources can be found in the Web Links module in Chapter 6 on our Companion Website at www. prenhall.com/schell.

Information on both lists can be found in the Web Links module in Chapter 6 on our Companion Website at www.prenhall.com/ schell.

For more information, see the Web Links module in Chapter 6 on our Companion Website at www.prenhall.com/ schell.

Read-Alouds

Daily or regularly scheduled read-alouds for students at all grade levels is strongly encouraged and, in fact, required in some districts. One of the keys to a good read-aloud is in the selection. The selection should be inviting and enticing for students so that with each reading, they listen carefully, imagine the story vividly, look forward to continuous readings gladly, and interact with the story naturally. Fortunately, there are multiple selection options for teaching the variety of topics that are required in your social studies curriculum. A sampling of titles for various topics, themes, and big ideas is included in Table 6.1. Most textbook publishers will either supply or recommend titles for reading aloud and professional journals, including *Book Links* and *Social Education,* regularly feature titles appropriate for the teaching of social studies. Your school librarian, colleagues, and students will often recommend titles that fit this criterion, so it is wise to consult them and invite them to share "good reads" with you on a regular basis. Resources such as California's *Pages of the Past: K–6 Literature Aligned to History–Social Science Standards* and *Tales of Time: 6–8 Literature Aligned to History—Social Science Standards* provide teachers with lists of teacher-recommended literature appropriate for various grade levels and tied directly to grade-level standards. More thematic book lists can be found in such resources as *Children's Literature in Social Studies: Teaching to the Standards* (National Council for the Social Studies, Bulletin 95, Krey), *Children's Literature and Social Studies: Selecting and Using Notable Books* (Zarnowski), and *Notable Children's Trade Books in the Field of Social Studies* (Children's Book Council & NCSS). The National Council for the Social Studies collaborates with the Children's Book Council annually to review and recommend new books that appropriately support social studies education.

There is no shortage of literature available for use in the reading program that supports student understandings of social studies content. So, beyond read-aloud selection, it is important that teachers present selections in an enticing manner and invite students into the story. Here are some ideas to consider in introducing a read-aloud selection.

Propose Intriguing Questions

If you begin a lesson with a question such as "What would it feel like to move with your family to a new place?" you can motivate students by capturing their imaginations. Then you could probe further with related questions such as "What would it be like to move from one part of your city to another part of the city? What if you moved from one state to another state far away? What if you moved from one country to another? What would you take with you? What would happen if you got lost on your way and ended up in an entirely different place than

(text continued on page 161)

Table 6.1   Book titles organized by topics, themes/concepts, and big ideas.

Topics	K–3 Titles	4–6 Titles
Native Americans	*Buffalo Woman*, by Goble *The Girl Who Loved Wild Horses*, by Goble *The Legend of the Bluebonnet*, by dePaola *Who Was Sacagawea?*, by Fradin	*If You Lived With the Sioux Indians*, by McGovern *If You Lived With the Iroquois*, by Levine *Indian School*, by Cooper *Indian Captive: The Story of Mary Jemison*, by Lenski
Ancient Egyptians	*Mummies in the Morning (Magic Tree House Series)*, by Osborne *Mummies Made in Egypt*, by Aliki *Temple Cats*, by Clements *The Magic School Bus Ms. Frizzle's Adventures: Ancient Egypt*, by Cole *Tut Tut: Time Warp Trio*, by Scieszka	*Ancient Egypt: Eyewitness Books*, by Hart *Cat Mummies*, by Trumble *Cleopatra VII: Daughter of the Nile, Egypt, 57 B.C. (Royal Diaries Series)*, by Gregory *The Gods and Goddesses of Ancient Egypt*, by Fisher
Age of Exploration	*Encounter*, by Yolen *Follow the Dream: The Story of Christopher Columbus*, by Sis *Kids During the Age of Exploration*, by MacGregor	*If You Were There in 1492: Everyday Life in the Time of Columbus*, by Brenner *Land Ho! Fifty Glorious Years in the Age of Exploration*, by Parker *Where Do You Think You're Going, Christopher Columbus?*, by Fritz
American Colonies	*A Picture Book of Thomas Jefferson*, by Adler *Mary Geddy's Day*, by Waters *Samuel Eaton's Day: A Day in the Life of a Pilgrim Boy*, by Waters *Tapenum's Day: A Wampanoag Indian Boy In Pilgrim Times*, by Waters *What's the Big Idea, Ben Franklin?*, by Fritz	*If You Lived in Williamsburg in Colonial Days*, by Brenner *Stranded at Plimoth Plantation*, by Bowen *The Lost Colony of Roanoke*, by Fritz *The New Americans: Colonial Times 1620–1689*, by Maestro *Thomas Jefferson: A Picture Book Biography*, by Giblin
Themes/concepts	**K–3 Titles**	**4–6 Titles**
Migration	*Amelia's Road*, by Altman *Apples to Oregon: Being the (Slightly) True Narrative of How a Brave Pioneer Father Brought Apples, Peaches, Pears, Plums, Grapes, and Cherries (and*	*Coolies*, by Soentpiet *Dear Levi: Letters from the Overland Trail*, by Woodruff *Esperanza Rising*, by Ryan *If You Traveled West on a Covered Wagon*, by Levine *Way West: Journal of a*

(continued)

Table 6.1   Continued

Themes/concepts	K–3 Titles	4–6 Titles
	Children) Across the Plains, by Hopkinson *Mississippi Mud: The Prairie Journals,* by Turner *Tomas and the Library Lady,* by Mora	*Pioneer Woman,* by Knight *The Stories of Juana Briones: Alta California Pioneer,* by Richter
Immigration	*Ellis Island,* by Quiri *Grandfather's Journey,* by Say *How Many Days to America? A Thanksgiving Story,* by Bunting *Journey to Ellis Island,* by Bierman *Silent Movie,* by Mordan *The Lotus Seed,* by Garland	*Black Potatoes: The Story of the Great Irish Famine, 1845–1850,* by Bartoletti *Coming to America: The Story of Immigration,* by Maestro *I Was Dreaming to Come to America: Memories from the Ellis Island Oral History Project,* by Lawlor *If Your Name Was Changed at Ellis Island,* by Levine *Immigrants (Library of Congress),* by Sandler *Immigrant Kids,* by Freedman
Families	*Allison,* by Say *All Families Are Different,* by Pelligrini *Aunt Flossie's Hats (and Crab Cakes Later),* by Howard *Families,* by Morris *My Two Grandmothers,* by Older *Tar Beach,* by Ringgold *The Keeping Quilt,* by Polacco *The Patchwork Quilt,* by Flournoy *Two Mrs. Gibsons,* by Igus	*Al Capone Does My Shirts,* by Choldenko *Sounder,* by Armstrong *The Watsons Go to Birmingham,* by Curtis *Because of Winn-Dixie,* by DiCamillo *Esperanza Rising,* by Ryan *Becoming Naomi Leon,* by Ryan *Lizzie Bright and the Buckminster Boy,* by Schmidt
Leadership	*Dinner at Aunt Connie's House,* by Ringgold *Harriet and the Promised Land,* by Lawrence *Harvesting Hope: The Story of Cesar Chavez,* by Krull *Martin's Big Words: The Life of Dr. Martin Luther King, Jr.,* by Rappaport *Rachel: The Story of Rachel Carson,* by Ehrlich *Teammates,* by Golenbock *When Marian Sang: True Recital of Marian Andersen,* by Ryan	*Follow the Drinking Gourd,* by Winter *Kids on Strike!,* by Bartoletti *Lincoln: A Photobiography,* by Freedman *Lives of the Presidents,* by Krull *Rosa Parks: My Story,* by Haskins *The Sky's the Limit: Stories of Discovery by Women and Girls,* by Thimmesh *Ten Kings: And the Worlds They Rule,* by Meltzer *Ten Queens: Portraits of Women in Power,* by Meltzer

Table 6.1   Continued

Big Idea	K–3 Titles	4–6 Titles
All citizens have rights and individual responsibilities.	*The American Flag,* by Patricia Ryon Quiri *Berenstain Bears' Trouble With Money,* by Stan and Jan Berenstain *Did You Carry the Flag Today Charlie?,* by Rebecca Caudill *Fables,* by Arnold Lobel *The Fourth of July Story,* by Alice Dalgliesh *From Sea to Shining Sea, A Treasury of American Folklore & Folk Songs,* by Amy Cohn *Martin's Big Words,* by Doreen Rappaport *Memorial Day,* by Lynda Sorensen *Mufaro's Beautiful Daughters: An African Tale,* by John Steptoe *The National Anthem,* by Patricia Ryon Quiri *Nobody Listens to Andrew,* by Elizabeth Guilfoile *The Pledge of Allegiance,* by Bill Martin *The Pledge of Allegiance,* by Stuart Kallen *The Statue of Liberty,* by Lloyd G. Douglas *Tale of Peter Rabbit,* by Beatrix Potter *We the Kids: The Preamble to the Constitution,* by David Catrow *We the People: The Constitution of the U.S.,* by Peter Spier	*F is for Flag,* by Wendy C. Lewison *Fireworks, Picnics, and Flags,* by Jim Cross Giblin *The Flag We Love,* by Pat Munoz Ryan *If You Lived 100 Years Ago,* by Ann McGovern *If You Lived in Williamsburg in Colonial Times,* by Barbara Brenner *The Declaration of Independence,* by Sam Fink *Veterans Day,* by Lynda Sorensen
Where people live influences how people live.	*Bread Around the World,* by Cynthia Rothman *A Chair for my Mother,* by Vera Williams *Fly Away Home,* by Eve Bunting *Going Home,* by Eve Bunting *Houses and Homes,* by Ann Morris	*The American Family Farm: A Photo Essay,* by George Anderson *Coming to America,* by Betsy Maestro *Dakota Dugout,* by Ann Turner *Dust for Dinner,* by Ann Turner

(*continued*)

Table 6.1   Continued

Big Idea	K–3 Titles	4–6 Titles
	Japanese Children's Day and the Obon Festival, by Dianne MacMillan *The Keeping Quilt,* by Patricia Polacco *The Lotus Seed,* by Sherry Garland *On the Mayflower: Voyage of the Ship's Apprentice and a Passenger Girl,* by Kate Waters *Sarah Morton's Day,* by Kate Waters *Samuel Eaton's Day,* by Kate Waters *Sugaring Time,* by Kathryn Lasky *Tapenum's Day: A Wampanoag Indian Boy in Pilgrim Times,* by Kate Waters *When I Was Young in the Mountains,* by Cynthia Rylant	*The House in the Mail,* by Rosemary Wells *How Many Days to America? A Thanksgiving Story,* by Eve Bunting *Whispering Cloth: A Refugee's Story,* by Pegi Deitz Shea
People move to improve their lives or because they are forced.	*Aunt Harriet's Underground Railroad in the Sky,* by Faith Ringgold *Dandelion,* by Eve Bunting *Giving Thanks: The 1621 Harvest Feast,* by Kate Waters *Harriet and the Promised Land,* by Jacob Lawrence *If You Traveled West in a Covered Wagon,* by Ellen Levine *The Keeping Quilt,* by Patricia Polacco *Mississippi Mud: Three Prairie Journals,* by Ann Turner *On the Mayflower: Voyage of the Ship's Apprentice & Passenger Girl,* by Kate Waters *Samuel Eaton's Day: A Day in the Life of a Pilgrim Boy,* by Kate Waters *Sarah Morton's Day,* by	*A Journey to the New World: The Diary of Remember Patience Whipple, Mayflower, 1620,* by Kathryn Lasky *A Narrative of the Life of Mrs. Mary Jemison,* by James Seaver *Pilgrim Voices: Our First Year in the New World,* by Connie Roop *Standing in the Light: The Captive Diary of Catherine Carey Logan,* by Mary Pope Osborne *Trail of Tears,* by Joseph Bruchac *The Captive,* by Joyce Hansen *Constance: A Story of Early Plymouth,* by Patricia Clapp *Don't Know Much About the Pilgrims,* by Kenneth Davis *Homes in the Wilderness: A Pilgrim's Journal of Plymouth Plantation in 1620,* by Margaret Wise Brown *Jump Ship To Freedom,* by

Table 6.1   Continued

Big Idea	K–3 Titles	4–6 Titles
	Kate Waters *Silent Movie,* by Avi *Three Young Pilgrims,* by Cheryl Harness	James & Christopher Collier *Kidnapped Prince: The Life of Olaudah Equiano,* by Ann Cameron & O. Equiano *A Lion to Guard Us,* by Clyde Bulla *Many Thousands Gone,* by Virginia Hamilton *Molly Banneky,* by Alice McGill *The New Americans: Colonial Times 1620–1689,* by Betsy Maestro *Now Let Me Fly: The Story of a Slave Family,* by Dolores Johnson *The People Could Fly,* by Virginia Hamilton *Stranded at Plymoth Plantation 1626,* by Gary Bowen *The Underground Railroad,* by R. Conrad Stein *Views of American Slavery, Taken a Century Ago,* by Anthony Benezet *Who's That Stepping on Plymouth Rock?,* by Jean Fritz *Across the Wide and Lonesome Prairie: The Oregon Trail Diary of Hattie Campbell,* by Kristiana Gregory *Frontier Home,* by Raymond Bial *I Was Dreaming to Come to America,* by Veronica Lawlor *Laura's Album: A Remembrance Scrapbook of Laura Ingalls Wilder,* by William Anderson *Only the Names Remain: The Cherokees and the Trail of Tears,* by Alex Bealer *The Oregon Trail,* by Leonard Everett Fisher *A Pioneer Sampler,* by Barbara Greenwood *Pioneers,* by John Artman *Spanish Pioneers of the Southwest,* by Joan Anderson *The Way West: Journal of a Pioneer Woman,* by Amelia Stewart Knight

(continued)

Table 6.1   Continued

Big Idea	K–3 Titles	4–6 Titles
People establish and use systems of government for order and group survival.	*We the Kids: The Preamble to the Constitution,* by David Catrow *We the People: The Constitution of the United States,* by Peter Spier	*The Amazing Life of Benjamin Franklin,* by James Cross Giblin *Ben Franklin of Old Philadelphia,* by Margaret Cousins *Colony of Virginia,* by Brooke Coleman *Governing and Teaching: A Sourcebook on Colonial America,* by Carter Smith *If You Lived in Williamsburg in Colonial Days,* by Barbara Brenner *The Jamestown Colony,* by Gail Sakura *The Many Lives of Benjamin Franklin,* by Aliki *Molly Bannaky,* by Alice McGill *What's the Big Idea, Ben Franklin?,* by Jean Fritz *Will's Story: 1771 (Young Americans Colonial Willamsburg),* by Joan Lowery Nixon *Alexander Hamilton: First U.S. Secretary of the Treasury,* by Veda Boyd Jones *George Washington,* by Zachary Kent *The World Turned Upside Down: George Washington and the Battle of Yorktown,* by Richard Ferrie *The Bill of Rights,* by Patricia Ryon Quiri *If You Were There When They Signed the Constitution,* by Elizabeth Levy *A Kids' Guide to America's Bill of Rights: Curfews, Censorship, and the 100-Pound Giant,* by Kathleen Krull *A More Perfect Union: The Story of Our Constitution,* by Betsy Maestro *The Senate,* by Veda Boyd Jones *Shh! We're Writing the Constitution,* by Jean Fritz

planned?" These questions could precede the reading of almost any story about the Pilgrims traveling to North America on the Mayflower, pioneers moving west during the period known as Westward Expansion, or immigrant experiences.

Introduce Interesting Artifacts

Artifacts do not have to be rare, expensive or necessarily old to gain interest in a classroom. Common objects may be used to shed new light on a story (as well as that object). For example, before reading a story about Japanese internment during World War II, such as *Baseball Saved Us* (Mochizuki), you might bring in a baseball and bat. Display the artifacts and engage students in a brief discussion about baseball. Do not assume that all students know about baseball. During the read-aloud, hold up the baseball or position the bat over your shoulder to accentuate parts of the story. Help students see the significance and feel the importance of one ball and one bat in the lives of many who made the most of unfortunate circumstances.

Artifact replicas are also useful tools to help students visualize foreign objects or ideas. Introducing students to a story about ancient Egypt, such as *I Am the Mummy, Heb-Nefert* (Bunting), inexpensive clay scarabs or mummy beads will help students visualize parts of the story that are not readily understandable. Many such items may be purchased inexpensively at museum gift shops or through on-line sources such as Colonial Williamsburg (http://www.history.org), Smithsonian (http://www.smithsonianstore.com), or Social Studies School Services (http://www.socialstudies.com).

Another option is to ask students to bring to class certain items that will relate to your read-aloud. For example, if you are reading a story about the Pony Express, such as *They're Off!: The Story of the Pony Express* (Harness), you might ask students to bring into class something that they received recently in the mail. Before reading the selection, invite students to share what they brought (letters, magazines, postcards, photographs, cards, etc.), map the places from which these mailings originated, and explain the importance of receiving information from afar. Note the variety of kinds of mail today as was true then.

Display Visuals, Including Photographs, Charts, Posters, and Documents

It has been said that a picture is worth a thousand words, and this may hold true in your classroom. Depending on the reading selection and your reading, there may be no pictures for students to view before or while listening to the story. Oftentimes, when reading beautifully illustrated picture books, we will not show the pictures during the read-aloud on purpose. This is because we want our students to paint

History Connections

The Pony Express operated along the 1900 miles between Missouri and California. They delivered mail for just a short time— 18 months from April 1860 to October 1861.

Many classrooms are now equipped with document cameras that allow for immediate large-screen projection of book pages. Consider when showing the pictures is appropriate during a read-aloud and when it is not.

Source: *Cover from* I Am the Mummy Heb-Mefert *by Eve Bunting.*

pictures in their minds—this is one way to engage the reader in the reading process. However, depending on the students, the topic, and the selection, students may not be able to visualize parts of the story because they are unfamiliar with the time period, setting, items, or situations. They are therefore unable to paint those pictures in their minds, or worse yet, they create imaginative pictures in their minds and imprint those visions at the expense of learning what objects, landscapes, or settings really look like. For fiction, this may be fine, but for historical fiction and nonfiction texts, it is not.

For example, in reading *Island of the Blue Dolphins* (O'Dell), you might bring in photographs of sea otters and abalone (if not real abalone shells, if you have access to these). Reading *Mojave* (Siebert), you might display photos of desert plants, animals, and scenes. It is important that you do not assume that students know what certain landscapes look like and feel like just because you may have experienced them. Many students have had limited experiences and have not visited zoos, museums, or marine facilities, so they do not know what certain animals look and sound and smell like. It is an easy process, however, to research photos or images on the Internet and print out or project these images for class use.

Similarly, primary documents help invite students into reading. Before reading *We the People* (Spier), *We the Kids* (Catrow), *The Declaration of Independence* (Fink), or *The Signers: The 56 Stories Behind the Declaration of Independence* (Fradin), it would be inspiring to present replicas of the U.S. Constitution or Declaration of Independence to students. The more worn, torn, and crinkly the paper, the more students seem to be "wowed."

Chances are you will have at least one student who will ask, "Is that the *real* thing?" when they see the replicas.

Use Maps to Identify Where the Story Takes Place

Maps are very useful in helping students at all grades better understand where a story takes place. Even at the primary grades, a simple map can help students see that the story takes place on a continent far from North America, or near a large body of water, or close to the equator where the climate is hot. Maps are especially helpful when characters in a story move from place to place. It is helpful for students to get a general understanding of the "territory" of the story in terms of the continent, state, climate, etc. If a story takes place in Africa, such as *Mufaro's Beautiful Daughters* (Steptoe) or *Why Mosquitoes Buzz in People's Ears: A West African Tale* (Aardema), begin by identifying the continent on a map and ask students to share what they already know about this place. Invite students to add to this body of knowledge, confirm what they think they know, or clear up some misconceptions by listening to this story.

Many publishers will provide you with free maps—just ask!

During and after read-alouds, there are a variety of ways to keep students engaged in the story. Consider strategies to help students process information, interact with the story, and better understand the information presented through the literature. In some cases, simply providing students with blank paper or blank journals to draw scenes from the story is all you need to keep students engaged in the story. Many students are able to multitask like this, but some are not. You will want to keep an eye on students and make sure you are not sacrificing their attention to the story with these activities. It is also important to make activities optional during readings. Activities before and after you are reading aloud, however, should not be optional. In either case, here are some suggestions.

Let Students Map the Story

With laminated desk maps or blackline masters that students can write or draw on, allow students to track the progress of the story. Reading selections such as *Stowaway* (Hesse), *I, Crocodile* (Marcellino), or *How to Make an Apple Pie and See the World* (Priceman) invites students to follow their journeys, and maps help them do just that. For example, Priceman's *How to Make an Apple Pie and See the World* takes the reader from the comforts of home to Italy for wheat, France for eggs, Sri Lanka for cinnamon, England for milk, Jamaica for salt and sugar, Vermont for apples, and back home to bake the pie.

Consider allowing students, while you read, to draw icons along the route that reflect events in the story, or to simply draw lines indicating the best routes. For your kinesthetic learners, provide modeling clay for them to mold objects representing items in the story and then place these miniatures in the appropriate places on the map.

There are some great reading selections that take students all over the map without a particular story sequence. For example, *Throw Your Tooth on the Roof: Tooth Traditions From Around the World* (Beeler), *On The Same Day in March: A Tour of the World's Weather* (Singer), or *Talking Walls* (Knight) introduce students to places all over the globe. In these cases, students can still "stop" at each place and interact with their maps eventually creating a pattern map of the world. In the end, encourage students to draw conclusions about the patterns of their marks on their maps.

Use Hands-On, Minds-On Activities

Some students enjoy sitting and listening to a good story while their imaginations run wild with details of the story. Others become fidgety and require something to keep their hands busy. You are likely to know which students are often restless. Providing them something to keep their hands busy while you read will more likely keep them listening and focused on the story. For example, while reading *The True Confessions of Charlotte Doyle* (Avi), you might provide students with a copy of the ship's diagram presented in the book. Also provide students with a cardboard tray, a box of toothpicks, and a bottle of glue. Give students the option to build a 17th-century sailing ship like the one in the story while listening to the story, or not. Many students may decide to participate in this creative project while listening to the riveting story. Others may choose to just sit and listen, and watch the others construct miniature ships. One teacher distinctly

Book Links

Avi is one of our favorite authors who brings history to life through historical fiction, including *The Secret School, The Fighting Ground, Night Journeys, Captain Grey, Don't You Know There's a War On?, Finding Providence,* and *Crispin: The Cross of Lead.*

remembers reading this story to a class of fourth-grade students who, at certain points, stopped construction, stared at her with mouths wide open, and anxiously waited to hear what would happen next. As with most travels at sea, there are lulls in the story where the student-crafted ships receive lots of attention, and there are moments of excitement when ship-making becomes abandoned and attention is focused solely on the story.

Use Dramatic Recreation

Stopping at points during the story or after you finish reading, consider having students recreate scenes (favorite scenes, important or pivotal scenes, confusing scenes, etc.). Invite students to work in groups to recreate or retell a particular scene or event in the book. Discuss the various interpretations of the same thing and contributing factors to these variations. Or, have students stage an event in the story, then have the actors freeze in one moment. During that moment, invite students in the audience to ask questions of the characters. The actors respond to the questions in the role of the character attempting to explain the actions, thought, motivations, and feelings of that particular character.

Rewrite the Story

After each day's read-aloud, have students reconstruct that chapter or portion of the story in their own words. Depending on your goals for this rewrite, direct students to summarize or retell the story as they heard it; rewrite the story changing a major character or event, but not the entire storyline; or improve upon the story by rewriting it altogether (but based on the original).

SHARED READING

Shared reading allows teachers and students to work together as they read and discuss a literature selection. Students follow along reading the text and viewing the illustrations through big books or shared texts. In shared reading lessons, you might focus on text features, language, vocabulary, or other reading skills. Oftentimes, the reading selection is rich and engaging, and students read and reread the text several times. Shared reading lessons are excellent opportunities for the integration of social studies through careful selection of social studies standards–aligned literature selections.

Text features such as headings, illustrations, diagrams, captions, bold words, glossaries, and indexes are designed to help the reader understand the text. Students often require instruction in using these features.

More and more publishers are producing beautiful books that introduce creative approaches to nonfiction text, historic fiction, and literature with social studies concepts. Picture books such as *Martin's Big*

Words (Rappaport) and *So Far From the Sea* (Bunting) require repeated readings as students become intrigued by the style and content of the art, identify primary source information through the use of quotes, and consider the unique presentation of information. For example, both books use chronology to present a series of events that provide historic context to their stories of the civil rights movement and Japanese internment. These are but two examples of the many social studies titles available to teachers at all grade levels that cover a variety of social studies topics.

INDEPENDENT READING

Independent reading has become a staple in most classrooms across the nation. Attention to time, choice, and facilitation for consistent independent reading has improved reading fluency for many students and moved a generation of readers in the direction of lifelong learning. As already noted, there is no shortage of appropriate and available reading selections to help support students in understanding history, culture, geography, economics, government, and citizenship. There are social studies titles that span literature genres, author studies, and themes, and deserve a place in every classroom library where most students select their independent reading titles.

Some teachers, particularly those using a Reader's Workshop model (Atwell, 1987) for independent reading, have created book bins or book baskets based on reading levels, themes, topics, authors, genres, or Big Ideas (Frey & Fisher, 2006). See Table 6.1 for suggested titles in these organizational categories. Teachers have then required students to make selections, over time, from each of the genres or topics or Big Ideas. No matter how you organize your book collection for students to select and then dive into reading, be sure to include rich social studies titles. Then, requiring students to read from a variety of authors, topics, or genres will still allow for a natural integration of social studies content.

In developing a classroom library chock-full of social studies resources, you will want to consider the following question: *Do I select and present only the books that support my grade-level standards or content in social studies, or do I include titles that are about different time periods, people, and places?*

The answer to that question will depend on you and your students. Because you will want to support the detailed and in-depth study of social studies content that relates to your content standards, it will be advantageous for you and your students to limit your selection to the topics presented in your standards. For example, if your grade level is required to study early American history, your classroom library may provide titles related to Native American cultures, exploration, colonization, the Revolutionary War, starting a new nation,

Genres are categories of literary forms (novel, lyric poem, epic, historical fiction, for example). Students need experience with all kinds of genre.

Reader's Workshop allows for choice, time, and guidance in reading. Mini lessons focus students on elements of reading, and teachers often conference with individuals or small groups of readers while the rest of the class reads independently.

Remember, during independent reading, students should be reading books they *can* read and *want* to read, based on the big ideas the class is studying.

These second-grade students self-selected titles from the themed book basket "People Who Made a Difference."
Source: *Emily Schell*

A well-stocked social studies library includes age-appropriate and engaging magazines, including *National Geographic Kids*.
Source: *Emily Schell*

and westward expansion. That is still quite a range! Students interested in the Oregon Trail may read a fascinating book in October and anxiously await the unit that comes in April. Or, a student who learned about explorers in October may want to learn more and do so through books that allow her to study through January, though the chronological presentation of early American history has moved beyond the age of exploration.

On the other hand, expanding student access to historic periods and characters that are not part of that grade level's standards has its benefits, too. Imagine a student moving into the state of California as a sixth grader and being told that March 31st is a state holiday in honor of Cesar Chavez. If this student has no idea who Chavez was, and certainly will not learn about Chavez as part of his ancient civilizations curriculum, where else might he turn to learn more about this historic character? We'd like to think that the school or community library is an easily accessible resource, but oftentimes it is not. Therefore, you should consider adding selections to your classroom library that do not necessarily align with your grade-level standards for students to access and enjoy.

Additionally, working across grade levels, we continue to hear complaints from social studies teachers that students do not have enough prior knowledge on historic periods or places from which to draw. Literature can do that for students who should not have to wait until the standards require attention to particular eras, places, or events. While in fourth grade, Emily's son became fascinated with stories about World War II. Emily wanted him to concentrate on reading about early California history because that is what he was studying in school (and she was not thrilled about his sudden interest in war), so she tried to steer him into the direction of some excellent titles on California settlers. He persisted and eventually Emily gave in and he became immersed in reading several of Scholastic's My Name is America (the "boys' version" of the Dear America series, which presents historical fiction through a series of diary entries) books about World War II soldiers and Japanese-American internees. To Emily's surprise, he really was ready to learn about and discuss real issues of conflict, race, and citizens' rights. Both of them grew in their understandings of people and our world as a result of those readings. Then, later in the year when his class was studying about California's role in World War II, he had lots of prior knowledge to share!

Find ways to negotiate appropriate readings with your students. Reading abilities, topics, and interests should be important factors in those negotiations.

Book Links

Some excellent books about Cesar Chavez and migrant farmworkers include *Harvesting Hope: The Story of Cesar Chavez* (Krull), *The Fight in the Fields: Cesar Chavez and the Farmworkers Movement* (Ferriss & Sandoval), *Cesar Chavez: A Struggle for Justice* (Griswold del Castillo), *Cesar Chavez: A Hero for Everyone* (Soto), *First Day in Grapes* (Casilla), *Amelia's Road* (Altman), and *Tomas and the Library Lady* (Mora).

How can people make a difference in our world? These students are reading a variety of books in their book club to further discuss this essential question.
Source: *Emily Schell*

LITERATURE CIRCLES

One successful method for integrating literature and social studies, which can be used during the social studies/literacy block, literacy period, or social studies period, is with Literature Circles (Daniels, 2001).

As with Reader's Workshop, there are many variations, definitions, and different approaches to literature circles. In general, we know that literature circles are student-centered, rely on reading and reader response, and involve small reading groups. Here are the major components of most:

- Students select their own reading materials, though often from a selection provided by the teacher.
- Small, temporary reading groups are formed according to the choices students make for reading materials; all members of the group are reading the same book; different groups read different books.
- Groups have scheduled meetings to discuss their reading.
- Roles are given to members of the group to summarize, question, illustrate, or illuminate information from the reading.
- Students determine discussion topics and have natural conversations about the text, author, etc., and make personal connections or ask text-related questions.
- The teacher may facilitate the work of the students, but does not direct the group work.

Information about the operation of literature circles in general can be found in the Web Links module in Chapter 6 on our Companion Website at www. prenhall.com/schell.

- Students self-evaluate their progress, and teachers use observations to add to the evaluation.
- When books are completed, new book choices are made and new groups are formed.

Literature circles allow for students to study social studies topics in depth, drawing personal connections, and in a small, supportive group environment. Social studies topics, such as communities, could include these choices for second-, third-, or fourth-grade students using literature circles:

- *The House on Maple Street* (Pryor)
- *Right Here on This Spot* (Addy)
- *When I Was Young in the Mountains* (Rylant)
- *Blue and Gray* (Bunting)
- *This Is Where I Live* (Wolfe)
- *Cactus Poems* (Asche)

These selections span time, place, and literary style. And students will enjoy reading and discussing these books!

Some teachers have used literature circles to allow students to explore different facets of a period. For example, in learning about the southern colonies, teachers have offered students these titles from Joan Lowery Nixon's Young Americans: Colonial Williamsburg series:

- *Caesar's Story, 1759*
- *John's Story, 1775*
- *Ann's Story, 1747*
- *Maria's Story, 1773*

Each story takes students back to 18th century Williamsburg to learn about the life and challenges of children who actually lived at that place in that time. The names are real, but the stories are intended to present typical lifestyles and situations of this period. All of the stories are told from the child's perspective. For example, in *Caesar's Story*, Caesar tells about his life as a slave living in his master's house and caring for his master's needs. Maria, in *Maria's Story*, is the daughter of the colony's printer and tells about her daily chores, conflicts, and ultimately the loss of her parents. Ann in *Ann's Story* dreams of becoming a doctor like her father, but learns that such dreams are unsuitable for a young lady of her time. Although focused on their own lives, these characters reflect customs, laws, and events of the 18th century and provide interesting windows on studies about this period—beyond biographies of Thomas Jefferson and George Washington. With choice and flexibility, students work in their literature circles to cross-reference information from their social studies textbooks and empathize with children their ages from a "foreign" time and place.

History Connections

When George Washington was elected President, there was a king in France, a czarina in Russia, an emperor in China, and a shogun in Japan. Only the office of President remains today.

Literature circle selections can be varied to focus students on social studies topics while addressing the varied reading levels, interests, and needs of your students. See Figure 6.3 for a variety of titles recommended for literature circles connected to a unit on the American Revolution.

Figure 6.3 Literature circles titles: A unit on the American Revolution.

Novels

The Fighting Ground (Avi)
This is a minute-by-minute account of a day in the life of a young boy who stole away to fight in the American Revolution.

Johnny Tremain (Forbes)
A 14-year-old orphan boy is the focus of this classic novel set in Boston at the start of the Revolutionary War. He becomes an apprentice to a silversmith and eventually a patriot.

Winter of Red Snow: The Revolutionary War Diary of Abigail Jane Stewart (Gregory)
This story in the "Dear America" series presents a diary-like account by 11-year-old Abigail of life in Valley Forge from December 1777 to July 1778. She describes the action as General George Washington prepares his troops to fight the British.

Toliver's Secret (Brady)
When her grandfather is injured, 10-year-old Ellen Toliver replaces him on a top-secret patriotic mission. Disguised as a boy, she manages to smuggle a message to General George Washington.

George Washington Spymaster: How the Americans Outspied the British and Won the Revolutionary War (Allen)
This book recounts the work of spies and counterspies while relating the events of the war.

Easy Read (Chapter Book)

Eyewitness: American Revolution
Highly visual, this book offers information about the war in themes.

George the Drummer (Benchley)
A view of the incidents at Lexington and Concord, Massachusetts, which were the start of the American Revolution, as seen from the eyes of George, a British drummer boy.

If You Lived at the Time of the American Revolution (Moore)
Like other books in this series, interesting facts and stories are told about life during this historic period.

Phoebe the Spy (Griffin)
A young black girl spies for General Washington during the American Revolution.

Sam the Minuteman (Benchley)
An easy-to-read account of Sam and his father fighting as minutemen against the British in the Battle of Lexington.

The Secret Soldier (McGovern)
This tells of a woman who dressed up as a man in order to fight against the British.

Revolutionary War on Wednesday (Magic Tree House Series) (Osborne)
This fictional story takes Jack and Annie back in time to 1776, where they encounter George Washington on the Delaware.

Picture Books

They Called Her Molly Pitcher (Rockwell)
A camp follower went onto the battle field to help soldiers and ended up assisting in battle. They called her Molly Pitcher and she was rewarded for her acts of bravery.

The Boston Tea Party (Kroll)
One of the events that started the war with Britain is retold in this illustrated story.

Mary Geddy's Day (Waters)
This photo essay tells about the daily life of a young girl living in the colonies as talk about declaring independence looms.

Paul Revere's Midnight Ride (Krensky)
Longfellow's famous poem is retold with beautiful illustrations that recreate the story of Revere's ride.

Give Me Liberty: The Story of the Declaration of Independence (Freedman)
This picture book gives detailed information about the events that led to colonists' discontent and decisions to break away from Great Britain.

The Liberty Tree: The Beginning of the American Revolution (Penner)
This illustrated picture book provides information about the many events that led to the American Revolution and focuses on the symbol of the liberty tree.

These suggestions for using literature to support your teaching of social studies are not offered in any sort of hierarchical order. With the diversity of needs, schedules, and restrictions on teachers, some suggestions will work in some situation, but not others. We offer a variety of suggestions in hopes either that teachers find a solution to their challenges of integrating literature and the reading curriculum with social studies, or that this sparks creative thinking and planning so that the needs of the teacher and students are met while maximizing the limited time available for teaching and learning multiple subjects effectively.

TEACH SOCIAL STUDIES APART FROM TEACHING READING

Incidentally, we strongly object to this "use" of social studies as an end-of-the-day punishment or option. Think about the message that this sends to students about the importance and purpose of social studies.

Present social studies separate from reading. Traditionally, reading occurs at the beginning of the day when students are "fresh" and social studies occurs at the end of the day when students are sometimes given the option to go to physical education instead of having social studies. Whether this end-of-the-day "option" is presented or not, there exists the possibility that the day's activities run long and that time becomes unavailable for planned lessons in this important content area. Therefore, we suggest that careful planning accompany a clear commitment to the teaching and learning of social studies. Long-range planning and an adhered-to pacing guide will help teachers know what targets to meet at certain times of the year. Though some flexibility is important, hold fast to your goals for social studies achievement.

Some teachers have told us that they present social studies at the end of the day because it is the subject that students most look forward to, and that students recognize the need to stay on schedule so that the class does not have to shorten or forego social studies. When students help drive your day like this, then you have done things right! Susan Hewitt, a fifth-grade teacher in Lakeside, California, explained that she wants her students to leave school every day with new ideas, questions, and enthusiasm about something they learned. Therefore, she purposely presents social studies as the last subject of the day because her students leave the classroom anxious to tell their friends and families about this gross, interesting, bizarre, or fascinating story that they heard about life in early America. Susan, incidentally, is a fabulous storyteller, and her room is decorated with books that relate to what they are studying in social studies.

Some of the things that a good storyteller needs to think about include **volume** (Could I hear the teller?); **validity and reliability** (Did the characters seem believable and real to me?); **personality** (Did the teller keep my interest and attention?); and **clarity** (Did the story create images in my mind?)

Even when social studies is presented completely separate from reading and language arts, the inclusion and use of literature is important. Many teachers use the beginning or end of the social studies period to read aloud stories that deepen understanding of the topics. This practice adds dimension to the social studies period. Others integrate literature selections into their lessons when appropriate. For example, a teacher might read *Molly Bannaky* (McGill) during a lesson about indentured servants, or *Right Here on this Spot* (Addy) during a lesson on how communities change over time. Engaging texts such as these focus students' thinking and discussion on social studies content instead of vocabulary, language, and genre. This allows students to see and enjoy literature purely for its content rather than its form.

Conclusion

While planning and organizing your curriculum to teach multiple subjects, you can make opportunities to effectively integrate reading and social studies and enhance students' understandings and appreciation of both content areas. Whether you integrate social studies content into your reading program, or reteach and reinforce reading skills during your social studies program, this planned approach will help students see the purpose for learning how to read as well as the benefits of reading to learn. Oftentimes, you will motivate readers through intriguing and captivating stories related to real life. Other times, you will inspire good readers to consider social studies topics and new genres through your integrated approach to teaching these important content areas.

A variety of engaging and on-topic literature, which spans reading genres, is available to support your efforts in integrating literature and social studies. Consider your reading objectives and align those with your social studies objectives to engage students in effective learning activities that lead to achievement in both.

History's Finer Points

Perhaps you have heard the story about George Washington chopping down a cherry tree. When his father asked who cut down the tree, George Washington told him, "I cannot tell a lie; I did it with my little hatchet." Why do you know this story? Why do thousands of children continue to hear this story in classrooms throughout the United States when the story is, in fact, a fabrication? Truth be told, it was Parson Mason Locke Weems (1756–1825), the editor of George Washington's biography *The Life of Washington*, who created and added this story to the biography. Why? Parson Weems stated that a good biography, especially that of our nation's first president, should teach lessons to children about good morals and behavior.

Document Based Question: Is this ironic? In this case, children learned this story and were taught to be truthful and honest. Did the ends justify the means?

Quiz yourself on this chapter's important concepts on our Companion Website's Chapter 6 self-assessments at www.prenhall.com/schell.

Questions to Consider

1. What types of literature are essential for use in the social studies classroom?
2. When should specific instructional approaches (read-alouds, shared readings, literature circles, and independent reading) be used?
3. How can social studies content be integrated into the literacy block?

Exercises

1. Start a book collection. Either identify titles that you want to have in your collection or begin shopping at garage sales, used book stores, and such to build your classroom library. It's never too early to start!
2. Identify a big idea for your assigned grade level. Based on this big idea, identify at least 10 pieces of children's literature that could be used. Identify which books would be best as read-alouds and practice using these books.

References

Atwell, N. (1987). *In the middle: new understandings about reading, writing, and learning*. Portsmouth, NH: Heinemann.

California Department of Education. (2001). *History–social science framework for California public schools*. Sacramento, CA: Author.

Curriculum and Instruction Steering Committee. (2000). *Pages of the past: K–6 literature aligned to history–social science standards*. San Diego, CA: San Diego County Office of Education.

Curriculum and Instruction Steering Committee. (2002). *Tales of time: Middle school literature aligned to history-social science standards*. Stockton, CA: San Joaquin County Office of Education.

Daniels, H. (2001). *Literature circles: Voice and choice in book clubs and reading groups*. York, ME: Stenhouse Publishers.

Frey, N., & Fisher, D. (2006). *Language arts workshop: purposeful reading and writing instruction*. Upper Saddle River, NJ: Merrill Prentice Hall.

San Bernardino County Superintendent of Schools. (2005). *Schools of California Online Resources for Educators (SCORE) History–Social Science*. Retrieved October 6, 2005 from http://score.rims.k12.ca.us. Author.

San Diego County Office of Education. (2005). *Schools of California Online Resources for Educators (SCORE) Language Arts*. Retrieved

October 6, 2005 from http://www.sdcoe.k12.ca.us/SCORE/cla.html. San Diego, CA: Author.

Wiggins, G., & McTighe, J. (1998). *Understanding by design*. Alexandria, VA: Association for Supervision and Curriculum Development.

Children's Literature

Aardema, V. (1978). *Why mosquitoes buzz in people's ears: A west African tale*. New York: Puffin Books.
One little mosquito sets of a chain of events that ultimately offers a lesson about telling the truth.

Addy, S. H. (1999). *Right here on this spot*. Houghton Mifflin.
What happened right here on this spot one thousand years ago? One hundred years ago? Ten years ago? This book takes the reader back in time to see how one plot of land has changed over time.

Alder, J. W. (Ed.). (1998). *In the path of war: Children of the American revolution tell their stories*. Cobblestone.
This collection of stories tells about the American Revolution from the perspectives of children.

Allen, T. B. (2004). *George Washington, spymaster: How the Americans outspied the British and won the revolutionary war*. Washington, DC: National Geographic.
Events of the American Revolution are presented through a series of spy and counterspy missions involving General Washington and British leaders.

Asche, F. (1998). *Cactus poems*. Gulliver Green.
Photographs and fun poems present a variety of images in the desert—from cactus to lizards to tortoises.

Altman, L. J. (1987). *Amelia's road*. New York: Lee & Low Books.
A young girl reflects upon her life as a child in a migrant family of farmworkers.

Avi. (1997). *The true confessions of Charlotte Doyle*. New York: HarperTrophy.
13-year-old Charlotte recollects her 1832 transatlantic voyage filled with fear, excitement, and danger.

Beeler, Selby. (2001). *Throw your tooth on the roof: Tooth traditions from around the world*. Boston: Houghton Mifflin.
This informative picture book reveals traditions around the world that relate to children's teeth. What did you do when you first lost a tooth? And why did you do that?!

Borden, L. (2002). *America is . . .* New York: Margaret K. Elderry.
This picture book poetically describes our nation reflecting its diversity of people, history, land, work, and potential.

Bunting, E. (1997). *I am the mummy Heb-Nefert*. San Diego, CA: Harcourt Brace.

A mummy looks back on her life as a beautiful Egyptian princess. Bunting's poetry evokes rich imagery and tantalizes your senses capturing glimpses of this ancient world before the mummy is moved to a sterile museum exhibit.

Bunting, E. (1998). *So far from the sea*. New York: Clarion.

A family revisits the site of a WWII Japanese internment camp and transitions between two worlds, two eras, two perspectives.

Casilla, R., & Perez, L. K. (2002). *First day in grapes*. New York: Lee & Low.

A young boy's family follows the crops for work on farms and associates memories with seasonal crops.

Catrow, D. (2002). *We the kids: The Preamble to the Constitution of the United States*. New York: Dial Books.

Catrow uses his political cartooning skills to create a colorful picture book that illustrates the preamble for young readers. Kids are asked to consider the meaning and big ideas behind our founding documents so that they understand that these are for citizens of all ages.

Farris, C. K. (2003). *My brother Martin: A sister remembers growing up with the Rev. Dr. Martin Luther King, Jr.* New York: Simon & Schuster Children's Publishing.

The sister of Martin Luther King, Jr., tells stories from their childhood growing up in Atlanta, Georgia. Young readers can relate to the pranks and events of his early life.

Ferris, S., & Sandoval, R. (1998). *The fight in the fields: Cesar Chavez and the farmworkers movement*. Orlando, FL: Harvest.

A detailed companion book to the PBS documentary provides lots of information about the life and convictions of Chavez and his followers.

Fink, S. (2002). *The Declaration of Independence: The words that made America*. New York: Scholastic.

Fink interprets the words of the Declaration of Independence using political cartoons.

Forbes, E. (1987). *Johnny Tremain*. New York: Yearling Books.

A 14-year-old orphan boy is the focus of this classic novel set in Boston at the start of the Revolutionary War. He becomes an apprentice to a silversmith and eventually a patriot.

Fradin, D. B. (2002). *The signers: The fifty-six stories behind the Declaration of Independence*. New York: Walker & Company.

Short biographies share interesting information about each of the 56 signers of the Declaration of Independence. Readers learn of the sacrifices and risks taken by each of these founders.

Fritz, J. (1976). *And then what happened, Paul Revere?* New York: Putnam.

This biography of Paul Revere tells the story about his historic ride on horseback warning the American colonists that British troops are advancing.

Gerstein, M. (2003). *The man who walked between two towers*. Brook-field, CT: Roaring Brook.

This picture book presents the story of Phillip Petit's daring tightrope walk between the Twin Towers in Manhattan in 1974. The story compares that memorable event to the towers themselves—which still live in the memories of Americans who knew them.

Gregory, K. (1996). *Winter of red snow: The revolutionary war diary of Abigail Jane Stewart, Valley Forge, Pennsylvania, 1777*. New York: Scholastic.

An original to the Dear America diaries series, this presents a young girl's perspective of the American Revolution as her life was changed forevermore.

Griffin, J. (1989). *Phoebe the spy*. New York: Scholastic.

Thirteen-year-old Phoebe is asked to serve as a spy during the Revolutionary War and works to save George Washington's life.

Griswold del Castillo, R. (1998). *Cesar Chavez: a struggle for justice*. Houston, TX: Pinata.

A biographical account of Chavez' life and struggles to bring justice to farmworkers.

Harness, C. (2002). *They're off: The story of the pony express*. New York: Aladdin.

This well-written picture book tells about the Pony Express.

Hesse, K. (2002). *Stowaway*. New York: Aladdin.

A young boy stows away on Captain James Cook's tall ship, the *Endeavour*, in England around 1768. His tales of adventure are both frightening and exciting, but reflective of the risks and customs of the period.

Hoose, P. (2001). *We were there, too!: Young people in U.S. history*. New York: Farrar, Straus and Giroux.

This book features a large collection of historical narratives about children who have contributed to U.S. history.

Kent, D. (1994). *American Revolution: 'Give me liberty, or give me death!'* Berkeley Heights, NJ: Enslow.

Kent seeks to present a balanced perspective on the American Revolution from both sides—the Loyalists as well as the Patriots.

Knight, M. B. (1995). *Talking walls*. Gardiner, ME: Tilbury House Publishers.

Knight presents a pictorial tour around the world to visit walls and learn about their history and significance.

Krull, K. (2002). *Harvesting hope: the story of Cesar Chavez*. San Diego, CA: Harcourt.

A beautifully illustrated biographical account of Chavez' life and work.

Marcellino, F. (1999). *I, crocodile*. Michael Di Capua.

This fun picture book tells a story from the perspective of a crocodile taken from Egypt by Napolean to France. It's a humorous story!

Masoff, J. (2000). *American Revolution, 1700–1800: Chronicle of America*. New York: Scholastic.
Using high-interest photographs and intriguing text, this book presents information about the American Revolution.

McGill, A. (1999). *Molly Banneky*. Boston, MA: Houghton Mifflin.
Based on a true story, this large picture book tells of Banneky, who became an indentured servant in colonial America, married her slave, and made a life for herself and her family. The story ends with her grandson, Benjamin Banneker.

McGovern, A. (1991). *The secret soldier: The story of Deborah Sampson*. New York: Scholastic.
For one-and-a-half years, Deborah Sampson served in the Continental Army during the Revolutionary War while disguised as a male soldier—women were not allowed to serve as soldiers. This book tells the story behind this historic event.

Mochizuki, K. (1995). *Baseball saved us*. New York: Lee & Low Books.
This picture book tells what life may have been like for some Japanese American citizens interned in camps during World War II. Playing baseball helped characters in the story cope with their living conditions and loss of freedom.

Mora, P. (1998). *Tomas and the library lady*. New York: Alfred A. Knopf.
A young boy finds solace and a friend in the library before his family moves to yet another migrant camp.

Murphy, J. (1995). *A young patriot: The American revolution as experienced by one boy*. Jefferson City, MO: Troll Communications.
This book tells the experiences of 15-year-old Joseph Plumb Martin, who enlisted in the Continental Army in 1776.

Murray, S. (2002). *American Revolution: Eyewitness book*. New York: DK Publishing.
Photographs, illustrations, and text present information about the American Revolution in such categories as life in British America, winter soldier, France becomes an ally, and Yorktown.

Numeroff, L. (1991). *If you give a moose a muffin*. New York: Laura Geringer.
In keeping with her other patterned books that began with *If you Give a Mouse A Cookie,* this series of events begin with a moose who wants a muffin and ends up . . . well, you'll see!

O'Dell, S. (1960). *Island of the blue dolphins*. Boston: Houghton Mifflin.
Inspired by a true story, O'Dell tells the story of a 12-year-old American Indian girl who is stranded with her brother on an island off the coast of California. Karana makes a life for herself after her brother dies and lives there for 18 years.

Priceman, M. (1996). *How to make an apple pie and see the world*. New York: Dragonfly Books.

A young girl decides to bake an apple pie, but the market is closed, so
she travels the world for her ingredients and returns home to bake.

Rappaport, D. (1998). *Martin's big words*. New York: Hyperion.

This beautifully illustrated picture book tells about the life of Martin
Luther King, Jr., using his words and the words that influenced
his legacy.

Scieszka, J. (1995). *The true story of the three little pigs by A. Wolf*. New
York, NY: Picture Puffin.

This alternative to the traditional fairy tale of the three little pigs
tells the same story, but from the perspective of the wolf.

Scieszka, J. (1994). *The frog prince continued*. New York, NY: Picture
Puffin.

This tale relates the rest of the story after the princess kissed a frog
who became a prince. As Scieszka tells, they did not live happily
ever after after all!

Siebert, D. (1992). *Mojave*. New York, NY: HarperTrophy.

This picture book presents a lengthy illustrated poem telling all
about the physical and cultural geography of the Mojave Desert.

Singer, M. (2001). *On the same day in March: A tour of the world's
weather*. New York, NY: HarperTrophy.

On the same day, see what life and the weather is like in various
cities around the world.

Soto, G. (2003). *Cesar Chavez: a hero for everyone*. New York: Aladdin.

A brief narrative tells about the experiences of Chavez.

Spier, P. (1987). *We the people: the Constitution of the United States of
America*. New York: Doubleday.

Spier's cartooning skills illustrate the preamble to the U.S. Constitution and allows for thoughtful reflection and discussion about
this important, powerful, lasting, and living document.

Steptoe, J. (1987). *Mufaro's beautiful daughters*. New York: Lothrop,
Lee, & Shepard.

This is a beautifully illustrated picture book presenting a common
fable that demonstrates the importance of inner beauty through
compassion and kindness.

Wells, R. (1997). *Bunny Money*. New York: Dial.

Ruby and Max set out to find a birthday present for grandma with a
wallet full of dollar bills. They learn that money does not go a
long way!

Putting the Pieces Together:

Curriculum Planning and Organization

Source: *Emily Schell*

Big Idea

Planning, organization, and reflection lead to more effective teaching and learning of social studies.

Essential Question

"I need to teach a unit on ancient China. Where do I start?" Ms. Hofmann asked herself. She had completed a 2-week institute that year, which introduced her to a great deal of scholarship, resources, and ideas for teaching about China. She opened her overstuffed notebook and read over the notes she had taken during lectures. The content was fascinating, and she knew her students would love the stories about the kings and emperors who lived so many years ago. She flipped through some handouts and remembered a few activities that she had learned and wanted to implement in her classroom so that students would consider the multiple perspectives of the diverse people who lived throughout the Middle Kingdom during the various dynasties.

Ms. Hofmann turned to a stack of books that she had compiled, and wondered whether she should use these for read-alouds or independent research projects. Maybe, she thought, she could use some to create reader's theatre scripts because she knew how much her students enjoyed doing reader's theatre.

Remembering her school's focus on writing informational text, Ms. Hofmann began brainstorming ideas for engaging her students in writing about ancient China, creating charts, graphs, and maps to enhance the informational text.

Finally, she let out a big sigh. How would she take all that she had learned, all that she knew about good teaching, and all these great resources, as well as her district-adopted textbook, to help her students learn what they needed to know about ancient China?

"All that they need to know about ancient China?" she thought. "What exactly *do* they need to know and be able to do?" Ms. Hofmann decided to start with the end in mind. She looked to her state standards and unpacked them to determine exactly what her students were required to learn in this unit on China as well as for the rest of her early world history curriculum. She then started to plan accordingly while aligning resources that would help students understand the big ideas that she uncovered during her unpacking of the standards. Soon, Ms. Hofmann was prepared and excited to start teaching her unit on ancient China. In fact, she was already prepared for teaching the following unit on ancient India as well!

INTRODUCTION

With a great deal of information about what to teach and how to teach, it is now time for you to put all of this together in order to teach. Where do you start? How do you make sense of all this information for you and your students? How will you develop meaningful plans for teaching social studies?

We suggest you begin with the end in mind. Know where you want to end up at the end of the school year. For example, Ms. Hofmann knew that by the end of the year, she wanted her students to know about prehistory and the civilizations from the ancient period. She knew that ancient China was one of those civilizations for her students to learn about. By the end of the year, she wanted her students to be able to understand and compare and contrast China, Greece, India, Egypt, Israel, and Rome during the ancient periods. Therefore, she needed to teach particular information about the civilization that developed in China. All the while, she needed to teach students to think critically about this time period, the geography of the region, an emergence of economies, the development of government, and more. While focusing in on this unit about ancient China, the teacher remained aware of the big picture for her grade-level content, the final destination for her students, and the important connections between the instructional units she prepared for her students.

Ms. Hofmann could have started her school year by mapping out her curriculum, rather than planning unit after unit and realizing the connections halfway through the school year. Let's take a look at how you can work smarter by starting with the end in mind when planning for your entire year's curriculum, individual instructional units, and lesson plans.

CURRICULUM MAPPING

Frameworks and content standards articulate what students should know and be able to do in our classrooms. Rarely do these come with instructions that tell us how long to teach each standard or objective, where we should take certain topics into depth, or how to organize the sequence of our instructional plans. Therefore, we have a great deal of work to do with these guiding documents.

Effective instructional planning is based in the standards and maximizes available resources. Therefore, it is important for you to plan your instruction with the various and important standards and goals in mind. Now that you have learned about national, state, and local guides as well as sound educational practices that promote the integration of the curriculum as well as engagement of literacy skills and resources, it is time for you to put together all of the many pieces of an effective social studies program in order to teach.

Remember Chapter 4?

History Connections

During the Tang Dynasty (around 900 A.D.) the Chinese "farmed" fish exclusively for the emperor's consumption. Sources date Chinese fish farming as far back as 3500 years ago. Today China farms more freshwater fish than any other country.

Many teachers are willing to share their curriculum maps and lesson plans. If they are offered to you, take them!

For links to state content standards, see the Web Links module in Chapter 7 on our Companion Website at www.prenhall.com/schell.

Figure 7.1

Source: *www.cartoonstock.com*

We recommend that you focus your attention on your grade-level standards and expectations and map out a plan for organizing and teaching that content and those skills so that you end up where you need to be in the end. Analyze your state-mandated or voluntary grade-level content and skills, consider the developmental levels of your students, and keep in mind what you know about teaching social studies for meaning. In other words, ask yourself these questions:

- What frames the content for my grade level?
- Is the content organized chronologically or thematically?
- Are there patterns across the content that allow for me to teach with big ideas and essential questions?
- Are the historical thinking and analysis skills integrated into the content or presented separately from social studies content?

Asking yourself these questions helps you develop a teaching plan or curriculum map.

- Are history, geography, economics, and civics and government content well integrated or presented as separate studies?
- How and when will my students be held accountable for this learning?

When you have a good grasp of content knowledge to help you guide your curriculum mapping process, it is time to begin. Mapping the curriculum from beginning to end, and from the end to the beginning—backward mapping—prepares you for developing solid instructional units. Mapping out the curriculum allows you to achieve several goals. These goals include a better understanding of the standards and content-specific objectives, organization and pacing of the curriculum, and focused assessment related to specific goals and objectives.

To begin the process of curriculum mapping, analyze the body of content standards for your grade level in social studies. Then compare and contrast these standards to additional sources of information that support effective teaching and learning at your grade level and in social studies. You may find that you need to add to your content to scaffold understandings, or you may need to condense parts because of overlap with other grade levels or subject areas. This process works best with grade-alike colleagues who bring varying perspectives and expertise to teaching. As a result of this collaboration, strengths and weaknesses of the standards become apparent. You will have a better understanding of the standards and identify concerns and questions that you may encounter while teaching.

Once you know the general topics or content to teach at your grade level, analyze the organization of your standards-based content. Most social studies teachers agree that history is best taught either in chronological order or thematically. Depending on your content, grade level, and other factors, decide on the best organization for your curriculum.

Next, identify the content by units and order of teaching. Depending on your grade level and specific content, decide on a reasonable order in which to teach your content, which will be presented through instructional units. You know your content and grade level, and you know whether or not teaching certain content at certain holidays will enhance your students' understandings (e.g., Pilgrims around Thanksgiving; American presidents around Presidents' Day; Women's Suffrage during Women's History Month). Additional factors may influence your order of teaching, such as availability of resources, team teaching schedules, or organization of your textbook and materials (although the textbook order should not be the driving force in your decision-making process).

Once you have identified the instructional units (e.g., Native Americans, Exploration, Colonization, Revolution, Nation-building, Immigration), and placed them in order, you must determine how much time to devote to each instructional unit. Start by determining the number

Oftentimes, new teachers describe anxieties about their own lack of historical and geographic content knowledge. Many textbook publishers provide background information for you in the teacher's guide. We also suggest quick references, such as books from the Everything series (*The Everything Civil War Book: Everything You Need to Know About the War That Divided the Nation; The Everything American History Book: People, Places and Events That Shaped Our Nation*) and For Dummies series (*World History for Dummies; U.S. History for Dummies*).

Why do you think that teachers want to teach in chronological order?

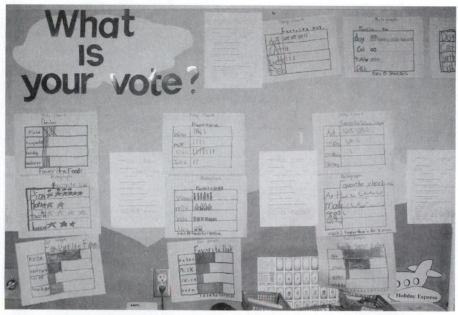

What is your vote? Students voted on various issues, then charted and analyzed their responses in this second-grade classroom.
Source: *Emily Schell*

of weeks that are available for teaching social studies. Then decide how many weeks should be dedicated to each identified instructional unit. Some units may require more time than others. For example, in teaching about early American history, a unit on exploration may require less time than a unit on colonization. Because you have a finite number of weeks during which to teach, you will have to make some hard choices about how long to spend on each instructional unit in order to get to the "end" or goals for your grade-level content. During this process, you will want to use a school calendar to see where you want to start and end instructional units. Working around winter and spring breaks, intersession periods, holidays, and school programs is never easy, but it is important to do this planning well in advance. Sometimes this means spending less time on some units than others. When faced with these decisions, keep your end goals in mind.

If possible, share your curriculum maps for your grade level with other grade levels. If you can see what your students learned the previous year(s) as well as what your students will encounter in following years, you can help connect and enhance your students' long-term learning in social studies. See Figures 7.2 and 7.3 for examples of social studies curriculum maps developed using the California History–Social Science Content Standards (CDE, 2001).

Figure 7.2   Grade 2 People Who Make a Difference Curriculum Map.

Month	Sept./Oct.	Nov.	Dec./Jan.	Feb./March	April–June
Weeks	1–4	5–8	9–14	15–21	22–28
Big Idea	We have a place in this world.	Families have history.	Where people live influences how people live.	People make a difference in the world.	The actions of a nation are guided by its beliefs and laws.
Strand	Geography	History; Chronology	Geography; Economics	History; Character	Government; Citizenship
Topic	Locations, maps, symbols, map skills	Ancestry, families	Community, state, nation, world; resources, production, interdependence	Heroes; historical events; biographies	Laws and consequences; national interactions
Standard	2.2	2.1	2.2; 2.4	2.1; 2.5	2.3

Source: *Emily Schell, San Diego County Office of Education (2001).*

BACKWARD PLANNING

After your year-long course of study is mapped out, and a pacing guide has been developed to help you stay on track to get through your year's worth of content and skills, you are ready to plan your instructional units. Like your curriculum map, we recommend that you plan your units by starting with the end in mind. A visual display of the process of

Figure 7.3   Grade 5 Making a New Nation Curriculum Map.

Month	Sept.	Oct./Nov.	Dec./Jan.	Feb. – April	May/June
Weeks	1–3	4–11	12–17	18–27	28–32
Big Idea	People adapt to the geography of their environments.	People move to improve their lives or because they are forced.	People establish and use systems of government for order and group survival.	Economic, political, and social differences may lead to rebellion and war.	Cooperation and conflict often result when people of different cultures come into contact with each other.
Topic	Geography; American Indians	Early Explorers; Early Colonization	Colonial Era; Rebellion	American Revolution; New Nation	Immigration; Resettlement
Standard	5.1	5.2	5.3–5.5	5.6, 5.7	5.8

Source: *Emily Schell, San Diego County Office of Education (2001).*

Figure 7.4   Backward planning process.

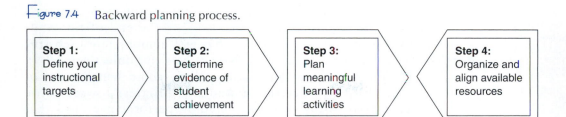

backward planning, as outlined by McTighe and Wiggins (1998), can be found in Figure 7.4.

First, analyze your standards-based curricular goals and objectives for the unit you are planning. Because social studies requires students to learn specific content knowledge as well as develop certain skills, one suggestion for analysis of the standards or goals is to unpack the statements into these two categories. For example, this third grade standard (Georgia Department of Education, 2004) reads:

The student will describe the four types of *productive resources:*

   a. natural (land)
   b. human (labor)
   c. capital (capital goods)
   d. entrepreneurship (used to create *goods* and *services*)

You might unpack this standard by separating the knowledge and skills in this manner:

Knowledge: natural resources; human resources; capital resources; entrepreneurship

Skills: define types of resources; describe productive resources; give examples of resources; compare and contrast types of resources; explain uses of resources

As you can see, unpacking the standard leads to the identification of specific topics and essential vocabulary as well as ideas for learning activities. Know your targets by asking:

- What do I want my students to know as a result of this unit?
- What skills will students develop during the course of this unit?
- How do I describe these goals clearly and concisely to my students so they understand where we should be at the end of this unit?
- What essential knowledge will students need to access to make sense of this information?
- Do my instructional goals align with strategies identified in the curriculum map?
- Have I introduced any Big Ideas that are pertinent to this content?

See Chapter 9 for more information on the use of assessments.

Second, develop assessments that will show you each student's progress toward those goals and objectives. By the end of this unit, you will want to have some evidence that will demonstrate each student's achievement of the standards-based goals and objectives. However, during the unit, you will want to have some benchmarks or indicators that help you determine students' progress toward those goals. Balance your assessments by including performance tasks that are informal and show students' progress (e.g., reflective writing, discussion groups), as well as tasks that are formal and summarize student achievement (e.g., essays, research reports, projects). In determining your assessments, remember to focus on ways to measure student progress and achievement of the stated goals and standards. Ask yourself:

- What do I want to know and see from each student?
- What are the best methods for students to demonstrate what they know and can do based on the goals and objectives?
- How many assessments do I need to determine what students know and can do?
- How will I balance informal and formal assessments?
- How will I assess students with diverse learning styles, skills, and abilities?
- How can I prepare and support students?
- How will these assessments promote student progress in social studies?
- At what time(s) during the unit will I administer these assessments?

Finally, after you have determined acceptable evidence for student achievement in your instructional unit, you must decide on meaningful learning activities that will help students succeed in those assessments. In other words, determine what students will need in order to learn this content, develop these skills, and demonstrate their understandings of the stated goals. Your understandings of effective teaching and learning will tell you that students need engaging learning activities that have a purpose, connections for students, and multiple opportunities to read, discuss, visualize, write, draw, and comprehend. This is where you get to use those great research-based strategies you have learned, ideas for engagement that you have developed, and wonderful resources you have gathered. These become organized into lesson plans that collectively make up the day-to-day structure of the instructional unit. While developing these lesson plans, consider:

Asking students to visualize and then illustrate or draw helps you understand their thinking process.

- How will students learn what they are expected to know?
- How will I engage students in the studies of this unit?
- In what ways might students relate or connect to this information?
- What research-based strategies will be most effective with my students and in these studies?

- How will I differentiate my instruction to meet the diverse needs of my students?
- How will I scaffold or provide access to the curriculum for my English learners?
- What vocabulary requires attention in this unit?
- How much time will I have to effectively teach this unit?
- How will I use the textbook and other resources to support the goals and objectives for this unit?
- What lessons will I develop?
- In what sequence will I teach these lessons during this unit?
- How will these lessons support the assessments already determined in the second step of the backward planning process?

One additional step will complete this process of unit planning. Although you may have thought about and identified useful texts and resources during the last step, this step requires you to locate and manage your resources for the instructional unit. Effective teaching and learning of social studies requires the use of multiple forms of text, visuals, artifacts, and other varied sources including multimedia. Consider what you have available in your classroom and at your school site. Search the Internet for useful resources as well. The resources you use for a unit of study should align to your stated targets or goals, assessments, and learning activities. Too often, teachers teach according to their available resources and as a result miss their own targets for instruction. During this final step of the unit planning process, ask yourself:

- What parts of the textbook are required for the lessons determined in Step Three?
- What ancillary materials are needed for the lessons in this unit?
- What websites will I recommend to students to support these lessons?
- Do I need to contact guest speakers or obtain outside resources?
- What literature resources are available to support this unit?

LESSON PLANS

Instructional units are made up from a series of lesson plans. An instructional unit may have any number of lesson plans, depending on the goals and design of the unit as well as the length of the lessons. In developing lesson plans, you plan and describe the learning activities that are determined in Step 3 of the backward planning process. As with the backward planning process, you should always keep the standards-based goals or targets in mind and integrate the assessments as necessary to determine students' progress toward those goals. Effective social studies lessons require preparation, organization, modeling for students, and

One of the features of the No Child Left Behind law is that we focus on research-based approaches. Understanding the research base helps you meet these federal guidelines.

As you can see, the process of planning curriculum requires thinking about a number of questions.

Step 3 of the backward planning process can be found in Figure 7.4.

George Washington
Source: *Gilbert Stuart, Museum of the City of New York*

student engagement in learning. Consider these elements of good social studies lesson plans:

- Has clear, standards-based objectives
- Shares objectives with students
- Includes meaningful assessments and checks for understanding, providing immediate feedback
- Accesses prior knowledge, builds background, and connects learning
- Fosters critical thinking skills and student engagement in learning
- Makes efficient use of teacher and student time and resources
- Uses a variety of materials and strategies
- Provides for individual differences
- Utilizes appropriate materials and resources
- Uses appropriate pacing and transitions

At the end of this chapter, we have provided examples of two different unit plans. Remember that unit plans describe what students will know and be able to do over multiple lessons. Typically unit plans incorporate several weeks' worth of information. Figure 7.5 contains the plan for a second-grade unit of study on heroes, or people who make a difference. Figure 7.6 contains the plan for a fifth-grade unit of study on U.S. expansion.

In addition, you'll find sample lesson plans (Figures 7.7 and 7.8). We have provided one lesson plan for each of the two units described. As you review these lesson plans, you'll note some common features of lesson plans.

Figure 7.5   Heroes unit from grade 2.

Big Idea:

People can make a big difference in the lives of others.

Standard:

Students understand the importance of individual action and character and explain how heroes from long ago and the recent past have made a difference in others' lives (e.g., from biographies of Abraham Lincoln, Louis Pasteur, Sitting Bull, George Washington Carver, Marie Curie, Albert Einstein, Golda Meir, Jackie Robinson, Sally Ride).

Purpose/Meaning:

Students should understand that a person's ideas and actions, guided by character traits, may result in lasting improvements for their own lives as well as the lives of others.

(continued)

Knowledge:

- Individual action and character are important
- Heroes lived long ago and in the recent past
- People become heroes for different reasons
- Heroes make a difference in others' lives
- Biographies tell the stories of real people's lives
- Abraham Lincoln, Louis Pasteur, Sitting Bull, George Washington Carver, Marie Curie, Albert Einstein, Golda Meir, Jackie Robinson, and Sally Ride are heroes

Skills:

- Distinguish long ago from recent past
- Explain connections between the present and the past
- Judge the significance of a person's character and actions
- Pose relevant questions about heroes
- Distinguish fact from fiction
- Evaluate the actions of people from the past
- Place people and events in historical context

Assessments:

1. Students will create and present a comic book featuring factual information about a hero from long ago or the recent past. (formal, summative performance task)
2. Students will complete graphic organizers identifying the actions and character traits of a hero. (informal, formative learning activity)
3. Students will orally describe the major events in the life of a hero. (informal, formative learning activity)

Learning Activities:

1. Students will brainstorm ideas about the term *hero*.
2. Students will analyze and categorize the ideas from the brainstorm.
3. After listening to a read-aloud about one well-known hero (Abraham Lincoln), students will discuss the traits that made him a hero.
4. After listening to a read-aloud about a less-known hero (Rachel Carson), students will compare and contrast the traits that made her a hero with the traits of the well-known hero.
5. Students will share examples (stories) of people they know who share at least one trait in common with a hero (referring to brainstorm list and category charts).
6. Students will read biographies of heroes.
7. Students will use index cards to identify and sequence the major events in the life of a hero they read about.
8. Students will read comic books about fictional heroes and compare/contrast the fictional hero's traits with the traits of real heroes.
9. Students will plan and develop a comic book about a real hero from long ago or the recent past.
10. Students will present their comic books to the class, place their comic book on a wall-size timeline, and mark on a map the location of where this hero lived.

Resources:

- *People and Places (California Vistas)*. New York: Macmillan/McGraw-Hill (2007).
- *Rachel: The Story of Rachel Carson*. A. Ehrlich (2003). Orlando, FL: Silver Whistle/Harcourt.
- *Rachel Carson: Preserving a Sense of Wonder*. T. Locker (2004). Golden, CO: Fulcrum.
- *A Picture Book of George Washington Carver*. D. Adler (2000). New York: Holiday House.
- *A Picture Book of Martin Luther King, Jr.* D. Adler (1990). New York: Holiday House.
- *A Picture Book of Amelia Earhart*. D. Adler (1999). New York: Holiday House.
- *The Children's Book of Heroes*. W. Bennett (1997). New York: Simon and Schuster.
- *Sitting Bull*. L. Penner (1995). New York: Grosset & Dunlap.
- *The Story of Sitting Bull*. L. Eisenberg (1991). New York: Yearling.
- *Sally Ride*: *Shooting for the Stars*. S. Hurwitz (1989). New York: Ballantine.
- Big Chalk (search biographies for K–5): http://www.bigchalk.com
- Women of the Century: http://school.discovery.com/schooladventures/womenofthecentury
- America's Story—Meet Amazing Americans: http://www.americaslibrary.gov/cgi-bin/page.cgi

Figure 7.6   U.S. Expansion unit from grade 5.

Big Idea:

People move to improve their lives or because they are forced.

Standard:

Students trace the colonization, immigration, and settlement patterns of the American people from 1789 to the mid-1800s, with emphasis on the role of economic incentives, effects of the physical and political geography, and transportation systems.

Purpose/Meaning:

The American story is constantly changing as people move into, out of, and within the nation's borders. U.S. borders continued to expand during the late 18th and early 19th centuries as people sought new opportunities and took advantage of new technologies.

Knowledge:

- People formed colonies in North America
- After the colonial period, land was divided into states and territories
- Pioneers settled new territories, which ultimately became states
- People needed incentives to move to new territories and settle and farm untamed lands
- Settlers changed the physical and political geography in the United States
- New forms of transportation offered incentives for new settlers to move West

Skills:

- Read historical maps
- Differentiate between political boundaries (colony, state, territory)
- Conduct cost-benefit analysis from various points of view
- Understand multiple perspectives
- Compare and contrast historical evidence and opinions/arguments
- Draw conclusions about why people made the decisions they made
- Apply historical and geographic information to understand context

Assessments:

1. Students will create a series of maps of North America identifying colonies, countries, states, and territories during three different years between 1789 and 1850. Each colored, completed map will include a title, key, legend, compass rose, and cartouche. There will be at least three maps total.
2. Students will write a one-page document to accompany each map. Each document (e.g., diary entry, log, letter, broadside, article) will be written from the perspective of a person who may have lived during the time represented on the map. The sum of perspectives presented will represent a diversity of voices from this period (e.g., men, women, children, military, tradesmen, religious, political, Native American, African American, European American, wealthy, poor). Each document must include geographic, historical, and economic information that helps explain why people are moving (immigrating, migrating, or traveling).

Learning Activities:

1. Students create a journal and record these questions to explore and answer throughout the unit: Why did some people move West? How did the United States expand across North America? How did new technologies change people's lives? What are a government's boundaries?
2. Students create a timeline of people and events that spans 1789 to 1850. Small groups will work together to read, gather information, and present to the class information about one major event on the timeline. Each group's information will be summarized by individual students and added to their individual timelines (e.g., Louisiana Purchase; Lewis and Clark Expedition; War of 1812; Fulton's steamboat; Richard Allen founds African Methodist Episcopal Church; Erie Canal is built; Andrew Jackson is elected; Indian Removal Act; Mexican-American War; Fremont's Rebellion in California; Gold Rush).

(continued)

3. Students will participate in an interactive PowerPoint presentation showing the geography of the United States during this time and a variety of transportation modes used to transport people and goods into and throughout new territories (e.g., overland wagons, flatboats, steamboats).

4. Students will view online exhibit and study a variety of maps and illustrations from this period and listen to descriptive excerpts from the journals of Lewis and Clark. The teacher will present information about Native Americans and others using the land for trapping, hunting, and trade. Students will hold small group discussions about the land, its value, U.S. plans for the land, and ownership of lands.

5. Students will trace overland trails and read accounts, including *The Way West: The Journal of a Pioneer Woman* (Amelia Stewart Knight), of pioneers. Students will work in pairs to discuss the varied experiences of pioneers, incentives for moving and settling, and geography.

6. Students will participate in a simulated experience of traveling along the Oregon Trail in "families" created in class. Fate cards will be drawn throughout the simulation for students to learn about their fates, which will mirror the fates of many early pioneers and settlers.

Resources:

- *Making a New Nation.* (2007). New York: Macmillan McGraw-Hill.
- historic maps (1700s; Louisiana Territory; pre- and post-Mexican-American War)
- blackline masters of maps of North America
- Lewis and Clark journal excerpts
- Library of Congress web-based exhibit (http://www.loc.gov/exhibits/lewisandclark/)
- *Lewis & Clark on the Trail of Discovery: The Journey that Shaped America (A Museum in a Book).* Rod Gragg. (2003). Nashville, TN: Rutledge Hill.
- *The Way West: The Journal of a Pioneer Woman.* Amelia Stewart Knight. (1993). New York: Simon & Schuster.
- *Mississippi Mud: Three Prairie Journals.* Ann Turner. (1997). New York: HarperCollins
- *Apples to Oregon: Being the (Slightly) True Narrative of How a Brave Pioneer Father Brought Apples, Peaches, Pears, Plums, Grapes, and Cherries (and Children) Across the Plains.* Deborah Hopkinson. (2004). New York: Atheneum.
- *Lewis & Clark Voyage of Discovery.* Stephen Ambrose. (1998). Washington, DC: National Geographic Society.
- PowerPoint slideshow with images of U.S. landscapes, pioneers, transportation of the early 1800s
- Class simulation of traveling along Oregon Trail (adapt from Interact simulation and Oregon Trail software game)

Objectives

These are the goals that you have as the teacher for the lesson. As we have noted before, objectives should meet the SMART criteria:

- Specific (S)—the objective focuses on only one topic and is expressed in clear, precise terms.
- Measurable (M)—the objective is expressed in terms of an observable behavior.
- Achievable (A)—the objective corresponds to the capabilities of the individuals concerned and can be achieved under the existing conditions (time, resources).
- Relevant (R)—the objective corresponds to the identified needs of the learner.
- Timed (T)—a time line has been set that indicates when the objective should be met.

Electronic versions of the unit planning tool and lesson planning tool can be found in the Web Links module in Chapter 7 on our Companion Website at www. prenhall. com/schell.

Figure 7.7   Lesson plan: day 1, Heroes.

Objectives	Today, students will define what it means to be a "hero." This week, students will identify and discuss real heroes from biographies.
Anticipatory Set	Ask students what they think about when they hear the word *hero.* Chart responses as students brainstorm ideas about heroes.
Modeling and Guided Practice	1. Review chart with brainstorm of ideas about heroes. 2. Ask students to help you determine what some of these ideas have in common. For example, there may be several **names of people** on the chart. Ask students to help you identify and circle the names of people with a colored marker. Continue to identify categories, such as **personality traits**, **actions**, or **ideas**, and classify students' ideas about heroes with different colored markers. 3. Summarize the categories, or traits, of heroes. Ask students to think about people they know or know about who have any of these traits. 4. Ask students to turn to a partner to share the names and information about people they know who share these qualities of a hero. 5. Introduce a picture book about Abraham Lincoln and tell students, "I am going to read to you a story about a person that you may know about. As I am reading this biography of Abraham Lincoln, I want you to think about whether or not this man was a hero." 6. Read aloud the biography, stopping to ask students what traits they might have thought about while listening to this story about Lincoln. 7. Ask students to turn to a partner to discuss whether or not Lincoln can be considered a hero. 8. Call on some students to share what they discussed with their partners. 9. Display additional biographies that students will be able to read during independent practice. 10. Review the America's Story website at the Library of Congress, which students will be able to visit during independent practice. 11. Explain to students that they will spend the next 15–20 minutes exploring biographies of heroes and completing a graphic organizer that summarizes the person's qualifications to be a considered a hero.

Independent
Practice
	1. Students read biographies and explore websites to learn about heroes.
	2. Students complete a graphic organizer that requires them to:
	  • Who: identify the name of the hero
	  • How: describe the qualities of this hero
	  • What: explain why the person is considered a hero
	  • Why: describe how this hero changed his or her life and affected the lives of others
	  • Where: locate where this person lived
	  • When: identify important dates in this person's life

Closure	Students share their graphic organizers in small groups. Teacher draws students' attention to their original brainstorm and category charts and asks, "What do we need to add or change about our ideas about heroes?" Teacher makes necessary edits to the charts. Teacher explains to students that tomorrow they will read another biography to learn more about a different kind of hero.

Figure 7.8   Lesson plan: day 4, U.S. Expansion.

Objectives	Students will analyze and evaluate North American expedition maps from 1803 and 1814. Students will gain a greater understanding and appreciation of maps as important representations of what is on the land.
Anticipatory Set	Ask students to spend 5 minutes drawing a map of their city. Using their maps, ask students to work in pairs to trace the route between their home and the school.
Modeling and Guided Practice	1. Lead students in a discussion that identifies the features, uses, and frustrations of maps. Connect discussion to activity from anticipatory set. Relate discussion points to students' use of other maps. 2. Project animated presentation of 1803 and 1814 maps of North America found at http://www.loc.gov/exhibits/lewisandclark/kiosk-before.html. Ask students to note the features, uses, and frustrations with these maps. 3. In small groups, ask students to discuss the features, uses, and frustration noted about these maps. 4. Read two or three descriptive excerpts from the journal kept by Meriwether Lewis during the Lewis and Clark expedition. Ask students to imagine that they were accompanying Lewis and Clark on this adventure. Ask them to think about the Nicholas King map they have available on the expedition and write a brief journal entry that describes the features, uses, or frustrations with the map. 5. Ask students to share their entries in pairs and discuss the value and accuracy of maps—then and now.
Independent Practice	1. Provide students with additional readings (textbook, on-line exhibit, trade books, references) about maps, mapmaking, the Lewis and Clark expedition, and the geography of North America. Provide students time to use these resources for research. 2. Ask students to develop a map representing North America during this period of time. Using accounts of the period, remind students to add important features as seen in the online animated presentation. 3. Remind students that a document will have to accompany this map. This may influence what the students choose to represent on the map.
Closure	Read a selection from one of the many resources providing descriptive language about the land and people's interactions with the land from this time period. Remind students about the multiple perspectives involved at this (and every) historical period. Ask for students to share their maps and documents with the class. Provide feedback on what is presented.

Objectives can be written to help students with knowledge, skills, or attitudes. Key terms associated with each of these types of outcomes are presented in Figure 7.9.

Anticipatory Set

The anticipatory set is the hook. It should be designed to activate students' background and prior knowledge and serve to capture their interest. There are a number of possible anticipatory set activities, including:

- Provocative questions—"How might the world be different if the U.S. Civil War was never fought?"

Figure 7.9   Considerations for social studies objectives.

Knowledge	Skills	Attitudes
Explain	Be able to	Accept
Describe	Demonstrate	Respect
Explore	Show	Value
Identify	Participate	Behave
List	Develop	Judge
Tell	Create	Recognize
Express	Make	Appreciate

- Review of previous lesson(s)—"Remember our discussion about the framers of the U.S. Constitution. . . ."
- Quickwrites—"Take a few minutes and write a letter to Dr. Martin Luther King Jr. about the progress we have made on civil rights since his death."
- Use of text pages—"Let's take a look at this page. What do you notice? What do you think that the author is going to tell us?"
- Storytelling—"There we were, riding along in a covered wagon. I could taste the dust and I was thirsty. There was no water in sight. . . ."
- Picture, illustration, or cartoon—"What is this and how might it relate to what we're studying?"
- Startling or unexpected statement—"Columbus didn't 'discover' America—but he did bring diseases to the 'new land.'"

Modeling and Guided Practice

This component of the lesson plan provides students the opportunity to experience modeling, scaffolding, and coaching from someone who is more knowledgeable than the learner. The teacher may provide students input through lecture, film, tape, video, pictures, etc. Along the way, the teacher regularly checks for understanding. This determination of whether or not students have "got it" is necessary before proceeding to guided practice.

Guided practice provides students an opportunity to demonstrate their new learning by working through an activity or exercise under the teacher's direct supervision. Guided practice is not simply assigning a worksheet, problems, or questions to be completed in class. Instead, the teacher must ensure that students are provided activities that facilitate their acquisition of the necessary skills and knowledge.

Independent Practice

Once students have developed a level of skill and fluency with the content and concepts, they are ready to independently practice. This allows students to apply their knowledge and skills to new situations or information and to ensure that they are able to use the skill or information in new contexts.

Figure 7.10   Lesson planning tool.

Objectives	
Anticipatory Set	
Modeling and Guided Practice	
Independent Practice	
Closure	

Closure

Closure is the act of reviewing and clarifying the key points of a lesson. Closure is used to:

- Signal students that the lesson is ending.
- Form a coherent mental model for students so that they can consolidate information, eliminate confusion and frustration, and so on.
- Reinforce the major concepts or ideas to be learned.

In other words, closure is the act and art of reviewing and clarifying important components of a lesson, relating these to previous and future learning, and making connections such that students see a coherent whole.

Conclusion

Lesson planning, especially using backward planning, is critical to the success of the social studies classroom. Given the limited time teachers have for planning and for teaching, it is essential that we use efficient and effective processes for planning. In this chapter we introduced curriculum maps, unit plans, and lesson plans. Taken together, these tools ensure that content standards are aligned and taught and that valuable instructional time is maximized.

History's Finer Points

How do teachers know what to teach?

In the 1700s, children were schooled with hornbooks and primers that taught them how to read and recite prayers. Aside from reading and catechism, older boys studied mathematics, Latin, and philosophy. Thomas Jefferson promoted a general education, and later Horace Mann facilitated the growth of public education in America.

A child's report card in 1890 reflected achievement in the following subjects: deportment, spelling, reading, writing, arithmetic, geography, language, history, algebra, physiology, philosophy, rhetoric, and botany.

Text-Based Questions: What are the core subjects for all students in American public schools today? How has education in America changed over time?

Quiz yourself on this chapter's important concepts on our Companion Website's Chapter 7 self-assessments at www.prenhall.com/schell.

Questions to Consider

1. What is backward planning and curriculum mapping?
2. How does instructional planning help a teacher?
3. Why should teachers map the curriculum for the entire year?
4. What is the difference between a unit plan and a lesson plan?

Exercises

1. Collect curriculum maps from a wide variety of teachers. Review these maps and discuss them with your peers.
2. Design a unit plan for a set of standards at the grade level you teach. How many days will you devote to this unit? Which instructional materials will you use? What objectives are important to consider? What evidence (assessment information) will you accept that students understand the content?

3. Develop daily lesson plans using the format in Figure 7.10 for the unit plan above. How will you hook students into the learning? What will you model for students? What range of guided practice will students need to master the information? How will you ensure, through independent practice, students' application of the information you teach?

References

California Department of Education (2001). *History–social science framework for California public schools.* Sacramento, CA: Author.

Georgia Department of Education (2004). *Georgia performance standards for social studies.* Atlanta, GA: Author.

Haugen, P. (2001). *World history for dummies.* New York: Hungry Minds.

McTighe, J., & Wiggins, G. (1998). *Understanding by design.* Alexandria, VA: Association for Supervision and Curriculum Development.

Oberlin, L. H. (2001). *The everything American history book: People, places and events that shaped our nation.* Holbrook, MA: Adams Media.

San Diego County Office of Education (2001). *History-social science standards-based implementation models.* San Diego, CA: Author.

Vaughan, D. (2000). *The everything Civil War book: Everything you need to know about the war that divided the nation.* Holbrook, MA: Adams Media.

Weigand, S. (2001). *U.S. history for dummies.* New York: IDG Books Worldwide.

Chapter

8

Real-World Teaching and Learning

Source: *Emily Schell*

Big Idea

The relationship between social studies and the real world is inseparable.

Essential Question

How does social studies relate to the world around us?

Sitting together on the school bus on their way back to school at the end of the day, veteran third-grade teacher Mrs. Osborne explains to her student teacher the events for the rest of the week. You see, Mrs. Osborne and her third-grade students traditionally spend at least 1 week outside of their classroom exploring local history and geography, which is what their state content standards demand. This week, they are learning in a local city park, which has a variety of museums for students to visit and enjoy. Here, they are expanding their studies about the local community to learn from exhibits, docents, and each other. The teacher plans and facilitates the learning activities in and around the museums while demonstrating to students—and her student teacher—the importance of learning outside of a classroom.

The student teacher comments, "I loved going on field trips when I was in elementary school. I can tell that our students love it, too. They sure did have a lot of fun today!"

"What else did you notice or think about during our first day of field studies today?" asked Mrs. Osborne.

"Well, I was surprised at how much they already knew when they spoke with the museum docent. I know the docent was impressed, too. He told me that most classes are not as prepared to come here and learn. I like the way he found out what they knew and then led them into the exhibits to learn even more about the people who first settled in our community. The pictures, old maps, and artifacts really maintained the attention of the students. I noticed that the students were engaged and excited about learning, but do they remain this way all week long? I do not remember going on any field trips that lasted more than one day when I was in school. Do you have support from the principal and parents to take kids out of school for a whole week for social studies?"

Mrs. Osborne responded, "You ask some good questions. First, it is important to identify a real purpose for taking students out of your classroom to learn. In this case, we cannot access these exhibits and primary sources of information without going to the museums. Furthermore, we could invite the docents into our classroom, but they do not

If you were Mrs. Osborne's student teacher, what other questions would you have about her plans to provide opportunities for students to learn social studies outside of the classroom? How might you use your local community to enhance social studies for your students? What plans would you need to make?

have the same impact without their exhibits. Second, you must recognize the integration of multiple disciplines that become taught, practiced, and assessed through our field studies. Did you notice the listening, speaking, reading, and writing skills that were exercised today? Did you hear Joaquin say, "This wall looks like a big page from our social studies book!" as he read the information cards, or captions, for his group? Tomorrow, when we visit the art museum, we will look at paintings and focus on perspectives and interpretations of landscapes and historic people and events. Although our focus remains on social studies, pay attention to the integration of other subject areas throughout the week. Also, I want you to answer your question about student excitement and engagement. Watch the students carefully, especially those who tend to be less engaged in our classroom. At the end of the week, we will talk about your observations more."

INTRODUCTION

Good social studies teachers like Mrs. Osborne seek ways to help students connect to the real world in their teaching. Sometimes this means expanding the four walls of the classroom and physically taking students into the community for meaningful learning activities. Keep in mind what you read in the last chapter about opportunities to take students on virtual field trips using modern technologies. At other times, this means creating an environment in the classroom and engaging students in learning activities that reflect the reality of life beyond the school.

Most educators agree that the purposes for education in America include preparation for citizenship and the workforce. The National Education Goals in Goals 2000: Educate America Act (U.S. Department of Education, 1993) and No Child Left Behind (U.S. Department of Education, 2002) identify these goals and provide support for teaching and learning that promotes lifelong learning and preparation for higher education and the workforce, as well as citizenship education. With these goals in mind, it makes sense to organize our classrooms to reflect the roles and responsibilities required of citizens and social participants. These goals, in fact, reiterate the national definition of social studies, which states, "Social studies is the integrated study of the social sciences and humanities to promote civic competence" and that "the primary purpose of social studies is to help young people develop the ability to make informed decisions for the public good as citizens of a culturally diverse, democratic society in an interdependent world" (NCSS, 1993).

Let us explore some ideas that teachers have developed as ways to achieve these goals for their students through classroom management, problem-based learning, service learning, field studies, and guest speakers.

CLASSROOM MANAGEMENT

How did you learn the rules and regulations for your classroom when you were a student in the elementary grades? Chances are, your teacher took the time and effort to establish the rules and procedures, then explained to you and your classmates her expectations for your behavior during the school year (Frey, 2005). Accompanying this explanation was probably a description of consequences for those who did not follow the rules established for the class. Finally, you probably remember the rules because they were posted on the wall of your classroom to remind you that these rules existed. Right?

Let us give some thought to this traditional approach to classroom rules. Whose rules are these? How were these rules developed? Why are these the rules for this classroom? What do these rules mean to the students? How do they learn what these rules really mean—before they are found to be violating one of them? For example, do 10-year-olds know what it means to show respect to their teacher and to their classmates? Do students agree to these rules? If not, what are their options for challenging or changing a rule? Do students really care about these rules or is this just another first-day-of-school exercise?

Rules are important for any group of people who need order and safety to coexist. Varying definitions of the term *rule* include the words *principles, behaviors, governing,* and *problems.* Because a classroom is a rich source of problems and requires that principles become used to guide the decisions and behaviors of students who are directly influenced by these problems, it is a natural environment for rules. Rules are then used in the governing, or controlling, regulating, or directing, of activities that occur in the classroom. This is where students often lose sight of the purpose of rules. Rules for the sake of rules do not hold much value for anyone. Rules that allow people to conduct their business, thrive in their work and lives, and create a safe environment for all are rules worth making and upholding. So, let your students discuss the importance and purpose of rules before engaging them in a process that allows them to identify, evaluate, and understand the rules that they are being asked to follow.

Reflecting a democratic process used in the society in which we live, some teachers invite their students to develop their own class rules through one of the following methods.

There is a difference between rules and procedures. There are consequences when rules are not followed. If students don't follow procedures for entering the classroom, submitting papers, or such, they need to have more teaching about the procedures.

Class Rules

At a most basic level, the teacher leads students in a discussion about class rules. She might ask, *"What is a rule? Why do we need rules? Where do rules come from? What happens when people follow the rules? What happens when people do not follow the rules?"* After students gain a better understanding of rules, they brainstorm with the teacher a list of

Figure 8.1

Source: *www.cartoonstock.com*

rules that they believe are needed for the class to be positive, productive, and safe for everyone. The teacher lists all ideas during the brainstorm and then allows students to discuss which rules they believe are most important for their class. Depending on the age of the students and preference of the teacher, students either vote or work together to prioritize and select the most important rules for the class. Sometimes, students will classify some ideas into one general category. For example, "Don't run in class," "Keep the floors clear to walk," and "Put backpacks and lunches away" might be combined to state, "Keep the classroom a safe place to learn." This becomes an opportunity for the

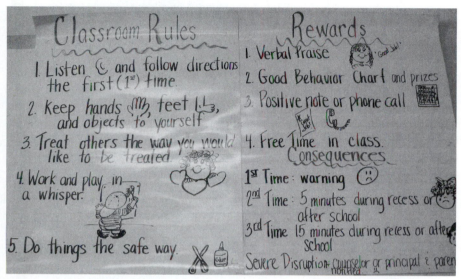

Classroom rules with Rewards and Consequences posted in this second-grade classroom become a common document for students, parents, and the teacher to use throughout the school year.
Source: *Emily Schell*

teacher to facilitate student understandings of the real purpose and value of class rules.

Most teachers prefer to phrase their rules in a positive way so that students do not feel constricted by a list of "do not do this" and "do not do that." Still, others feel the need to make some rules explicit and clear, so they might phrase some using the terms *do not* or *never*. You will have to decide what is best for your classes. You will maintain control over this process as you facilitate student discussions and remind students of the purpose, value, and importance of the rules they are deciding on. In doing so, you can gently remind students about situations they might have encountered in other classes, or describe for students some situations that you have encountered as a teacher so that everyone's prior experiences are used to inform the development of meaningful class rules.

Once consensus is reached and students agree that they understand the rules and can follow these rules, they are ready to be posted in the classroom. Engaging students in this process, too, helps them see that these are their own rules. Assign different rules to different table groups to write on sentence strips or construction paper for posting in the room. These groups can illustrate the rule and present to the class the new official rule of your class. Later, the groups might be asked to present a skit that shows what this rule looks like in a real-life situation. Or, the groups might be asked to create a song or poem that better explains the purpose and value of the rule.

Listing all of the "don'ts" might invite students to look for exceptions.

Harry Wong's book *First Days of School* provides a number of good ideas about starting the year. For more information about this book and the supporting website, see the Web Links module in Chapter 8 on our Companion Website at www. prenhall.com/schell.

Remind students throughout this process that these are **their** rules. They created this set of rules through brainstorm, discussion, evaluation, and agreement. Therefore, they are responsible for working together to uphold these rules throughout the school year. You might decide that students agree to these for the entire year, or you might propose that halfway through the school year, the class will revisit and discuss these rules. Students might find that the rules need to be revised (perhaps one needs to be added or rewritten). Doing this reflects the processes used by other groups (organizations, teams, governments, etc.) who value each person's ideas, input, and perspectives on what should guide everyone's behaviors within the organization. Let students know this fact. Also let them know that the rules are only useful if each person agrees to work towards upholding the rules for the good of the group.

Democracy operates in much the same way—we agree to uphold the rules for the good of the group.

Our Bill of Rights

Students at all grade levels are ready to learn about how our nation works. After a basic introduction to the U.S. Constitution, students should understand that this document carefully describes the basic laws and organizational structure of our country. This document explains how our country is governed. Using this example as a model, you might present the school rules that are necessary for the governing or structure of your school. After a brief history lesson about the amendments to the U.S. Constitution articulating individuals' rights in the Bill of Rights, you might lead your class in a discussion about the rights that belong to the students in this class.

Remind students that they are still responsible for the school rules, but might have different ideas about what rules should guide their behaviors and work inside our classroom.

Begin the discussion by asking students, *"What is a right? What rights do you have? How do you know that you have these rights? What are you able to do because of these rights? What will happen if you abuse these rights?"*

Lead students to understand that rights are not automatic and that they must work hard to maintain their rights. Offer some examples from history of rights that people have identified and fought hard to earn (e.g., abolition of slavery, freedom to profess any religion or no religion at all, women's right to vote, school integration). Then pose the question, *"What rights do you need to be successful as a student in this classroom this year?"* Allow students to share their ideas and record these ideas on the board. After time to discuss these, ask students to select the rights that they believe are most important for the entire class. Try to focus on 3–10 rights so that students do not have a long, meaningless list. Again, look for opportunities to combine some ideas so that rights are generally described. This allows for greater interpretation when necessary during the school year. As students make poor choices in their behaviors, they might be asked to identify which right they are neglecting or violating through their behaviors. For example, a student who talks incessantly during instructional time might be asked to review the class Bill of Rights to determine which right he or she is denying

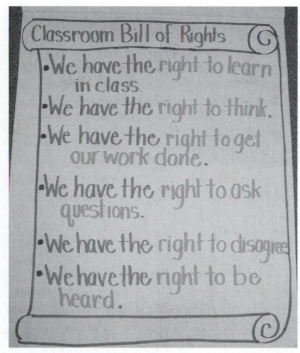

Bill of Rights from classroom wall.
Source: *Emily Schell*

other students in the class. The student would then have to interpret such rights as "We have the right to learn in class" or "We have a right to think and get our work done" to understand that talking keeps others from working and learning in class.

Teachers often prefer this method because it focuses on the benefits of positive behaviors and reinforces the importance of upholding the rights of others in order to protect one's own rights. In some cases, however, teachers have bad days or bad weeks when it seems that the students need harsher, more direct rules to guide their behaviors. In these cases, it usually works to create a mini-simulation in which students are stripped of the rights that they have agreed to uphold, but began to abuse. The teacher then introduces martial law, or a system of strict rules that take effect when a military authority takes control. Usually, martial law reduces the personal rights granted to the citizens, and harsh punishments are imposed. Or, the teacher might introduce students to a dictatorship—a different form of government in which a ruler, or dictator, assumes sole power over the people and the state. It is the dictator who makes the rules and carries out the laws in a manner that suits the dictator. The teacher takes care to identify historic, or real, examples of when and how these kinds of changes came about in our world, then takes on the role of the leader who makes all the decisions herself

Making the connection between a learners' bill of rights and the U.S. Bill of Rights helps students understand why these are important components of our democracy.

History Connections

The principles of martial law in the United States were derived mainly from the experience of the American Civil War, together with "Dorr's Rebellion" in Rhode Island in 1842, and the labor unrest of the late 19th and early 20th centuries.

Book Links

There are a number of books that explore the U.S. Constitution and Bill of Rights, including *A Kid's Guide to America's Bill of Rights: Curfews, Censorship, and the 100-Pound Giant* (Krull, 1999), *In Defense of Liberty: The Story of America's Bill of Rights* (Freedman, 2003), and *The Bill of Rights* (Quiri, 1998).

regarding the rights of the students. After one or more days of this simulation, the teacher debriefs with the students and helps them understand that they chose these rights themselves, but did not work hard to uphold their rights, so they were taken away. She might then explain that we live in a democratic society in which this could very well happen, but it is not likely because citizens work so hard to protect and uphold their rights. The teacher might state that because we, as a nation, value individual rights, she would like to reinstate their rights with the understanding that they might be taken away for good if neglected or abused in class again. Our very youngest of students understand these concepts and learn from such an example.

Even if the class works hard to uphold their class Bill of Rights, you should facilitate a discussion with students periodically to articulate the hard work, the benefits, and the value of such a self-directed system of classroom management and class rules.

Our Rights and Responsibilities

Similar to the class Bill of Rights lesson, teachers can lead students in a discussion about rights. After students have a good understanding of rights, ask them what they know about responsibilities. Ask, *"What is a responsibility? What responsibilities do you have? Why do you have responsibilities? What would happen if you ignored your responsibilities? Who else has responsibilities? Why? What happens when others ignore their responsibilities?"* Eventually, help students understand that rights and responsibilities are like two sides of a coin—they are inseparable.

T-charts are one type of graphic organizer that help students visualize information.

Instruct students in small groups to complete a T-chart, in which one column is titled "Rights" and the other "Responsibilities." Have students discuss and record what they believe are their rights and responsibilities in the classroom. Allow ample time for discussion, questions and answers, and small-group consensus. When their time is up, record the groups' ideas on one large T-chart as you rotate from group to group asking each to identify one right from their list until all groups' ideas are recorded. Then, use the same process for combining and recording the groups' ideas for responsibilities.

Allow students to ask questions if they are unsure about what any of these ideas mean. Ask students if they disagree about any of these ideas. Ask, *"Are there any rights on this list that you do not feel should be your right or another student's right in this class? Are there any rights on this*

Source: *Cover of* In Defense of Liberty *by Russell Freedman.*

list that you are not willing to uphold for yourself and for others? Are there any responsibilities on this list that you think you cannot or should not be responsible for?" When there is consensus, explain to students that you will type up this list of their rights and responsibilities to present in class the next day. Remind them that this is their last chance to ask questions or argue about any of these ideas that they do not fully understand or do not agree with before it becomes typed up as an official document. Explain that once these are agreed on, typed up and finally signed, they officially become the guiding principles for their behaviors and work in class for the rest of the year. Glance over the list with the students to ensure that these rights and responsibilities are complete and will help create a safe, positive, and productive environment in which everyone can learn.

That afternoon, type up the document, including a preamble to the effect of:

We the students of Room 5 at Rosa Parks Elementary School,
in order to form a more perfect classroom,
create a safe and positive environment,
provide opportunities for everyone to learn and share,
and build a better community for us to enjoy and contribute toward,
do establish and agree to these rights and responsibilities
for an excellent and successful school year.

Another approach is to model this document after the Declaration of Independence and declare the rights and responsibilities for the students of the classroom with an introduction, such as:

We hold these truths to be self-evident, that all students are created equal, that they are endowed by their families with great intelligence, talents, potential, and rights. Among these rights are Life, Liberty, and the Pursuit of Happiness. And to secure these rights, they will work together and act responsibly, laying a foundation for a successful school year.

Add the list of rights and responsibilities for students to read and discuss during class the following day. To reinforce student understandings of these rights and responsibilities, you might engage students in activities to act out examples of these, write fables using their ideas as the morals for the stories, illustrate promotional posters, or create 1-minute public service announcements for the various rights and responsibilities.

Finally, ask students to formally come to the front of the room and sign their name to the master copy of the document. Provide brief historical references to the signing and signers of the Declaration of Independence and U.S. Constitution. When the master copy is signed, post in the classroom and make photocopies for each student to refer to in his or her binder.

Full-text versions of many historical documents such as the Declaration of Independence are available on-line. For a list of sources, see the Web Links module in Chapter 8 on our Companion Website at www.prenhall.com/schell.

Representative Government

Individual rights and responsibilities do not always promote cooperation and collaboration. One way to develop a classroom management system that depends on group cooperation is to set up a representative government system in your class. Explain to students that they all belong to table group communities. Each community must elect a representative who will speak for them when decisions need to be made. Begin by allowing students to work together to elect their representative. Explain that elections will be held each month for a new representative in each community. Then, instruct students to discuss in their groups what they believe should become the class rules. Remind communities that all members can help the representative by writing down the ideas, facilitating the conversation, contributing good ideas, etc. Most important, let students know that you will only hear the proposed class rules from the representatives and not from the other community members. Make sure they understand what this means.

After groups have had time to share ideas and decide on the rules they think are most important, call the representatives to the front or center of the classroom so that the rest of the class can observe your meeting with the representatives. Conduct the meeting by listening to the ideas of the representatives, asking for suggestions, combining ideas, and eliminating repeating ideas. Generate a set of rules that the representatives then vote upon on behalf of their communities. Then, excuse the representatives.

Allow the representatives to return to their communities to report what they observed, how they felt during the meeting, and how they feel about the results of the vote. Then, allow the community members to tell their representative what they observed and how they felt they were represented in the meeting.

Throughout the school year, as issues are raised and decisions need to be made, allow students to discuss their ideas in their communities, and then invite the representatives to share the ideas of their groups before decisions are made with that representative body. Of course, draw connections to the development and issues of a representative government in our country and contrast this to a system in which the voices of the people are not heard and decisions are made without the input or consideration of the citizens.

Any time you develop and post a set of rules with your class, remind them throughout the school year the importance and benefits of a common document from which we guide and evaluate our behaviors in a community setting. Draw references to the founding documents that still require interpretation in our Supreme Court, legislative offices, and elsewhere. Integrate examples from the news that challenge individuals' and groups' rights and raise questions about the intent of the laws determined from our founding documents. Let students see these documents as representative of ideas from long ago, but also as living, changing, important documents that we all share as citizens of this nation, this state, and this local community.

Time invested in the development of class rules with students at the beginning of the school year will go a long way in establishing your classroom management system. Students know when their opinions and ideas matter because they are valued and included in the ongoing work of their class. To use this as an exercise and then not follow through with these established rules, rights, and responsibilities would send the wrong message. When issues arise in class, draw students' attention to the class rules—however they are stated—and allow them to interpret and evaluate progress as well as infractions with you.

Also, build in regular activities that allow students to revisit their ideas to write editorials, deliver speeches, illustrate posters, act out

History Connections

Most scholars believe that representative government was first used in the 16th century when Deganawida (also known as "The Great Peacemaker") established the League of the Five Nations of the Iroquois in what is now New York State. Their tradition of representation is the basis for modern democracies.

Share news articles throughout the school year to provide examples of representative government.

commercials, debate issues, create a mock trial, or find examples of these behaviors in historical characters as they read, reflect, learn, and grow as citizens.

Banking Behaviors

A formal system of creating a society in miniature was created by MicroSociety. Information about this program can be found in the Web Links module in Chapter 8 on our Companion Website at www.prenhall.com/schell.

Consider developing a classroom management system that rewards students for positive behaviors and fines students for negative behaviors as established in class. Begin by brainstorming with students what they think deserves "credit" in the bank accounts that you have established for them in your "Class Bank." They will probably note such behaviors as completing homework on time, 100% attendance, and class jobs. Then, brainstorm with students what they think they deserve "debits" in their bank accounts. They will often include such behaviors as late homework, tardies, talking too much, and messy desks. Working with students, or on your own, rank these behaviors on two separate charts and assign a dollar value to each behavior.

To create a banking system in your classroom, you can either print out fake money (teachers often use their own photo at the center and generate "Brown Bucks" or "Dawson Dineros") to use and distribute, or you can provide a checking or savings account register for each student. Some teachers have created a credit card system where they punch notches along the perimeter of the card or rubber-stamp spaces to increase value. In all cases, a monetary value is attributed to behaviors—positive and negative—and students learn that there are consequences for following as well as breaking class rules and expectations for work.

When checking account registers are used, these can be fixed to the tops of students' desks using Velcro and remain there for use throughout the school year. Cards and bonus bucks tend to get lost or stolen and sometimes create more issues than teachers want to deal with. With a checking account register, each entry adds to a running record of each student's behaviors. In the first column, the teacher writes the date for the entry, then the reason for the credit or debit, and then the amount. Students may be held accountable for balancing their own checkbooks with the help of calculators and fellow students assigned class jobs of "accountants." Parents or guardians visiting the class may be invited to add a determined amount of funds while participating in Back to School

Book Links

There are a number of books that explore banking systems, such as *In the Money: A Book About Banking* (Loewen, 2006), *Out and About at the Bank* (Attebury, 2006), and *What Do Banks Do?* (Basel, 2006).

Source: *Cover of* Out and about at the Bank *by Nancy Garhan Attebury.*

Night or parent conferences. Administrators or other staff members may be encouraged to also add to students' funds if they are caught being good outside of the classroom. As the bank president, you can adapt the system to meet your objectives and needs. Students requiring a special behavior modification contract might see adding funds to their accounts as incentive to meet their contract goals.

Of course, students will want to use their funds for something. This is also where you can decide what best meets your objectives and needs. Some teachers reward students by sharing lunch with them in the classroom instead of sending them to the lunch arbor or cafeteria. For this, the teacher might establish a $25 charge for the Thursday Lunch Bunch, and limit the number of reservations for each lunch sitting (a great lesson in supply and demand, too). A nice tablecloth makes the lunch even more special! Some teachers have a class store that opens once a week or once a month. Students can use their funds to purchase pencils, stickers, erasers, and treats. Some teachers invite parents and community organizations to donate items for monthly auctions. Students then bid against each other for the items they wish to purchase. When you have sports memorabilia from a local team, books, or other high-interest items, it helps to display these and inform students that you will auction these off in a couple of months so that students who really want these items can work especially hard to earn the funds for the auction. Auction and sale items do not have to be expensive. Creating a "Free Homework Coupon" (exempting the student from one regular homework assignment—not to be used for a major project or exam) or a "2-Minute-Early Pass" (allowing the student to be excused for recess, lunch or home 2 minutes early, but without leaving campus or disturbing anyone else on campus) is of little cost to you. If used in an auction, chances are these will be purchased by your most responsible students anyhow (another great lesson on market value)!

To extend the banking behaviors systems, help students utilize their math and technology skills to generate graphs, tables, or spreadsheets that show how and when they earned funds, spent funds, and so forth. Students can learn to create budgets and project spending. Some teachers use a system where they pay their students for coming to school and doing their work, but also charge them rent for the use of their desks, computer time, etc. These students learn a thing or two about budgets and cost-benefit analyses!

There are a number of ways to manage your classroom in such a way that students learn about and practice skills that relate to the problems, decisions, and issues in the real world. Whether you create a classroom management system that mirrors government systems, business models, or sports organizations, allow students to question, learn through trial-and-error, and reflect on their decisions and actions. Identify historic examples as you study, and allow students to see the relationship between what they practice in class and what happens in the real world.

PROBLEM-BASED LEARNING

If we want to emulate the real world in our classrooms and engage students in critical thinking through problem solving, we need to fill our classrooms with real problems, real issues, real concerns that relate to the social studies content our standards demand. At the core of the problems presented through historical studies are oftentimes the same issues faced by our communities and students. History is filled with examples of problems, and in most cases, historians tell us how people worked to successfully, or unsuccessfully, address those problems. But, oftentimes, our students do not yet know how people approached these problems and what happened as a result of their decisions. So, we have the opportunity to generate real intrigue and interest in our students when we present a problem and challenge students to solve the problem.

For example, while students are studying about the events that led to the Revolutionary War, identify with them the taxes that were imposed on the colonists, one by one, after the expenses mounted from the French and Indian War. Help students understand the historical, geographic and economic context for this period in time. Then, divide students into three- to four-person work groups. Assign one third of the groups to represent and loyally support Great Britain. Assign one third to represent

There are special lesson plans available for free on teaching students about banking systems. For information, see the Web Links module in Chapter 8 on our Companion Website at www.prenhall.com/schell.

Problem-based learning also helps students understand cause and effect, a common text structure that authors use.

Students work as individuals to illustrate a problem they see in their classroom. This was preceded by brainstorming and will be followed by presentations, discussions, and problem-solving steps in this community of learners.
Source: *Emily Schell*

and remain faithful to the American colonists. Assign the final third to take no sides, but consider options that exist for solving the problems seen on both sides. Set a date in time in which to imagine we are all living, such as December 1775, and challenge students to develop and propose a solution to the problems that were mounting between the colonists and Great Britain. Pose the question, *"What should be done to restore the relationship between the colonists and Great Britain?"* Explain that each group will be responsible for presenting a reasoned and informed proposal at an international summit in 1 week. Give students time to research, hypothesize, and formulate a proposal as if they were in this situation in 1775. Provide support for students to investigate and even weigh the events that did unfold historically. However, challenge students to come together as a group to present their best possible solutions to the problem. As a class, discuss the merits and flaws of the proposed ideas based on information that was available during their research: for example, if a group overlooks the expenses of the French and Indian War in order to make their point that Great Britain was just greedy for money from the colonists and should pay back the colonists for any taxes paid.

As a result of studying the events that led to the American Revolution in a problem-based learning format, students should recognize that history is filled with complicated problems, just as we see in our world today. They should also recognize that there were many options for many people who held different amounts of information, different values, and varying

History Connections

Have you heard the saying "the shot heard round the world?" It's from the Battle at Lexington Green in 1775 and the start of the American Revolution.

Problem-based learning is related to project-based learning and inquiry-based learning. To find out more about all three of these, see the Web Links module in Chapter 8 on our Companion Website at www.prenhall.com/schell.

perspectives about the events that occurred. Students might find that they have some ideas that should have been considered in 1775, and may have led to better circumstances for many people. Overall, students should be eager to study in depth what really happened and continue to generate ideas about how this problem might have been handled differently.

Problem-based learning is a natural activity with historical content, but can also be used to create scenarios that allow students to develop and apply their geography or economic reasoning skills. Students learning how to read a map may be placed in pairs or teams and told that the local visitor's bureau needs a new map to share with visitors showing the best routes to the best sites in the city. Students then work to research and develop maps that suggest the best sites and routes for visitors. Or, students could be told by the principal that maps of the school are needed to place in the office for visitors. Students can use their economic skills to propose fundraising ideas or create a plan for starting a class business. There are limitless ideas for placing students in the role of solving a problem. When all students are challenged to develop solutions to the same problem, they quickly learn that there are often many possible solutions to one problem. These students are then ready to evaluate proposed solutions to determine the most time efficient, cost efficient, practical, creative, and so on.

SERVICE LEARNING

More information about service-based learning can be found in the Web Links module in Chapter 8 on our Companion Website at www.prenhall.com/schell.

There are various programs and organizations that promote service learning for students linking service and educational goals. Students across the grade levels are encouraged to look for opportunities to provide service to their communities, and teachers seek to build connections between these service opportunities and the grade-level curriculum. Ultimately, the organized service project developed and carried out by a class of students enhances students' understandings and appreciation for the curriculum goals as well as their community needs.

For example, students have developed community gardens in response to the need to improve healthy diets or feed the poor in their communities. Although a service to the community, the gardens might be developed in conjunction with economic lessons about the interdependence of producers and consumers. To enhance students' understandings of this concept, they might first survey community members to learn what types of fruits and vegetables are most desired by local consumers. Then, they might conduct research on growing conditions, seasonal plants, and costs of planting and maintaining a garden. Next, they could determine responsibilities and develop schedules for planting, protecting, and caring for the garden. In the end, the students would work hard as producers providing service to their community of consumers while also better understanding economic as well as health, science, and math concepts.

Look for opportunities within your school, district, and community to develop service learning projects with your students. This will allow students to identify issues within their own communities, brainstorm solutions, act on their best ideas, and evaluate their roles as good citizens who contribute to the public good. Throughout these service learning projects, students should be encouraged to consider the many careers available for service to communities.

FIELD STUDIES

What do you remember about field trips when you were in elementary school? Chances are, you remember where you went and some of the fun aspects of the trip. But what did you learn? It is important for teachers to recognize the value of experiential learning through field studies, and to plan trips that result in successful learning opportunities for students. The fun factor is essential, but should not be the sole or guiding reason for field studies. Select sites that support or enhance your teaching and student learning while maximizing the use of local resources.

You'll want to keep a log of community resources that you might be able to visit with your class.

When you present a field study as "only for the students who are good," you have already sent a message to all students that this is more for reward than for educational value. A well-planned field study includes all students because it is an extension to the learning that occurs within the classroom. Consider how you perceive and present field studies to your class, recognizing that many may have the experience from past classes that this is solely a day of fun away from the school. If students have this mindset, you can change this for them through careful planning. Establish clear standards-based goals and objectives for your field studies, and then plan the field studies in three parts by asking yourself, *"What will we do before the trip, what will we do during the trip,* and *what will we do after the trip?"* Figure 8.2 contains some common topics and ideas for use before, during, and after the trip.

Before the field study, prepare students by immersing them in the content that will be further studied during the trip. Even if this field study introduces students to a unit of study, prepare students to understand the site they will visit, what the learning expectations are, and what to focus on while there. For example, if you are visiting a museum exhibit with mummies, introduce students to the history and culture of ancient Egypt so that students know that mummification was one aspect that related to the social customs and religious beliefs of ancient Egyptians. Before the field studies, explore the mummification process through literature, illustrations, and videos. Otherwise, a first look at mummies in a museum may result in "Ooo! That's gross!" or "How weird!" instead of "Look at those canopic jars—which one do you think holds the intestines?" and "The details in this funerary art show a lot of information about what people thought was needed in the afterlife." Equip students with necessary vocabulary and background information to make the most sense of the new environments in which they will learn outside of the classroom.

This is critical—students must be prepared for the field experience to make it worthwhile. The field experience cannot be a novel experience!

During the field study, students should be actively engaged in learning. Plan ahead by visiting the site and inquiring about the rules of the

Figure 8.2   Planning a field trip.

Topic	Field Study Location	Before the Trip	During the Trip	After the Trip
Community Helpers	Fire Station	Start KWL Chart: What do we know about firefighters? What do we want to learn? Discuss how firefighters help the community; generate and list questions for fire fighters	Tour the fire station with fire chief; allow students to ask questions from list created in class; simulate exercises firefighters conduct to train and practice for fighting fires; think-pair-share exercise focused on concept of teamwork in a fire station (What examples of teamwork do you see in the fire station? Why is teamwork important?); student groups interview one firefighter about his/her contributions to the community	Student groups share what they learned during their interview with a firefighter; review concept of teamwork and ask students what other community helpers use teamwork to make a difference in our community; complete KWL Chart (What did we learn about firefighters?); students write and illustrate thank-you cards for the fire station including at least three things they learned about firefighters
Colonial Americans	Museum of Art Portrait Gallery	Read stories about American colonists; learn about various occupations and lifestyles of colonists; explore the work of limners; write about why people would want to have their portraits painted	Short (15-minute) docent-led tour of the American portrait gallery; lead students in visual literacy analysis of portrait (What do you see? What do these things imply about the person? What questions do you have about this person?); pairs move to one portrait to complete visual literacy worksheet; students select a portrait to sketch (paper, pencils, clipboards)	Students share sketch with a partner and discuss why they chose this portrait to sketch and what they learned about this person's lifestyle; students write a letter from the perspective of the limner and another from the person in the portrait evaluating the work; class generates list of questions about life in the colonies based on field studies

site, as well as about areas in which the students may cluster in small or large groups for discussions and activities. Depending on the purpose of your field studies, where you visit, and what restrictions exist for the site, plan to engage students in more than casual observations or passive tours of the site. Docents may be helpful, though in some cases, they may have an adverse effect on students and learning. Consider whether or not you need to have a docent tour of your site, and explore your options. Consider some of the examples of student engagement during social studies–based field studies found in Figure 8.3.

After the field study, it is important to follow up on the learning that took place outside of the classroom. This will reinforce the learning and provide a larger context for learning. Often you will pose an essential question before and during the field studies, only to return to the same

Figure 8.3   Examples of student engagement in the community.

Grade	Standard	Site	Learning Activities at the Site
2	Understand the role and interdependence of consumers and producers of goods and services	Grocery Store	• Tour of the grocery store by store manager • With partner, identify and list on paper (on clipboard) five goods (each from a different area in the store) that they would like to purchase as a consumer; for each item, record what it is, what it costs, who produces the good, and where the good is produced • With partner, discuss where these goods came from (use the maps on the clipboard) and determine how they got here from those places (forms of transportation) • Share with the store manager what they learned about consumers and producers of goods. Ask what services are provided in the grocery store.
3	Describe the American Indian nations in the local region long ago and in the recent past.	Museum of Man	• Review the questions generated in class and found on student worksheets about local American Indians from long ago: *What did they eat? Where did they live? What did they wear? What did they believe? How did they learn? Who were their leaders?* • Students work in pairs to explore the exhibit and answer these questions in writing. • Class meets to review answers found. • Students are given role cards (father, mother, child, elder, hunter, chief, etc.) and asked to go back and explore the artifacts and information in the exhibit from the perspective of that person. For example, children will focus on games, and hunters on animals and weapons. • Provide students time to write and illustrate a "day in the life of" that person from long ago. • Introduce an American Indian speaker who will listen to volunteers read their entries and make comments. The speaker will then compare and contrast life long ago with life in the recent past of his tribe.
6	Cite the significance of the trans-Eurasian "silk roads" in the period of the Han Dynasty and Roman Empire and their locations.	Museum of Art	• Focus students on map showing the Silk Route. Discuss global context for map and major trading places along the route. • Lead students through the exhibit pointing out the artifacts from distinct cultures, as well as those with influences of other cultures. • Invite students to return to a favorite item to sketch and write a description card for (including date, location, and materials). Then, have students find another item from another culture along the route to sketch and describe. Finally, challenge students to sketch either of the two items again, infusing at least one cultural element from the other item. Create a third description card identifying a real location between the places of each of the two original items. • Allow students to showcase, or share, their creations and show on the large map the location that lies between the two places of the original artifacts.

question for clarification and assessment. Ideally, the discussion around that essential question will grow and expand, leading to a deeper understanding of the topic or issue. For example, in the examples given in Figure 8.3, you might pose these questions:

- How do we get the things we need?
- Why should we learn about people from the past?
- What are the benefits of trade among people from different cultures?

The answers to these questions neither start nor end with the field studies proposed in these examples.

Learning activities that engage students during their field studies may carry back into the classroom as students transform notes or sketches into final drafts or entries into a larger portfolio of work for the unit. Unit assessments should include information learned during field studies. Relate continued learning activities to the field studies to reinforce the point that learning occurs in a variety of places, in a variety of ways, and with a variety of people.

More information about assessments is presented in Chapter 9.

Depending on your curriculum, field studies do not have to be expensive or far from school. Oftentimes, places to study are within walking distance or include observation walks in a nearby environment. Post offices, police stations, fire stations, bakeries, restaurants, grocery stores, historic homes, libraries, parks, community centers, universities, airports, train stations, and businesses (newspaper offices, pet store, farms, banks, etc.) are rich learning environments.

GUEST SPEAKERS

Field studies are not often possible for many teachers for a variety of reasons. Instead of or in addition to field studies, in efforts to connect students to the larger community, you might consider inviting guests into your classroom to speak, lead a lesson or activity, display artifacts, or answer questions from students.

Remember that you can invite guest speakers into your classroom through technology as well!

Consider the many options available through contacts of families and colleagues at school as well as partnerships developed through your district. Also, consider why you would ask a guest to come into your classroom. Is it because you want a unique perspective presented? Is it because you want authentic voices and experiences presented during studies of events, places, or issues? Does a guest have artifacts and information that you do not have? Are your students learning through oral histories and do you require a subject for students to interview? Your purposes for inviting a guest should match your curricular goals and objectives and enhance student learning. Otherwise, guest speakers, like field trips, can become another fun or interesting distraction that detracts from the academic focus of your work.

In most cases, inviting a guest into your classroom demonstrates the importance of connecting in-class studies with the real world outside of the classroom. If we are preparing our students to become good citizens and plan for a productive work life, we can invite into our classrooms real examples of citizens, workers, scholars, volunteers, and officials who demonstrate what that means in society today. Contributing to the welfare of a community, traditions of a culture, decisions of a government, or scholarship of historic work, guests can bring to life the areas being studied from a textbook. Furthermore, students become introduced to career paths that they might not otherwise consider because of their limited exposure to areas of work and community.

When looking for and contacting guests to come into your classroom, be sure to communicate clearly your goals, objectives, and concerns about this area of study. For example, you might have a guest speaker from the local Buddhist temple coming to share information about Buddhism because this is part of your curriculum standards, your students are curious about the religion, and you want students to see that this religion is still practiced widely today. However, you may have reservations about this guest speaker because you know that teaching about religion in public schools is controversial and you want to make sure this speaker provides information, but does not seek to indoctrinate or engage students in any form of worship. You might meet with this guest speaker ahead of time or at least have a phone conversation clearly identifying your goals, objectives, and concerns. It will help to follow up the meeting or conversation with a written letter. Ask the guest if he or she has visited other classrooms, ask for references to call, and speak with other teachers who have observed this speaker with students. Not all speakers are engaging and interesting, either. Prepare yourself and your students and remain focused on the purpose of the guest. Share your expectations, time limits, class rules (hands raised to ask questions, no side conversations, etc.), and appreciation with the speakers as well.

Any time you take students into the community or you invite the community into your classroom, you are taking on added work and frustrations. Ideally, you will consider your options well, plan, organize, and prepare thoroughly, and recognize the unique value of connecting your students to the real world to enhance their understanding and achievement in social studies.

> Remember that every guest speaker needs to be approved by the principal. This ensures the safety of the students in the classroom, as well as reducing your personal liability.

Conclusion

Teaching in the real world is exciting and rewarding. Think about this for a minute: Burnout does not result from hard work. Rather, burnout results from work that doesn't seem to make a difference. When you have a smoothly operating classroom, with clear rules and procedures, an interesting curriculum that engages students in inquiry and problem-solving, and when students can see the connections between the content you're teaching (the standards) and their world, you will make a difference. As a result, teaching gives significantly more energy than it takes. You'll leave school every day excited and ready to learn alongside your students. All it takes is some planning and procedures.

History's Finer Points

Sometime before the age of 16, George Washington transcribed 110 Rules of Civility and Decent Behavior in Company and Conversation. Copying these expectations for punishment was a common instructional practice in schools during the 18th century. See if these expectations still hold up today:

- 1st Every action done in company ought to be with some sign of respect to those that are present.
- 4th In the Presence of Others Sing not to yourself with a humming Noise, nor Drum with your Fingers or Feet.
- 5th If You Cough, Sneeze, Sigh, or Yawn, do it not Loud but Privately; and Speak not in your Yawning, but put Your handkercheif or Hand before your face and turn aside.
- 24th Do not laugh too loud or too much at any Publick Spectacle.
- 40th Strive not with your Superiers in argument, but always Submit your Judgment to others with Modesty. (Washington, 1988)

Document-Based Question: Which of these behaviors would you like to see exhibited by your students? How can you help them develop these behaviors?

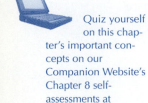

Quiz yourself on this chapter's important concepts on our Companion Website's Chapter 8 self-assessments at www.prenhall.com/schell.

Questions to Consider

1. What are the components of an effective classroom management plan?
2. How can you establish rules and procedures with your students?
3. What is problem-based learning, and how can it be used in the social studies classroom?
4. What is the role of field trips, field study, and guest speakers?

Exercises

1. Interview several teachers about their classroom management plans. Identify components of the plans that are consistent with your educational philosophy.

2. Develop a draft classroom management plan using the ideas you gathered from classroom teachers and this chapter.

3. Identify places in the community that would be good learning environments for students. Determine which standards could be addressed in each of these environments.

4. Create a log of possible guest speakers for the unit you developed in the previous chapter.

References

Frey, N. (2005). *The effective teacher's guide: 50 strategies for engaging students in learning*. San Diego, CA: Academic Professional Development.

National Council for the Social Studies. (1993). *What is social studies?* Silver Spring, MD: Author.

U.S. Department of Education. (1993). *Goals 2000: Educate America act*. Washington, DC: Author.

U.S. Department of Education. (2002). *No child left behind*. Washington, DC: Author.

Children's Literature

Attebury, N. G. (2006). *Out and about at the bank*. Minneapolis, MN: Picture Window.

Basel, R. (2006). *What do banks do?* Mankato, MN: Capstone Press.

Freedman, R. (2003). *In defense of liberty: The story of America's Bill of Rights*. New York: Holiday House.

Krull, K. (1999). *A kid's guide to America's Bill of Rights: Curfews, censorship, and the 100-pound giant*. New York: HarperCollins.

Loewen, N. (2006). *In the money: A book about banking*. Minneapolis, MN: Picture Window Books.

Quiri, P. R. (1998). *The Bill of Rights*. New York: Children's Press.

Washington, G. (1988). *George Washington's rules of civility and decent behaviour in company and conversation*. Bedford, MA: Applewood.

Chapter

9

Student Achievement and Assessments

Source: *Patrick White/Merrill*

Big Idea

Effective assessments measure student knowledge and skills while providing teachers with meaningful data to inform their instructional practices.

Two teachers met at a district assessment workshop. Ms. Juarez introduced herself as an elementary teacher who has worked in the district for 15 years. Mrs. Taft introduced herself as a social studies teacher who works at the middle school that receives students from Ms. Juarez's elementary school. During their conversation, Mrs. Taft complained that her students arrived each year without a necessary foundation of knowledge and skills for learning social studies. Ms. Juarez explained that she, like most colleagues in the elementary grades, never finds time to teach social studies because of the pressures to improve language arts and mathematics test scores. Mrs. Taft explained that she and her colleagues in the middle and high schools are under similar pressures to raise test scores in social studies, but that the students are unprepared for grade-level work when they have had little or no exposure to history, economics, geography, civics, and government from earlier grades. In fact, Mrs. Taft explained, the students are severely disadvantaged when they lack not only the necessary knowledge and skills, but also the confidence to learn a subject that has been neglected in their basic education.

Ms. Juarez thought about Mrs. Taft's comments, and she thought of all the unprepared students whom she had sent into middle school social studies during her years as a teacher. She had just assumed that students would pick up the information they needed once they got into secondary classrooms. Ms. Juarez now understood that she needed to attend to her responsibilities to prepare students for a well-rounded education. She asked Mrs. Taft, "What do you want students to know and do by the time they walk into your classroom?"

INTRODUCTION

It is not unusual for teachers to concentrate solely on the responsibilities and immediate pressures of their own work at their grade level or school level, especially when high-stakes tests are involved. When teachers work together across grade levels and across schools to determine what is best for students who move through the K–12 education system, they begin to identify and articulate areas of need for students. Because there is limited formal assessment of social studies in most states at the elementary levels (compared to language arts and mathematics), many elementary teachers do not make standards-based social studies a priority in their teaching objectives. Some elementary teachers do continue to teach social studies, but pay little attention to individual assessments. In this situation, students often see social studies as a subject that does not require their hard work and concentrated efforts to learn content and develop specific skills. Whether they work hard or not, the students have limited or no evaluation of their knowledge and skills to help them understand their progress as students of history and the social sciences. As a result, students move on to higher grade levels unsure of their abilities and unprepared to build on a weak foundation of knowledge and skills (Figure 9.1).

Formal assessments, such as high-stakes, standardized tests administered by states, are not and should not be the primary motivation for teaching social studies—or any other subject, for that matter. However, multiple-subject teachers have limited time and resources, which often become consumed by those content areas that are determined by legislators and school officials as "important enough to measure through consistent testing." When individual educators recognize the value and importance of social studies education for every young citizen in our schools, they make time, find or develop resources, and advocate for a meaningful, well-

Figure 9.1

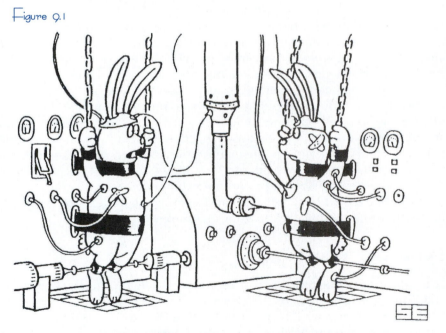

"If you think this is bad, you should see what they do to themselves."

Source: *www.cartoonstock.com.*

rounded education system. In these cases, teachers often seek out or develop formal and informal assessments that help them measure student progress and report the results directly to students and parents.

Whereas formal assessments are important at the national, state, district, school, and class levels, informal assessments are equally, if not more important to teachers, students, and parents who continue to wonder, "How is each student progressing?" Figure 9.2 contains a description of both formal and informal assessments. Note the various

Figure 9.2   Formal and Informal Assessments.

Formal Assessment		
Type	**Purpose**	**Procedure**
Standardized Testing	To measure a students' performance in a variety of skills and compare those scores to students in other geographic locations	Administered at set intervals; students answer questions from booklet on standard forms
Criterion-Referenced Tests	To indicate attainment of mastery on specific instructional objectives, usually by answering a percentage of questions correctly	Administered with lesson plans; students read items and answer on separate paper
Informal Assessment		
Type	**Purpose**	**Procedure**
Observations	To assess a student's use of language in a variety of instructional settings	Observe and record student's use of language, often written in logs or journals
Skills Checklists	To track a student's development by noting which skills have become or are becoming part of a repertoire	Set up a checklist of desirable skills in language arts and periodically observe the student to determine which have been attained
Portfolio Assessment	To document in a variety of ways how a student has developed as a language user	Teacher collects or students select samples of work, including "published" writing, taped oral readings, conference notes
Conferencing	To provide opportunities for the teacher and student to discuss development	Student and teacher meet at set times to review performance and discuss instruction that may be required for student to progress
Peer Reviews	To involve students in the evaluation process and to build their evaluative and interactive skills	Give students guidelines for evaluation; two or more meet to discuss one another's work; peer's grade is factored into final grade
Self-Assessment	To empower students by making them responsible for and reflective of their own work	Students continually evaluate their performance and progress via checklists, interactions, inventories, conferences, and portfolios

Note: From *Improving adolescent literacy: Strategies at work*, D. Fisher and N. Frey, 2004, Upper Saddle River, NJ: Merrill Prentice Hall. Reprinted with permission.

purposes, procedures, and tools available to us as educators. In this chapter, we explore the purposes for a variety of assessments at these different levels and suggest meaningful uses for assessment for all social studies students and educators.

PURPOSES AND USES FOR ASSESSMENTS

History Connections

According to the Oxford English Dictionary, assessment comes from the Latin *assidere,* which means to "sit by." Early uses of the word assessment meant to levy a tax.

Why should we assess students' knowledge and skills in social studies? Why administer tests, develop essay prompts, and assign projects? As an educator, you must ask these questions to develop a greater understanding and appreciation for assessments before finding or creating them, and then administering them to students. Otherwise, you may find yourself testing students for the wrong reasons, making incorrect assumptions about what students know and can do, and making inaccurate assumptions about your own teaching.

Consider the reasons that you have identified in response to the question "Why should we assess students in social studies?" Compare your responses to those found in Figure 9.3. Can you add reasons to one or both columns in this chart? The more you are able to recognize good as well as poor reasons to use assessments, the better informed you will be when making choices about curriculum and assessment plans for your instructional units.

Considering good reasons to use assessments, you must decide when you will assess students and how you will assess students. If you are

Figure 9.3   Reasons to use Social Studies assessments.

Poor Reasons to Use Assessments	Good Reasons to Use Assessments
May be used as punishment for students not participating in class or doing work	Identify specific knowledge and skills of students
Because they are in the textbook	Monitor students' conceptual developments
Brings closure to each chapter or unit	Evaluate and adjust pacing and content of lessons
Holds students accountable for the reading assignments	Hold students accountable for their learning
I need student work to put on the bulletin boards	Evaluate instructional strategies used
I did all the teaching, now I can see who paid attention and/or "got it"	Evaluate resources being used
Generate evidence to determine report card grades, which are due soon	Generate evidence of learning by making covert knowledge and skills overt
May be used as incentive for students to opt out of if they do their work, have good discipline, meet a goal, etc.	Allow students to evaluate their own progress and see the connection between effort and achievement

teaching a unit for the first time or using new materials, you might embed assessments every two or three lessons to evaluate your pacing and progress. If you are teaching a concept that you know is difficult for students to understand, you might embed assessments in every lesson to check for understanding and reteach as necessary. If you want to identify knowledge and skills at the beginning of a unit in order to preassess and tailor your plans to meet the needs of your students (i.e., build necessary background knowledge, develop vocabulary, review map reading skills, etc.), you might begin your instructional unit with assessments.

How you assess is another matter. At times, you will want to take the pulse of the class by throwing out the question, "Does everyone understand this?" This tends to be an ineffective method of assessment. Students may respond "Yes" or "No" for reasons that do not relate to whether or not they understand the material. These reasons range from fear to state what they do not understand to a desire to move quickly (or more slowly) through the lesson because of what comes next in the daily schedule. Similarly, asking content-related questions and receiving the correct answer from a minority of students in the class does not tell you whether or not the majority of your class is learning. Asking each student to take 5 minutes to complete a graphic organizer or quickly respond to a writing

Students participate in partner talk exercises while they read about historical characters and events.
Source: *Emily Schell*

prompt will give you more accurate information about all of your students. Asking students to turn to a partner and summarize the main idea of the lesson and then calling on students randomly will also give you a better indication of how well students are learning.

These examples of asking students to respond orally, complete a graphic organizer, or produce a quickwrite are examples of informal assessments. Informal assessments do not carry the pressure and anxiety often associated with formal assessments, such as a final exam, and are helpful to teachers and to students who need to monitor their progress toward the learning goals. These informal assessments are often embedded assessments, or assessments built into the lessons during a unit of study. Most informal assessments are also formative assessments, or assessments designed for the purpose of informing students and teachers about their progress. Research suggests that when classroom formative assessments are properly implemented, they become a powerful means to improving student learning (Black & Williams, 1998). If teachers and students do not regularly check for understanding and inform their own progress during a unit of study, misconceptions may interfere with learning or students may become overwhelmed and lost, causing them to give up or tune out of their studies.

Social studies often requires students to connect various stories, perspectives, topics, or concepts in order to understand an historic period, event, or character. When you chunk the information and organize these chunks through your lesson planning and presentation, you build in opportunities to check for understanding of these chunks. Additionally, you create opportunities for connecting these chunks by developing transitions between lessons. For example, planning a unit about the Age of Exploration, you might consider organizing your plans to include informal, formative assessments as seen in Figure 9.4. At the end of the unit, you might also administer a formal, summative assessment, which summarizes student learning for the entire unit. This summative assessment might be a test with multiple-choice items, a written essay, an oral performance, or a project. The results of a summative assessment, which aligns with the formative assessments used during the unit, should be predictable based on the results of the students' formative assessments. Students who did poorly on formative assessments should have analyzed, corrected, and learned from their mistakes in order to perform well on the formal summative assessment for that unit of study.

There are different purposes and uses for formative and summative assessments in social studies. You must determine what evidence you need to maximize and evaluate student learning in your classroom. The more accurate evidence, or information, you acquire during and at the end of units of study, the more valid your evaluations of student progress will be. When you can effectively evaluate student progress, you can make better decisions about your instructional practices, resources, and pacing.

Formative assessments are those that are done regularly during teaching and can inform instruction. Summative assessments are conducted at the end of the lesson to determine what students have learned.

Pacing guides, or curriculum maps, were discussed in Chapter 7.

Figure 9.4   Planning for informal, formative assessments during a unit of study about the Age of Exploration.

Lesson Sequence[a]	Content and Skill Development	Embedded Assessments to Check for Understanding	Transition From Past Lesson(s)
1	Develop concept and big ideas of exploration; historic, geographic, and economic context of 14th–16th centuries; timelines; world maps; map skills	Brainstorm and list ideas associated with exploration; develop timeline identifying 14th through 21st centuries; label continents on outline world map	Review concepts and big ideas used in prior units of study and relate to this unit addressing chronological sequence of units
2	Trade and technology in 14th–15th centuries; changes in Europe; vocabulary development	Label specific countries on outline world map (England, Spain, France, Portugal, China, India, Canada, Mexico); add major events/periods to timeline (Marco Polo travels to China, Columbus sails to Americas, Renaissance, Reformation, etc.); define essential vocabulary in notes	Review and edit ideas about exploration; review and discuss timeline created; review and discuss outline map; compare outline map to world map in atlas or textbook
3	Trade in Africa and Asia; Silk Route and goods traded; Zheng He and inventions; West Africa trade centers; gold, salt, and slavery; European trade routes	Compare and contrast Asian and African trade in Venn diagram; label major trade routes on outline map; identify a trade route and write about a day in the life of a trader; describe to partner examples of navigation technologies and trace major voyages on map	Share outline map with partner and check for accuracy with atlas or textbook; review and discuss timeline additions; use essential vocabulary to explain information learned
4	Old World meets New World; Christopher Columbus and his voyages; Columbian Exchange	Compare and contrast Europe and the Americas in a two-perspective dialogue essay; hot seat activity with students taking on roles of Columbus, church officials, kings, queens, merchants, crew; complete graphic organizer describing Columbian Exchange	Share writings with table partners; review and discuss trade routes on maps; analyze and discuss Venn diagrams
5	Spanish exploration; American empires; Spanish conquests	Label American empires on world map (Aztec, Inca, Maya); describe, compare and contrast Moctezuma II and Cortes; complete graphic organizer of social pyramid in New Spain; write about the differences between exploration and colonization	Discuss hot seat activity and summarize issues and various perspectives; share and revise graphic organizers

[a]The duration of a lesson may vary between 1 and 4 days.

In order to be an effective assessor of student knowledge and skills, you must develop a repertoire of assessment strategies that will help you determine, when necessary, exactly who is learning what. A variety of assessment strategies are contained in this chapter that may be used at various times during your units of study to assess student progress and learning. Administering the assessment is only the beginning, however. You must plan and prepare to evaluate the student assessments by your-self, with grade-alike colleagues, or have students evaluate work in class for themselves or their peers (Fisher, Lapp, & Flood, 2005). After the evaluation, students must receive and analyze the results of their assess-ments. In order for students to benefit from the evaluation, feedback should be immediate and specific (Marzano, Pickering, & Pollack, 2001). When the feedback is immediate and specific, the assessments become tools for learning that students can use to adjust their thinking, retrace their research, clarify misconceptions, identify needs, and further develop skills. Conferencing with students in small groups or individually helps students recognize that the data generated through assessments reflects what they know and are able to do according to a set of goals and stan-dards. Students then become more accustomed to the fact that assess-ments measure specific knowledge and skills and do not measure such features as neat handwriting or beautiful illustrations. Yes, we want stu-dents to display neat handwriting and create beautiful illustrations when required. However, these become vehicles for showing what the student knows and can do. These features do not compensate for lack of knowl-edge or skills. What has been deemed "good effort" in the past must be restated in the feedback as "lack of stated knowledge and skills." Effort, on the other hand, must be recognized and celebrated as the reason for success on assessments. When students begin to associate effort with achievement, they begin to realize how learning occurs, and they begin to dispel underlying beliefs that luck and other uncontrollable "forces" are responsible for their performances (Marzano et al., 2001).

When teachers work together to evaluate student work, they often generate data that help them inform their instructional practices. Working in grade-alike teams, teachers using the same curriculum goals or stan-dards can create common assessments that become administered in several classes. When the results of the assessments are analyzed among those teachers, they have an opportunity to discuss what worked and what did not work well in their classrooms during that unit of study as they com-pare and contrast the data generated from the common assessments.

Too often we have heard individual teachers state, "I taught the unit, but the students did not 'get it.'" After further probing, we found that some teachers were not clear about their teaching and learning ob-jectives, some teachers were using inappropriate assessments, and other teachers did not plan appropriately for the assessment of student learn-ing. For some teachers, assessment was literally an afterthought. After teaching a unit, they then looked for ways to assess the students' under-standings of what was covered in the unit. This method led to the ac-quisition or development of poor assessments that did not allow students to necessarily demonstrate what they had learned during the in-structional unit. As a result, the students and teachers looked at the grades from these assessments and wondered what went wrong. Students

A form for recording your student confer-ences can be found in the Web Links module in Chapter 9 on our Companion Website at www.prenhall.com/schell.

Making the link for students between ef-fort and achievement serves to motivate learning.

Remember, we should plan lessons with the end (or outcomes) in mind.

noted, "I thought I understood the content." Teachers reiterated, "I thought they understood the material during the unit." When neither students nor teachers know what will be assessed, there are bound to be poor results. When the students and teachers believe they have learned the required content and skills, feel prepared for an assessment, and then perform poorly, there may exist a problem with the assessment itself.

We also learned that in many cases, students do not take assessments seriously—oftentimes because they do not know they are being assessed or because they do not understand the purpose of the assessment. The purpose of the assessment should not rest with the mantra, "Because I have to put a grade next to your name." Instead, students should understand that assessments are measurements of their learning. The term *student achievement* is prevalent in the lives of teachers and should be prevalent in the lives of the students themselves. Ideally, students take pride in their work, their growth, their learning, and see assessments as opportunities to show what they have achieved.

As a result of working with many social studies teachers who are frustrated by the results they see from their assessment practices, we believe that teachers should consider the following:

- **Assessments should align with what is taught, which should align with your curriculum goals or standards.** If you do not know what assessments will be used before you begin teaching a lesson or unit, then chances are you will either develop a test after you have taught (based on what you taught and not based on your curricular goals or standards), or you will administer a test that loosely matches up with what was taught. In the first case, you will not assess what you set out for students to learn. Instead, you will assess what you covered in class lessons and believe the students understood. In the second case, you will find a test that may include items that assess information or skills that you did not teach (possibly because the information or skills were not part of your curriculum goals or standards), and you will generate data that does not accurately reflect what students learned.

  We recommend that you identify or develop your assessments before you begin teaching a unit. These assessments must clearly align with your curriculum goals or standards. Then, you may align your lesson plan content and activities with those assessments. In this way, your assessments, lesson plans, and resources all support the curriculum goals or standards that remain the focus of your unit. For example, if your standard calls for students to be able to distinguish between relative and absolute locations in their local community, before you begin planning and teaching, you might develop an assessment that requires students to write both relative and absolute locations of five major landmarks using a detailed map of the local community.

- **Textbook tests are not always the best assessments to use.** Some tests and assessment ideas presented in textbooks are excellent. Some

There are several electronic grade books available; examples can be found in the Web Links module in Chapter 9 on our Companion Website at www.prenhall.com/schell.

Knowing how you will assess students also helps you select instructional materials and literature.

are not. You will become more and more attuned to "good assessments" and "poor assessments" in time with greater attention and expertise. Do not assume that just because a test is found in a published program, or because the test booklet was expensive, that the tests are "good." Some test items are poorly written. Some are well written, but do not assess the knowledge and skills presented in the readings and teaching activities. Your assessments must match your curricular goals or standards, they must align with what you taught during the lessons or unit, and they must be well written in order to truly assess what students know and are able to do.

We recommend that you analyze the assessments that are available to you. Keep in mind that tests are only one form of assessment. You have many options. Discuss and evaluate available assessments with grade-level colleagues to determine whether these assessments are appropriate for your specific goals and standards. Many social studies programs provide assessments that can be easily divided or adapted to suit your needs. More and more publishers are providing test generators and test makers on CD-ROM, so you can develop your own tests by editing and adding items as needed. Finally, you should explore alternatives to what is available and also learn to develop effective assessments on your own. An excellent resource is *Test Better, Teach Better: The Instructional Role of Assessment* by W. James Popham (2003).

- **Students should know why and how they are being assessed.** Many students enjoy participating in social studies lessons, but do not enjoy the assessments administered. There are many reasons for these attitudes, and you may not be able to change all of your students' attitudes about assessments in general. However, you should share with your students your reasons and uses for assessment. When students understand that this is their way to "shine" and showcase what they have learned, they often have a more positive attitude about assessments.

We recommend that you present and approach assessments as celebrations of what students know and can do. Tell students that you know how smart and capable they are, and that you want to share evidence of this with others, including their parents, other students, and teachers, as well as the community. Share with students the reports you receive and comments you hear about how brilliant your students are, which becomes evident in a display of their work. In fact, find ways to consistently post your student's work in community spaces, including the school website. Remind students that they are generating the evidence that shows what they have achieved through their hard work and studies. Also, explain to students that their ideas are worth sharing beyond the four walls of your classroom. Use real-world examples of this as you discuss newspaper articles, news reports, public service announcements, museum exhibits, court hearings, movies, plays, and sports games as forms of assessment that showcase

A test generator is an electronic tool that allows you to customize assessments developed by the publisher.

Explaining to students that their performance helps you evaluate your work as a teacher is also helpful and well received by most students.

If you use the Internet for posting student work, be sure to check the district guidelines before doing so.

the research, work, training, skills, and knowledge of those presenting their "work" to the general public.

- **Students show their knowledge and skills in different ways.** When a student does not write a complete, detailed, and coherent essay about the topic presented, this does not necessarily mean that the student does not know a lot about the topic. Some students show what they know best through selected response tests, whereas others are better at showing what they know through writing or illustration. Some express their knowledge best orally and yet others through projects. We know a lot about multiple intelligences (Gardner, 1983, 2000), multiple learning styles (Armstrong, 1993), and differentiated instruction (Gregory & Chapman, 2002; Tomlinson, 1999). These theories about how students learn must also be applied to how students demonstrate what they have learned through assessment forms. Keeping this in mind, plan appropriately for your students' learning styles. If your objective is to find out what students have learned in social studies, do not let poor reading, writing, speaking, or artistic skills inhibit their performance on social studies assessments. Similarly, recognize the nature of what you are trying to assess. Most curricular goals or standards in social studies call for students to describe, locate, analyze, compare, trace, or evaluate. These require students to use different levels of thinking and therefore, different kinds of questions and tasks allow students to demonstrate these skills. Figure 9.5 provides suggestions for addressing varied levels of thinking and assessment tasks using Bloom's Taxonomy.

  We recommend that you provide multiple opportunities for students to show what they know and can do through a variety of assessments. Allow students to select (from a menu you have created) how they will demonstrate mastery of the learning goals or standards through writing, performances, projects, or selected-response tests. Hold all students accountable for the same content and skills, but allow them to showcase their knowledge and skills in appropriate ways. You may find that grading a variety of assessments is far preferable to reading 35 essays or grading 35 tests or listening to 35 oral presentations. When necessary, challenge students to develop and use their test-taking, writing, and oral skills for social studies assessments, but remember that you are evaluating social studies knowledge and skills, not language arts or visual and performing arts skills.

> Bloom's Taxonomy has been used to create educational objectives as well as for leveling questions teachers ask students.

When you consider what types of assessments you will use during your units of study, remember that good assessments share similar characteristics. The assessments should:

- provide information that tells students how well they have mastered the desired learning goals or standards.
- inform teachers about their instructional practices and help them improve their teaching.

Figure 9.5   Vary assessment demands and tasks using Bloom's Taxonomy.

Cognitive Learning Level	Intellectual Activity	Assessment Task Recommendations	Assessment Prompts
Knowledge	Arrange, define, label, list, memorize, name, order, recognize, relate, recall, repeat, reproduce, state	Multiple choice, matching, true-false, listing, completing graphic organizer, writing, oral report, label parts of illustrations, drawing	What is . . . ? Where is . . . ? When did ___ happen? Why did . . . ? Who was . . . ? How would you explain . . . ? Describe. . . .
Comprehension	Classify, describe, discuss, explain, express, identify, indicate, locate, recognize, report, restate, review, select, summarize, translate	Multiple choice, matching, true-false, listing, developing graphic organizers, writing, oral presentations, drawings, projects, research	How would you describe in your own words . . . ? What facts or ideas show . . . ? Which statements support . . . ? How would you summarize . . . ? What was the main idea of . . . ? What does ___ mean?
Application	Apply, choose, demonstrate, dramatize, employ, illustrate, interpret, operate, practice, schedule, sketch, solve, use, write	Writing, role-play, map-making, project development, problem-solving, oral performance, multimedia project, character interpretation, illustration, labeling, research	How would you use . . . ? What would happen if . . . ? What examples can you find to . . . ? What questions would you ask of . . . ? What other ways could . . . ?
Analysis	Analyze, appraise, calculate, categorize, compare, contrast, criticize, differentiate, discriminate, distinguish, examine, experiment, question, test	Socratic seminar, scored discussions, writing (editorial, persuasive essay, letter), debate, role-play, problem-based project, oral presentation (speech, commercial, news show), research, summarizing	What are the parts of . . . ? Why do you think . . . ? How would you classify . . . ? How is ___ related to . . . ? What evidence is there of . . . ? What conclusions can you draw . . . ?
Synthesis	Arrange, assemble, collect, compose, construct, create, design, develop, formulate, manage, organize, plan, prepare, propose, set up, write	Graphic organizers, outlines, labeling, illustration, project development, writing (summary, song, poem, news brief), oral performance, multimedia presentation	What would happen if . . . ? What alternatives were there to . . . ? What would you do if you . . . ? Formulate a theory about. . . . What could have been done to change . . . ?
Evaluation	Appraise, argue, assess, attach, choose, compare, defend, estimate, judge, predict, rate, core, select, support, value, evaluate	Writing (report, summary, evaluation, thesis statement), listing, matching, role-play, oral performance, Socratic seminar, scored discussion, debate, mock trial	In what ways do you agree/disagree with . . . ? How would you rate . . . ? Why did they do what they did? What was the value of . . . ? What is your opinion of . . . ? How would you evaluate . . . ? What was most important about . . . ?

- reflect the skills, materials, and content used during the unit. The assessment should not introduce new information or require students to develop new skills.
- be conducted in the classroom and not assigned for homework.
- measure both knowledge and skills required in social studies.
- reflect the interpretive nature of social studies. Although students will have to present some facts, they should also be able to analyze, evaluate, and interpret information to defend varying perspectives and arguments from history.

ASSESSMENT STRATEGIES

Most of what students learn in a social studies program is not readily visible or apparent to their teachers. Teachers must make overt what is covert about students' knowledge and skills (Popham, 2003). Therefore, teachers must create performance tasks for students to make overt what they know and can do in social studies. Analyzing student performances on these assessments, the teachers are then able to make inferences about each student's knowledge and skills. The most accurate inferences are, of course, based on information gleaned from a variety of performance tasks. This is why teachers assess—to determine how students are advancing toward the established goals and standards, and how well the students have each mastered the content and skills. Administering a paper-and-pencil test is only one method of assessment that can be used in the social studies class. Figure 9.6 presents a variety of strategies that might be used to assess students' progress (formative) as well as their achievement (summative). How do these lists compare to the kinds of assessments you remember from your days as a young student of social studies?

Figure 9.6   Formative and summative assessment strategies.

Formative	Summative
Cooperative line-up	Character interpretation
Fishbowl	Essay
Graphic organizers	Graphic organizers
Hot seat	Hot seat
Jeopardy or quiz bowl	Jeopardy or quiz bowl
Quickwrite	Multimedia presentation
Quickdraw	Oral performance
Rally table	Portfolio
Simulation	Project
Socratic seminar	Research report
Tea party	Scored discussion
Turn-to-a-partner	Simulation
	Written test

Musa writes about the problems he sees at school.
Source: *Emily Schell*

You might recognize some of these strategies from lesson activities. Well-planned lessons will embed some of these strategies as learning opportunities, but may also be used for assessment of student learning. For example, a teacher should not wait until the very end of a 6-week unit to assess what students have learned from each lesson of those 6 weeks. The teacher should check for understanding throughout the unit so that she can make necessary adaptations to her plans in order to reteach, adjust pacing, revise materials and resources, utilize different instructional strategies, and provide feedback to students so they know whether or not they are on track in their learning. At the end of the unit, the teacher may very well administer a summative assessment, which may take a variety of forms, to evaluate student achievement for the entire unit of study. With embedded and ongoing assessments during the unit, the students should be prepared to succeed on a summative test, because they know both their strengths and their challenges from the immediate feedback received after formative assessments during the unit.

Following are some examples of the kinds of assessments that might be used for either formative or summative assessment. Consider using, adapting, and adding to these ideas so that you can best access and assess what your students have learned in your class.

Character Interpretation

Assign or allow students to select a historical character from your unit of study. Students conduct research and develop a first-person monologue to deliver while acting and speaking as if they are that character. The expectations and rubric for this assessment may be adapted to meet the abilities of the grade level, length of study, and availability of research materials and costumes. The focus should remain on students' abilities to transport themselves (and their audience) to a different place and time through their historical knowledge, communication skills, dramatic talent, and creative abilities. Because a large group of students become the audience for each student presenting his or her character interpretation, audience members may serve as evaluators as well. Consider developing a rubric with or for students that they will use to help evaluate each other's performance.

For example, students studying about jobs might research and present information about the work of firefighters, librarians, postal workers, business owners, secretaries, and so on. Students studying about Ancient

There are a number of websites that create rubrics for teachers. For more information, see the Web Links module in Chapter 9 on our Companion Website at www. prenhall.com/schell.

Egypt might research and interpret historical characters such as Ramses the Great, Queen Hatshepsut, Nefertiti, Akhenaton, and Tutankhamen, as well as commoners, including scribes, artisans, carpenters, and enslaved workers. Students are then evaluated according to the information they present in their first-person monologue, their interpretation of those people, and the evaluative comments they make as they either compare and contrast from the character's perspective or comment on the social, economic, geographic, or political context of their character.

Cooperative Line-Up

This cooperative learning structure (Kagan, 1994) requires the teacher to propose a topic or question that has multiple responses. Each student responds in his or her head with an example for the topic or an answer to the question. The teacher then asks students to line up in a designated area from one point to another. The students must line up in order according to their answer. The teacher might ask students to line up in alphabetical, numerical, geographical, chronological, or some other order. The teacher might ask for half the class to line up at one time so that the other half can observe and help evaluate responses, or she might ask for groups to line up. Sometimes, the whole class can line up, then form a circle from the line to present to each other at the same time. In presenting, students step forward from their place in line and share their response to the topic or question.

The teacher must clarify her criteria for assessment before students respond. Teachers may assess for accuracy based in the content of the response, or may assess students' abilities to communicate with others and follow directions to line up. In some cases, the teacher may assess for students' abilities to demonstrate an understanding of chronology or geography (i.e., line up according to size of the state or country; line up according to distance from this spot—nearest to farthest).

For example, if the teacher asks students to think of a holiday (because the students are studying holidays), she might ask for five to seven students to line up in alphabetical order according to the name of the holiday they selected and have in their head. After allowing the students to organize themselves, they take turns to share aloud the name of their holiday and the rest of the class listens to ensure that they are in proper order. The teacher, meanwhile, may be assessing whether or not students can name a holiday accurately. The teacher might then ask for five to seven other students to come line up in chronological order—from January to December. After these students organize themselves and share the names of their holidays, another group might come line up in numerical order according to the date of the holiday (i.e., Valentine's Day is 14; July 4th is 4).

Use of questions rather than topics often generates more diverse responses in students. For example, while studying about supply and demand, you might ask students, "What items are in great demand by consumers today?" or "What items are difficult to purchase because of limited supplies?" If students are studying about immigration, you might ask, "What one item would you pack in your suitcase if you were immigrating to a new country?" and "What is an example of a contribution made by immigrants who settled in the United States?" The first question calls for a personal response that requires some historical understandings as well as analysis skills. The second question requires students to recall specific information from the unit of study. Both might be used to assess student understandings of immigration.

Essay

Beginning by grade 2, students can describe what they know and express their ideas in writing. With some guidance and structure, these descriptions and ideas can be used to write meaningful essays. Whether students write a simple three-paragraph essay or a detailed two-page essay, this form of assessment allows students to construct their responses to a question or writing prompt. The teacher should carefully craft an appropriate question or prompt that guides students in their thinking and response. If the question or prompt is too vague, students might not address the information or ideas that you intend to assess. If the question or prompt is too narrowly focused, the students will struggle to write the single "correct" response and neglect this opportunity to construct a well-written, unique response that showcases what they have learned and what they have thought about what they have learned. All essays require a clear rubric for evaluation of student work. The rubric should align the writing guidelines for the task as well with the curriculum goals or standards of the unit of study. For example, students learning world history might have the following standards-based goal at the outset of the unit:

> *Students compare different world cultures and civilizations focusing on their accomplishments, contributions, values, beliefs, and traditions. (Adapted from New York State Learning Standards for Social Studies, 1996)*

The unit of study may have focused on a sample task identified for that standard, which states that students should study the major cultural achievements of an ancient civilization (e.g., West African, Chinese, Japanese, European). The teacher may have selected Chinese civilization to study and established the following directions, question, and rubric for the essay:

> **Directions:** Answer the following question by writing a five-paragraph essay. Use examples and details to explain your answer. Review the scoring rubric before you begin writing your essay.

Question: How are ancient Chinese values and beliefs reflected in their traditions, accomplishments, and contributions?

Rubric Score	Criteria for Essay
3	• provides accurate and detailed descriptions of ancient Chinese values and beliefs • accurately describes several traditions, accomplishments, and contributions of the ancient Chinese • accurately explains how ancient Chinese beliefs and values are seen in the traditions and history of the people • writes a five-paragraph essay stating thesis or purpose in opening and closing paragraphs • consistently uses appropriate vocabulary and terms
2	• provides a limited description of ancient Chinese values or beliefs • describes one or two traditions, accomplishments, or contributions of the ancient Chinese • writes a five-paragraph essay • uses some appropriate vocabulary and terms
1	• states at least one value or belief • states at least one tradition, accomplishment, or contribution • writes an essay • attempts use of appropriate vocabulary and terms

Remember to focus your evaluation on the social studies content and skills instead of concentrating your evaluation on writing (e.g., spelling, grammar, sentence structure). Students should learn to communicate their ideas effectively through writing. At the same time, students should learn that good writers require specific knowledge and skills.

Fishbowl

Provide opportunities for students to participate in a discussion or small-group activity "inside the fishbowl" while peers watch and listen. Students inside the fishbowl are being assessed by the teacher and peers. Students outside of the fishbowl are required to take notes, share observations during the debriefing, ask questions after the fishbowl activity, or prepare evaluation comments for the students in the fishbowl or for the teacher. If you collect the evaluation comments from students outside of the fishbowl, you are able to evaluate the understandings of the students who were not inside the fishbowl. Students may take turns participating "in the fishbowl," but they do not have to be inside the fishbowl to be evaluated on their understandings. You can take notes to record the questions, comments, and evaluations of students "outside the fishbowl" as well.

You can probably imagine the conversation a group of fourth graders would have inside the fishbowl discussing the changes in the economy as a result of the Gold Rush. As Tino said, "They thought that they were

There are a number of genres common to essays, including persuasive, reports of information, summaries, and compare/contrast. The genre should be taught before students are expected to use it.

gonna get rich. Too bad, most of the gold was gone by the time the '49ers got to California. So many died getting there." To this, Angela added, "Some did make money, but the people in the cities were really the ones who benefited. The economy changed, especially in San Francisco because people needed to buy different things." This conversation continued with students asking questions of one another and summarizing what they had learned about immigration and migration as a result of the discovery of gold.

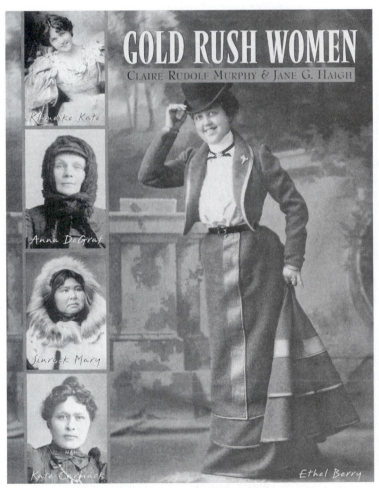

Source: *From Gold Rush Women by C. R. Murphy and J. G. Haig. Used with permission of Alaska Northwest Books, an imprint of Graphic Arts Center Publishing Company.*

Graphic Organizers

A variety of graphic organizers exist for students to use to organize facts. Provide students with appropriate organizers to complete while learning about a social studies topic, or use the organizer as an assessment for students to complete after studying the topic. More advanced students may be challenged to select or develop their own organizers to display information about a topic. Use a variety of organizers that help students see patterns in social studies, such as Venn diagrams to compare and contrast; flow charts to show progress; timelines to show chronology; webs to show description and detail; chains of events to show cause and effect; and pyramids to show distribution and hierarchy.

Sample graphic organizers were presented in Chapter 5. For sample graphic organizers that you can download, see the Web Links module in Chapter 9 on our Companion Website at www.prenhall.com/schell.

Hot Seat

Students studying about historical figures may be asked to sit in a "hot seat" and speak as if they are that person. While sitting in the hot seat, students are required to think and act like the assigned figure while responding to questions posed by the teacher and students. Students might rotate into the hot seat every 2 minutes, or the teacher might redesignate the hot seat to represent another individual from history. In one adaptation to hot seat, consider having two to five seats for students to portray a variety of figures, or perspectives, from the unit of study. The teacher should model effective questioning by asking questions that challenge the student in the hot seat to think deeply about the historical context, character traits of the person, and events or circumstances of that person's life. Before asking questions of students in the hot seat, students in the audience might be required to write their questions for review by the teacher. Some teachers like to inform students who will be in the hot seat the following day, whereas other teachers prefer to randomly select students from the class to take the hot seat. In either situation, this activity provides opportunities for fun and allows you to measure student understandings about the people and events of the period that you are studying.

The hot seat is a particularly useful assessment tool when students are studying biographies.

Jeopardy or Quiz Bowl

Popular game formats are enticing assessment strategies for students. Whether you use a format like *Jeopardy* during or at the end of an instructional unit, students will focus on specific content knowledge, vocabulary terms, and appropriate skills to prepare for and "play" the game. Students might work in pairs, triads, table groups, or two teams to take turns and answer with the questions ("What is . . . ") to answers that have been developed based on the curricular goals and standards. These games also serve as preparation for other forms of assessment, such as a written test. Teachers can easily make *Jeopardy* boards using

For information on electronic formats of these games, see the Web Links module in Chapter 9 on our Companion Website at www.prenhall.com/schell.

If students create projects based on different topics or different aspects of a topic, there is much more to learn through the peer evaluation process.

pocket charts or chart paper, and now there are computer formats available for projection and use in the classroom.

Multimedia Presentation

Students become motivated to showcase their social studies knowledge as well as their technology skills through PowerPoint and other multimedia formats. Students must research, summarize, write, rewrite, add illustrations, edit, and organize their topics before making presentations available in class. Students researching different aspects of a historical event, era, person, or place can present their multimedia work to the entire class, or make available at computer stations for students to review and respond to during center rotations or independent work time. However you organize the presentation of projects, consider the benefits of having students review and evaluate each other's work according to the rubric created for the project.

Oral Performance

There are a variety of types of oral performances to consider. Consider having your students prepare and present speeches, addresses, readings/narrations, monologues, dialogues, news reports, stand-up comedy, debates, or oral presentations. Because 30 consecutive oral reports about the same or a similar topic may become time consuming and even boring, consider your options. If your goal is to help students develop oral fluency, presentation skills, and communication skills while displaying their knowledge and skills in social studies, allow students to work in pairs or triads to develop and present information orally. Alternatively, allow students to select (from a short list of options) the format for their oral performance. Some students may prefer to deliver speeches. Others may prefer staging a debate. Most oral performances will require students to write their information and ideas on index cards to be used during the performances. Focus your evaluation of their performances on the social studies content and skills introduced during the unit of study.

When students do oral reports, use a timer. Not only do they need practice staying within timelines, but a timer limits the run-on presentations.

Portfolio

Portfolios are important repositories for student work. Adding entries to a social studies portfolio over time will help students see their growth in knowledge and skills. For example, initial assessments of map skills through hand-drawn maps at the beginning of the school year may be entered into the portfolio. During the school year and at the end of the year, as students learn more about mapmaking and as they focus on particular regions in their studies, their increased knowledge and skills should be reflected in their subsequent map entries. Similarly, increased understandings of chronology may be visible through beginning-, middle-, and end-of-the-year entries showing student-generated timelines.

Essays, projects, drawings, photographs, and other student work should be included in a portfolio to help students and parents recognize the diversity of assessments that demonstrate growth over a period of time. Ideally, these portfolios travel with the student to the following grade level so that the receiving teacher has a series of snapshots of what the student's strengths and weaknesses are. Additionally, the receiving teacher gets to see and refer back to the information that was covered in the student's prior school year.

Project

A variety of projects are typically used in social studies classroom, including dioramas, poster reports, models, and pop-up books. You can develop your own ideas and resources for projects in your classroom, knowing that projects do not have to be extensive or expensive. Projects are creations developed by students based in their knowledge and skills and focused on your learning objectives. Consider engaging alternatives to the written test and allow students to show what they have learned through the planning, development, and presentation of a project. Students often require guidance through the development of a project as they learn about planning and procedures. The results are rewarding for students who take pride in the creation of a unique product crafted from their own ideas, knowledge, skills, and efforts.

Some projects are assigned to individuals; others require partners or small teams. Identify and articulate your objectives before introducing projects in your social studies classroom. Some standards require students to work cooperatively to develop ideas and projects. You might combine the skills of working cooperatively with the knowledge gained from a unit on Celebrations Around the World. Your expectations and rubric for the project should be clear and reflect your assessment of both cooperative learning skills and knowledge of celebrations around the world.

Quickwrite

This type of informal, formative assessment allows students to "download" what they know and think in a simple, speedy manner. For a quickwrite, you simply ask students to write what they know or think about a topic during a short period of time. For example, you might say, "What was the Louisiana Purchase? During the next 2 minutes, write a description of the Louisiana Purchase." Timers are helpful for this strategy, and students become accustomed to timed writing. Students should be informed and reminded that the purpose of a quickwrite is for them to write down as many of their ideas as they can on paper during the allotted time. They should be reminded that this is a time when they should concentrate on the topic and not on spelling or constructing complete sentences. Some teachers provide students with notebooks or journals and use these as places for students to write and store their quickwrites.

Digital cameras are a great classroom investment. They allow for quick use and no developing costs.

History Connections

New Year's Day is celebrated differently around the world. For example, in Greece, children leave their shoes by the fireside on New Year's Day with the hope that Saint Basil, who was famous for his kindness, will come and fill their shoes with gifts. On New Year's Day in Japan, everyone gets dressed in their new clothes and homes are decorated with pine branches and bamboo—symbols of long life.

Quickwrites are also used as anticipatory sets to show what students already know about the topic.

Other teachers prefer to collect loose sheets of paper to assess regularly. Quickwrites may be used to help students recall and review information studied, or they may be used to take an inventory of background knowledge on a new topic. Quickwrites are often for the teacher to review and evaluate, but also serve as evaluation tools for the students themselves. Students should remain reflective of what they know and can do. This strategy helps students identify for themselves progress and areas of need.

Quickdraw

Similar to a quickwrite, students are given a question or prompt and asked to draw their response during a limited time period. Again, a timer is helpful and students are motivated to access and then draw their ideas quickly. You should remind students that artistic quality and detail are not the goals of this assessment. Instead, the objective is to "download" in a quick and concise manner their ideas or "pictures" of the stated topic. For example, you might ask students to spend 3 minutes quickly drawing a map of the world, the three branches of government, or types of American Indian dwellings. Quickdraws, like quickwrites, allow you and the students to get a quick snapshot of what the student knows most immediately and what the student lacks in understandings. Allow students to share and discuss their drawings with a partner, with the class, or with you so that misconceptions may be clarified and accurate knowledge may be validated. Learning and assessment should occur in nonlinguistic as well as linguistic forms. Ideally, both are used to reinforce and teach the other for deeper understandings.

Rally Table

This cooperative learning structure (Kagan, 1994) allows students to work together to show what collectively they know and can do. After you introduce the topic or question, each table group (two to four students are ideal) passes one sheet of paper around the table. On this paper, each student adds a response or answer before passing the paper to the next student. When each student receives the paper, he or she must read the responses already recorded so as not to repeat an answer before writing another. Students must be reminded to keep their ideas flowing during the rally table exercise so that they have several answers to add to the list—in case their answer is already recorded. Students should be instructed not to talk during a rally table so that each student has the opportunity to think and add responses for himself or herself. A set period of time should be designated for the rally table. When the timer ends, the student writing the final response can tally the number of responses or check for accuracy or repetition. Use these lists to review knowledge and skills used during the rally table. Misconceptions and strategies may be addressed with the whole class in a safe environment because there are no names attached to the responses. For example, you

Identifying misconceptions and inaccurate assumptions and explanations is a critical purpose for formative assessments. When you know about students' misconceptions, you can help them challenge them.

might ask, "What challenges were faced by immigrants?" or "What are the qualities of a hero?" or "Who is considered a hero?" Responses to these questions in a rally table will generate a variety of responses that should reflect the curricular objectives of the unit of study. The responses should help you and your students see whether they understand the objectives.

Research Report

Research reports have long been a tradition of the social studies classroom. This is one form of assessment, but it should not supplant other forms of assessment because much of the work in a research report relies on resources and independent learning. You can define your research report in a number of ways. For example, if you are studying about various cultures, people, places, or events, students may select (or be assigned) one of these cultures, people, places, or events to research and then report on. This is a way to jigsaw the content so that all students do not learn in depth about all of the cultures, people, places, or events. Instead, each student learns a lot about one of these and then learns a little about the others through exposure to classmates' reports. Sometimes, this is ideal and necessary because there is too much to cover. Depth is often preferred to minimal coverage of all the components.

As for the report itself, depending on your grade level and learning objectives, students might conduct research from a variety of reference materials and develop an organized written report, including notecards, table of contents, sections, maps, illustrations, etc. Or, the students may be required to access at least three sources of information, then write a one-page report or deliver an oral or multimedia report. The benefits of a research report include the opportunities for students to conduct independent research by accessing references beyond the textbook, as well as summarizing information to present in written or oral form. However, research reports cannot simply be assigned. Resources, clear criteria, time, and ongoing guidance are essential for research reports.

Scored Discussion

Discussions are excellent forms of assessment. However, it is often difficult to evaluate student contributions and understandings when there are multiple discussions occurring in the classroom. Informal discussions should occur regularly, especially with English language learners, and scored discussions should occasionally be held as well. In a scored discussion, students in the discussion group sit in a circle. The rest of the class sits outside of the circle and listens and observes the discussion. With the expectations for the discussion clearly outlined, students outside of the discussion circle evaluate, or "score," either the group or specific students during the discussion. For example, the discussion might be focused on the rights and responsibilities of American citizens. The expectations might be that no person dominates the discussion, that each person contributes to the discussion in a meaningful way, and that each person provides clear examples of rights and responsibilities. As the discussion occurs inside the circle, students outside the circle might be assigned to observe a specific student and record the number of times that person contributes, record what that person contributed and whether or not clear examples were given, and determine whether the person contributed in a meaningful way. After the discussion ends, you can lead the class in a debriefing session that allows the students inside the circle to share their evaluations of their contributions followed by comments from students outside the circle. Written documentation from students outside the circle may be collected and used to assess both the student inside the circle and the work of the scorer outside of the circle.

Scored discussions also help students develop their active listening skills.

Simulation

Simulations may be conducted as extensive or simple assessments of student knowledge and skills. Basically, students simulate a situation or environment and participate in a simulated experience using what they know about the situation or environment. In an extensive simulation, students may be asked to develop clothing, artifacts, and backdrops to simulate the place and time. Given a certain situation or time period, the students then take on a role to demonstrate their knowledge of the period and situation. For example, students learning about the American colonies might simulate a day in the life of a New England colonist. Or, students might simulate the arguments for and against revolution. Extensive simulations require a great deal of planning and preparation, as we have seen in schools where students restage pioneers moving west, the Constitutional Convention, or the United Nations hearings. Simple simulations require less planning and preparation, such as demonstrating understandings of the concept of trade by simulating trade in the classroom. In this example, the historic context is not the focus, but the knowledge and skills of basic economic concepts are. Other examples include students drawing pictures in an assembly line to simulate changes to work life during the Industrial Revolution, using the computer program "Oregon Trail" to simulate westward movement, and prohibiting students with January birthdays from voting in class to simulate discrimination and voting rights. Simulations should always be conducted with sensitivity to the lesson objectives and student maturity levels. These forms of instruction and assessment seek to tap into historical empathy and thinking skills, which are often difficult to teach and assess in traditional reading and writing formats. Serious consideration should be given to simulating such controversial and emotion-ridden experiences as enslavement, internment, relocation, and war. With limited time in the classroom, limited knowledge and varied maturity levels, many students may react inappropriately to the

History Connections

The United Nations was created on October 24, 1945, with 51 nations signing the charter. The UN has offices in New York, Geneva, and Vienna. Shirley Temple (the child actress) was appointed as U.S. Representative to the United Nations in 1969.

Simulating religious activity is not recommended in any public school classroom setting.

simulation and either belittle the experiences of people or misunderstand the context of events from the past by using a contemporary context. Use caution when considering when and how to use simulations to assess student understandings. As with most assessments, make sure to have a clear rubric to evaluate your students' demonstrations of specific knowledge and skills.

Socratic Seminar

Social studies teachers often enjoy using Socratic Seminars in their classrooms because they seek to see students ask meaningful questions, develop their ideas, and think critically instead of always searching for the correct answer. In a Socratic seminar, students read or view common documents, videos, photos, artifacts, or illustrations. After ample time to read or view, the students then bring their notes and ideas into a discussion group, where a facilitator outlines the ground rules for the seminar. These ground rules often include the following:

1. The facilitator is in charge of the seminar and will keep time, call on speakers, and keep the discussion focused on the topic.
2. Speakers may make a statement or ask a question when another speaker has finished speaking. Questions or responses may be directed at a specific speaker or to the group as a whole.
3. No speaker may dominate the discussion.
4. The purpose of the seminar is to gain a deeper understanding of the topic, not to get to any exact, correct answer.
5. Statements and questions should refer to the readings or viewings. In other words, statements should be phrased in reference to what everyone has read or viewed. Opinions may be included, but must relate to the common reference materials.

For more information on the use of Socratic seminars, see the Web Links module in Chapter 9 on our Companion Website at www.prenhall.com/schell.

You may serve as the facilitator or as an outside observer to assess students' understandings of the common materials as well as the context of the topic. You are also able to assess the critical thinking, listening, and speaking skills of students who are participating in the seminar. Depending on your class, you might have whole-class or small-group seminars so that assessment is manageable.

Tea Party

As in a traditional tea party, invite students to walk around the classroom, meet and greet others politely, and of course display their best manners. Before they begin, however, ask students to think about what they are studying in social studies. Ask them to think about something interesting they have learned and, as they mingle during the tea party, instruct them to share with others (as well as listen to others) the interesting knowledge they have gained. The teacher should circulate and observe the interactions of students while listening to the content of their polite conversations. This will give the teacher an idea about who is comprehending and synthesizing information and who is not. After a set time period, stop students and ask them to now think of some questions they have about the topic.

Turn to a Partner

A simple yet effective method of formative assessment and self-assessment for students requires students to turn to a partner and discuss or identify certain information. You might ask a specific question and ask each student to turn to a partner and answer the question. Afterwards, ask the partner to answer the same question to the student who answered first. As you reveal the correct answer, let students calibrate their responses to the answer. Using pairs provides a somewhat safe zone for students to attempt a response, listen to another's response, and then assess both responses. This method of formative, informal assessment may be used frequently and adapted in several ways. For example, you might ask pairs to negotiate the answer, then randomly call on students to assess their knowledge. Another adaptation requires students to turn to a partner to discuss the answer before writing the answer on the assessment.

This strategy also helps students review their knowledge before a high-stakes test, such as an end-of-chapter exam, that will be used for a grade.

Written Test

The most common form of assessment is a written test. Written tests traditionally include selected-response items, which ask the student to choose the correct answer from those presented. Selected-response items are often presented as multiple-choice, true-false, or matching items. Written tests also contain constructed-response items, which require students to construct their response to a question or prompt. Both types of items require knowledge and skill, but challenge students in different ways of thinking and responding. For example, some students cannot recall from memory the names of presidents or dates of events. However, given a selection of possible answers, students may be able to identify the correct names or dates. Similarly, students might know a great deal about a historical period or concept, but may not be able to demonstrate that knowledge through a series of selected-response items. If asked to answer a question, develop a list, or draw a diagram, that student might fare better in demonstrating thorough understandings of the period or concept.

The origin of the word *quiz* as it is used today is fascinating. Richard Daly, a Dublin, Ireland, theatre owner, made a bet in 1836 that he could get a nonsense word known throughout the town. At a performance later that night, he gave the audience cards with the word *quiz* written on them and asked people to post the word around town.

Conclusion

Assessment is essential to a meaningful social studies program. Each unit of study should focus clearly on the standards or learning objectives established, and the assessment should be based in those standards or objectives. In your planning process, we recommend that assessment plans immediately follow the identification of your unit goals. This way, your lesson plans include informal assessments and help you and the students recognize progress as well as misunderstandings or misconceptions before you get to the end of the unit. This process also allows you to stay on target in your teaching plans. Whether or not your state requires formal, high-stakes testing of social studies in the grade that you teach, consider the positive long-term effects of sound assessments that occur at each and every grade level in this content area. Students will move through the grades with a clear understanding of what they know and what they can do to better understand the world in which they live and contribute.

History's Finer Points

As more students gained access to our nation's public schools in the 1930s and 1940s, tests were used to determine each student's intellectual aptitude. Based on the results of these tests, students were assigned to an "appropriate" academic or vocational track. This method of assigning students to different curricular tracks in the 8th or 9th grade prevented large numbers of students from studying history as well as literature, science, and foreign languages. However, vocational tracks provided training and employment opportunities for many impoverished families.

Today, high-stakes tests are used in accountability systems throughout the nation to support the achievement of rigorous academic standards for all students, whether they intend to go to college or not. The development of many of these tests can be traced back to federal and state initiatives set forth in the 1989 National Education Goals. These goals sprang from reactions to reports showing that American students were poorly ranked in international tests.

Text-Based Question: What are some other purposes for assessment today?

Questions to Consider

1. What are the differences between formal and informal assessments? How are each used in the social studies classroom?
2. What role do assessments play in lesson planning?

Quiz yourself on this chapter's important concepts on our Companion Website's Chapter 9 self-assessments at www.prenhall.com/ schell.

3. When should formative and summative assessments be used? How are these assessments used?

4. Which assessment strategies are you comfortable using?

5. Which assessment strategies are you uncomfortable using? How will you learn more about these assessments?

Exercises

1. Interview several teachers about their assessment systems. How do they use assessments to inform their instruction?

2. Review your unit and lesson plans. How can you improve the formative and summative assessments you plan to use?

3. Use one of the assessment strategies outlined in this chapter to collect data on a group of students. What do these data tell you about students' learning?

References

Armstrong, T. (1993). *7 kinds of smart: Identifying and developing your many intelligences.* New York: Plume.

Black, P., & William, D. (1998). *Inside the black box: Raising standards through classroom assessment.* London: King's College.

Fisher, D., Lapp, D., & Flood, J. (2005). Consensus scoring and peer planning: Meeting literacy accountability demands one school at a time. *The Reading Teacher, 58,* 656–667.

Gardner, H. (1983). *Frames of mind: The theory of multiple intelligences.* New York: Basic.

Gardner, H. (2000). *Intelligence reframed: Multiple intelligences for the 21st century.* New York: Basic.

Gregory, G., & Chapman, C. (2002). *Differentiated instructional strategies.* Thousand Oaks, CA: Corwin Press.

Kagan, S. (1994). *Cooperative learning.* San Juan Capistrano, CA: Kagan Cooperative Learning.

Marzano, R., Pickering, D., & Pollack, J. (2001). *Classroom instruction that works: Research-based strategies for increasing student achievement.* Alexandria, VA: Association for Supervision and Curriculum Development.

New York State Board of Regents (1996). *New York state learning standards for social studies.* New York: Author.

Popham, W. J. (2003). *Test better, teach better: The instructional role of assessment*. Alexandria, VA: Association for Supervision and Curriculum Development.

Stiggins, R. (2001). *Student-involved classroom assessment*. Upper Saddle River, NJ: Merrill Prentice Hall.

Tomlinson, C. A. (1999). *The differentiated classroom: Responding to the needs of all learners*. Alexandria, VA: Association for Supervision and Curriculum Development.

Wiggins, G., & McTighe, J. (1998). *Understanding by design*. Alexandria, VA: Association for Supervision and Curriculum Development.

Children's Literature

Mercati, C. (2002). *Forty-Niners: The story of the California Gold Rush*. Logan, IA: Perfection Learning.

Murphy, C. R., & Haigh, J. G. (1997). *Gold rush women*. Anchorage, AK: Alaska Northwest Books.

Roop, P. (2002). *California gold rush*. New York: Scholastic.

How Do We Share What We've Learned in Social Studies?

Source: *Krista Greco/Merrill*

Big Idea

Educators benefit in a community of learners.

Essential Question

How can educators work together to improve the teaching and learning of social studies?

Ms. Gonzales approached her principal with apprehension. "I know we don't have much money in the budget for conferences. However, I would like to attend the national social studies conference, which will be held here in our city this fall. Is there any way I can participate in this conference?"

Ms. Gonzales' principal explained that although site funds are limited, she recognized this as a unique opportunity for her teachers to receive excellent professional development that might otherwise be unavailable because of restrictions and costs of travel. Furthermore, the principal acknowledged that opportunities for professional development in social studies were difficult to find. Ms. Gonzales and her principal sat down, estimated the costs for registration and substitute coverage, analyzed the budget, and worked out a plan for a representative from each grade level to attend the national social studies annual conference.

Besides costs, Ms. Gonzales was also hesitant to seek approval for attending this conference because she knew that her school's focus was on raising student achievement in reading comprehension. The principal also remained aware of her school's professional development focus. Prior to the conference, she met with the teachers who planned to attend. Using the on-line conference program, the principal helped teachers identify sessions that would help them address some of their concerns about teaching reading and social studies. They were all pleased to see a variety of sessions, workshops, and speakers focused on their very goal—to raise student achievement in reading comprehension! The principal reminded the teachers to make time for the exhibit hall as well and asked them to gather information about useful resources to bring back to the school site.

After the conference, the principal invited these same teachers to her office for coffee and to share what they had learned at the conference. At the end of the meeting, she asked, "Now how will we share this new information and these wonderful resources with the rest of the staff?"

The planning continued. . . .

GRASPING THE BRASS RING

When learning opportunities arise, it is imperative that we recognize and take advantage of them. Oftentimes, teachers are hesitant to ask for support when it comes to their own personal professional development. Financial and human resources are limited, and yet so many teachers remain mystified about their own students' lack of interest and achievement in the area of social studies. In many cases, funds are available for professional development and teachers simply need to appropriately request the funds. In other cases, there are ways to access resources inexpensively or through grants, private organizations, and special programs. In this chapter, we will explore some of these resources and avenues to professional development in social studies.

Remember, many professional development experiences such as conferences are also tax-deductible!

Figure 10.1

"I can't find the Geography Workshop."
Source: *www.cartoonstock.com.*

All teachers know that regardless of their preservice training and ongoing and meaningful inservice, staff development or professional development is required for effective teaching of social studies as well as any other subject. In other words, good teachers are also lifelong learners! Moreover, a large and diverse community of social studies educators that meets, discusses issues, brainstorms solutions, conducts research, and implements new ideas allows for sustained improvement in our classrooms.

There are a variety of ways to get involved and stay involved in order to remain current in the field of social studies, access professional development and available resources, and contribute to the ongoing learning of colleagues. You have heard that it takes a village to raise a child, and we believe that it takes a community to support an educator. We have both learned a great deal about social studies from each other and from the social studies community at large. We also recognize that we learn far more about teaching social studies when we, in fact, teach—especially when we teach other teachers. This can be true for you, too. Teachers are instrumental in the success of meaningful professional development, and there are ample opportunities for teachers to present their own ideas, research, and data through local, state, and national workshops, conferences, journals, and networks. Consider some of the following formal and informal opportunities to learn from and contribute to as you continue to learn how to make social studies meaningful, important, and dynamic in your own classroom.

See how much you can learn about yourself as a teacher when you share your teaching ideas with other adults. It is a very rewarding experience and one that we hope you'll engage in.

These teachers work collaboratively to discuss new assessment strategies they learned during a recent professional development workshop.
Source: *Emily Schell*

PROFESSIONAL ORGANIZATIONS

Membership in professional organizations keeps teachers informed about current issues, resources, and professional development opportunities. These organizations often hold an annual conference, and usually have a local or state affiliate. Most have a website, a newsletter, or a professional journal to share their latest research and teaching ideas. Dues vary, but entitle members to discounts on conference fees and resources. Dues may entitle the member to certain publications, including the organization's website or archives. Most organizations are run by leaders elected from the membership. With leaders who are also practitioners in the field, the organization's work tends to be closely tied to current educational needs. Following are descriptions of some noted social studies professional organizations.

NCSS

The largest organization of educators devoted solely to social studies in the United States is the National Council for the Social Studies (NCSS). This organization was founded in 1921 and serves to support educators in strengthening and advocating social studies. NCSS has members in every U.S. state, in the District of Columbia, and in 69 foreign countries. NCSS serves as an umbrella organization for elementary, secondary, and college teachers of history, geography, economics, political science, psychology, anthropology, sociology, and law-related education. NCSS is organized into a network of regional, state, and local councils and associated groups representing K–12 teachers, college and university faculty members, curriculum specialists and administrators, social studies supervisors, and leaders in the various disciplines that constitute the social studies. The mission of NCSS is to provide leadership, service, and support for all social studies educators. NCSS fulfills this commitment through publications, council work, grants, endorsements, curriculum development, and annual conferences.

Go to www.ncss.org for more information or to join the organization.

NCSS developed a sound definition for social studies, which we continue to use in all of our work in the field of social studies. This organization also created the national social studies standards.

NCHE

The National Council for History Education is a nonprofit corporation dedicated to promoting the importance of history in schools and in society. The council is led by a board of trustees and supported by the contributions of individuals and organizations. NCHE serves as an advocacy and educational network for K–12 educators, colleges and universities, museums, historical councils, and community groups. Founded in 1990 largely in response to the 1988 Bradley Commission on History in the

Schools report, and reinforced by the 1989 National Commission on the Social Studies report, *Charting a Course,* NCHE advocates for increased time and attention for history as the core for social studies. NCHE speaks with policy makers about the importance of these and encourages regular communications between schools and those who promote history education in the community.

Go to www.garlandind. com/nche/ for more information about the organization or to become a member. NCHE also has state affiliates.

NCGE

The National Council for Geographic Education promotes the importance and value of geographic education, facilitates communication among teachers of geography K–16, encourages and supports research on geographic education, develops and publishes teacher resources, and works with other organizations with similar goals. NCGE has an annual national conference for teachers to share, discuss, and gather instructional materials and ideas for their classrooms. The website offers national geography standards as well as lessons, grant information, and standards-based activities for an elementary school geography club.

Contact NCGE at www.ncge.net for resources and information.

National Geographic

Membership to the National Geographic Society is open to the public and is usually obtained through subscription to *National Geographic* magazine. However, National Geographic funds state geographic alliances, which solicit membership of educators in that region. Most alliances do not require a membership fee, but generate membership in order to build a network of educators dedicated to improving geographic literacy among students K–12. State alliances, which can be found through the National Geographic website, develop teaching resources, provide workshops and institutes, create school and community programs, assist teachers in writing grants, and coordinate student programs. National Geographic continues to sponsor the annual Geography Awareness Week (or Geography Action!) to raise national awareness about the importance of geographic education, provide grants for teachers, and coordinate the National Geographic Bee for students in grades 4–8.

Teachers can join the on-line Educational Network to receive e-mail information about news, resources, and programs, or simply bookmark the following website to find standards-based lesson plans and lots of geographic information: nationalgeographic. com/education.

Various organizations exist that support the teaching and learning of social studies, but that do not have a professional membership like NCSS, NCHE, NCGE, and the National Geographic Alliances. For example:

Colonial Williamsburg Foundation

This nonprofit organization operates the world's largest living history museum in Williamsburg, Virginia. Restored to its 18th-century roots, this historic area serves as an outdoor classroom for thousands of visitors, students, and teachers. The foundation works specifically with school groups that come to Williamsburg for field studies and also provides resources and electronic field trips—transmitted via satellite through cable television stations as well as the Internet—for students who cannot come to Williamsburg. For educators, the foundation offers a week-long institute that immerses teachers in the studies of 17th- and 18th-century Virginia life. Many teachers who participate in these summer institutes are sponsored by private citizens or local businesses or organizations. Colonial Williamsburg works with teachers to develop classroom resources and materials, which are often presented at state and national social studies conferences.

There are many smaller foundations, living history sites, libraries, organizations and museums that also offer professional development, resources, and student programs that you should investigate in your local region.

Information about Colonial Williamsburg programs and resources can be found at www.history.org.

Gilder Lehrman Institute for American History

This private nonprofit organization was founded in 1994 to promote the study and love of American history. The Institute creates history-centered schools and research centers, organizes seminars and programs, and produces useful publications and traveling exhibits. The Institute offers professional development to its network of teachers, national park administrators, and historians nationwide. Teachers of American history are invited to apply to attend week-long summer seminars presented at universities throughout the United States and in the United Kingdom. These seminars feature recent and respected scholarship in areas of U.S. history presented by noted historians while connecting educators with each other, primary sources of information, and discussions about teaching history.

Information about Gilder Lehrman resources, publications, history schools, and seminars can be found at www.gilderlehrman.org.

National Center for History in the Schools

Founded in 1988 through a grant from the National Endowment for the Humanities, NCHS develops and provides historical resources, professional development, and teaching materials for K–12 teachers. In partnership with various federal and state grants, NCHS has created more than 70 teaching units based in primary source materials, an online world history curriculum, and guides for history teachers. Based at the University of California at Los Angeles, the center developed the national history standards and continues to provide support for teachers implementing these standards.

Information and resources for NCHS can be found at www.sscnet.ucla.edu/nchs.

LOCAL OPPORTUNITIES

Sometimes you have to create your own opportunities for professional development and develop your own local networks. From raising important questions about social studies education in your grade level, department, or staff meetings at school, to creating a district or regional network of educators interested in promoting social studies education, you can make a difference. Create your own opportunities to share knowledge, skills, experiences, and resources with colleagues. Invite museum educators, administrators, and professors from institutions of higher education. Discuss issues, challenge practices, generate ideas, and share resources.

Working together, you might identify available grants and collaborate to write proposals and implement new programs. The federal Teaching American History Grants, National Endowment for the Humanities, and the National Geographic grants are just a few of the funding opportunities available to local education agencies. Most cities have local granting agencies as well.

CONTINUING EDUCATION

Local colleges and universities as well as school districts offer continuing education or extension courses for teachers seeking professional development and salary advancement. Often, these offerings include courses that support the teaching and learning of social studies. Request social studies courses from your local providers, and take advantage of those offered.

A growing number of these courses are now offered on-line through distance learning programs. This offers teachers a nice alternative to evening, Saturday, or summer courses. Depending on your learning style and availability for on-the-ground (traditional) courses, distance learning might be preferable. Regardless of the format, if you are provided with engaging learning opportunities to improve your teaching of social studies, you should take full advantage.

PROFESSIONAL READING

From professional books to journals and newsletters, there is a lot to read about social studies education. New research yields new recommendations for teaching materials, strategies, and methods. The implementation of these results in more studies, reports, and ideas. Teachers find their own comfort zones in on-line information, in-depth articles, or brief reports written by researchers, K–12 teachers, or curriculum specialists. Here are a few of the more popular and useful reading sources.

Social Education

Social Education is the official journal of NCSS, published seven times annually, and is a benefit of NCSS membership. The journal offers informational articles, lesson plans, and resources to support K–12 teaching of social studies. *Middle Level Learning* is a supplement focused on middle school content and lesson plans that is published three times per year and included with *Social Education*.

Social Studies and the Young Learner

This quarterly journal supports K–6 teachers in teaching social studies. Published by NCSS, this journal features literature titles, developmentally appropriate lesson plans, and issues that relate to elementary school social studies. This journal is also a benefit of NCSS membership.

History Matters!

NCHE publishes the newsletter *History Matters!* 10 times each year for members, and provides the lead article online for nonmembers. The full newsletter presents ideas, notes, and news about history education, including book reviews, a calendar of events, and information about grants, conferences, contacts, and teaching resources.

The Social Studies Professional

This official newsletter of NCSS provides the latest news, resources, professional development listings, grant deadlines, and information about local and state meetings for members. Published six times annually, this newsletter is a benefit of NCSS membership.

Theory and Research in Social Education

This quarterly journal is designed to stimulate and communicate research and thinking in social education. Conceptual or empirical studies of social education are presented through a series of articles to exchange ideas and research findings and expand knowledge and understanding about social education. Information about this publication can be found at the NCSS website.

The Social Studies

Visit www.heldref.org/tss.php for more information or to subscribe.

This bimonthly peer-reviewed journal is written by K–12 classroom teachers, teacher educators, and curriculum administrators. The journal provides a forum for teachers to share their instructional ideas and comment on current social studies issues. You will find articles on how to teach specific topics, themes, or eras using a variety of strategies such as using songs to teach the Civil War.

CHILDREN'S LITERATURE

As you have learned in previous chapters, a great deal of social studies may be taught and learned through informational and narrative books. Therefore, there are some important sources to consider in keeping abreast of the current titles, uses, and resources for children's literature. Frequenting your favorite bookstores that features a children's book section will be extremely helpful. Speak with the education staff about your grade level and interests. Building a good rapport with key personnel will help you find the most useful titles in teaching specific themes, concepts, and topics in social studies. Most bookstores have an e-mail list for you to join, and soon announcements about new titles and author visits will be in your inbox. When bookstores invite authors, storytellers, or educators to speak, be sure to visit and make contacts.

Online book shopping is also helpful, especially when the website stores your preferences for book topics. New titles that match prior queries will often pop up in your searches. Just browsing by certain search words (e.g., Revolutionary War; ancient civilizations; community helpers) in the children's book sections of the website will bring you to useful titles and information.

Book Links is an excellent monthly periodical that features useful trade books for the library and classroom. Although the magazine does not focus solely on social studies titles, rarely does an issue not feature an article or selection of new books that could be used for teaching and learning social studies. Similarly, a variety of websites exist that are useful to librarians and teachers interested in finding good literature selections, resources, and awards. For example:

- American Library Association (www.ala.org)
- Association for Library Service to Children (www.ala.org/ala/alsc/alsc.htm)
- Children's Literature website (www.childrenslit.com)
- Carol Hurst's Children's Literature Site (www.carolhurst.com)
- The Horn Book (www.hbook.com)

The International Reading Association and state or local affiliates often have workshops and conferences that feature presentations about using literature to teach social studies topics. If you are a member of a literacy organization, help your organization develop a social studies strand or emphasis in its professional development efforts.

If your school, district, or county has a children's book review committee, joining the committee will expose you to a variety of trade books. Most educators serve voluntarily on these committees to review new titles and present them to the committee for recommendation to schools for purchase. With an interest in social studies, you might serve on the committee to review only those titles that relate to social studies.

Finally, look for classes in children's literature that may be offered through a local college, university, or learning exchange. These classes often draw teachers with an interest in reading and learning about children's and young adult literature. Some instructors will even let you sit in on classes that feature your areas of interest.

A Personal Inventory

Few elementary teachers walk into their first teaching assignment with strong expertise in social studies. Good teachers take stock of what they know, what they can do, and what they have to work with. We recommend that you take a personal inventory to identify your strengths as well as your weaknesses in your content knowledge, skills, and resources. Perhaps you have great knowledge of history, but limited understandings of economics and geography. Perhaps you have a great deal of content knowledge, but limited skills in teaching social studies concepts to young learners. You may have strengths in literacy or technology that will be very useful in creating a strong social studies program in your classroom. Consider your motivations, passions, experiences, biases, and support resources (people as well as materials and equipment).

In taking a personal inventory, speak frankly with a colleague or take some time to write in a journal. Create a graphic organizer for yourself identifying your strengths and weaknesses, or incentives and concerns for teaching social studies. Or, use the Inventory and Needs Assessment (Figure 10.2).

The benefit to taking a personal inventory is that you personalize your plans for becoming a successful social studies teacher. You have learned a lot about what components can be used to create an effective, integrated, literacy-based, technology-enhanced social studies program. However, these ideas and resources may continue to swirl around in your head—like seeds in the wind without fertile grounds in which to become rooted, nurtured, and harvested—unless you give them a place to settle and flourish. Start with what you know, with your experiences and expertise, or with your dedication to powerful teaching and learning. We have no doubt that you will grow from there.

When you have been honest with yourself and documented your reflections in a personal inventory, you are then ready to identify your needs for your future as a social studies teacher. Identifying these needs now requires you to do something with this important information— seek appropriate professional development. There exist many professional development opportunities for all educators. Some professional development is better than other professional development. Some educators find better learning and resources at professional conferences, whereas others prefer taking continuing education courses. Some prefer to read, whereas others prefer to become engaged in school-based practical experiences. We recommend that you spend your career as a teacher seeking learning opportunities that are diverse, unique, and useful. Seek professional development from various perspectives and through different methods of delivery. After all, isn't this how you plan to teach your students?

Figure 10.2   Inventory and needs assessment.

Social Studies Inventory

	Completely	Somewhat	Not at All
I am confident in my general knowledge of history			
I am confident in my knowledge of geography			
I am confident in my knowledge of economics			
I am confident in my knowledge of civics/government			
I know where to find local, state, and national social studies standards			
I know how to "unpack" or analyze and interpret social studies standards			
I know a variety of research-based strategies to use in teaching social studies			
I know how to teach for understanding in social studies			
I know how to integrate literacy and social studies instruction			
I know a variety of assessments to use in evaluating student achievement in social studies			
I know how to use data from student assessments to inform and adjust my instructional practices in social studies			
I know where to go for resources and materials to teach social studies			
I am confident in my skills and abilities to teach social studies			
I am really excited about and looking forward to teaching social studies!			

Teaching Social Studies

My Strengths	My Weaknesses

Figure 10.3   Professional development plan.

Short-Term Plans

Goals	Where to Find Support	When to Get Support	How This Will Improve My Social Studies Program
To improve content knowledge in _____			
To develop skills in _____			

Long-Term Plans

Goals	Where to Find Support	When to Get Support	How This Will Improve My Social Studies Program
To improve content knowledge in _____			
To develop skills in _____			

PLANNING YOUR PROFESSIONAL DEVELOPMENT

You are in control of your own professional development. Although your site administrators and district or state requirements will recommend and require certain types of professional development, you will have plenty of room for personal choice. Professional development is limitless, and, as you have read, there are multiple opportunities for you to continue learning about effective teaching and learning in social studies.

Because of the overwhelming nature of teaching and because of the diversity and multitude of professional development opportunities in social studies, it is important that you make short-term and long-term plans for your own professional development. Take control of your own goal-setting, reflect on your needs and progress, and make your personal professional development plans work for you. We recommend that you take a personal inventory and needs assessment every year. Based on your personal needs, develop goals for the short term (within the next year) and for the long term (5 to 7 years). Ask yourself, "Where do I want to be in 1 year?" and "What do I need to be the best possible social studies teacher in 5 years?" Your responses may pertain to the acquisition of specific content knowledge (e.g., ancient history, politic sciences, state geography, Native American cultures) or pedagogy (e.g., developing historical thinking skills, using content-area reading strategies, assessing chronological and spatial thinking skills). Your means of professional growth may include readings, courses, observations, workshops, lectures, seminars, institutes, discussion groups, curriculum development, or other avenues of professional development. Knowing what is available will help you plan for your personal professional development. Participating in professional organizations will help keep you informed of various grants, conferences, workshops, speakers, and opportunities available.

In making your plans for professional development, consider using the Professional Development Plan found in Figure 10.3. Then work toward the attainment of your self-defined, well-informed, ambitious goals that will result in the best possible teaching and learning of social studies. Good luck!

Conclusion

Congratulations on completing your methods course in teaching social studies. You've learned a lot about the design and delivery of excellent lessons in history, social sciences, geography, civics, government, and economics. But you're not done learning. There is so much more that you can do to become an expert teacher. The world and its ever-changing societies will continue to challenge, inspire, and inform you and your work as an excellent social studies teacher. Take charge of and remain reflective of your professional development, and be that lifelong learner that your favorite teacher was.

History's Finer Points

Through the ages and across cultural borders, people have used proverbs to teach morals, or lessons. Proverbs offer advice and inspire wisdom. Most stand the test of time and provide insight for educators and education in the 21st century. For example:

- A book is like a garden carried in the pocket. (Arab proverb)
- A teacher is better than two books. (German proverb)
- A wise man hears one word and understands two. (Yiddish proverb)
- Necessity is the mother of invention. (Irish proverb)
- Praise the young and they will blossom. (Irish proverb)
- The work praises the man. (Irish proverb)
- To teach is to learn. (Japanese proverb)
- What belongs to everybody belongs to nobody. (Spanish proverb)
- Wonder is the beginning of wisdom. (German proverb)
- Knowledge is better than riches. (Cameroonian proverb)

Document-Based Question: What proverbs inspire and inform your work as a teacher? How will you use proverbs in your social studies classroom?

Questions to Consider

Quiz yourself on this chapter's important concepts on our Companion Website's Chapter 10 self-assessments at www.prenhall.com/schell.

1. Why should every teacher continue to develop as a professional educator?
2. What are ways that teachers can engage in professional development?
3. Which organizations exist to facilitate professional development in social studies?

Exercises

1. Complete the needs assessment in Figure 10.2. What are you good at? Which areas would like to focus on as an educator? In which areas could you share your knowledge with others?

2. Complete the professional development plan in Figure 10.3. Make a commitment to work on this plan, and revise this plan, as you enter this most amazing profession.

Index